God and the Constitution

God and the Constitution

Christianity and American Politics

Paul Marshall

ROWMAN & LITTLEFIELD PUBLISHERS, INC.
Lanham • Boulder • New York • Oxford

ROWMAN & LITTLEFIELD PUBLISHERS, INC.

Published in the United States of America
by Rowman & Littlefield Publishers, Inc.
A Member of the Rowman & Littlefield Publishing Group
4720 Boston Way, Lanham, Maryland 20706
www.rowmanlittlefield.com

12 Hid's Copse Road
Cumnor Hill, Oxford OX2 9JJ, England

Distributed by National Book Network

British Library Cataloguing in Publication Information Available

Library of Congress Cataloging-in-Publication Data

Marshall, Paul A., 1948–
  God and the Constitution : Christianity and American politics / Paul
Marshall.
    p. cm.
Includes bibliographical references and index.
  ISBN 0-7425-2248-2 (cloth : alk. paper)
  1. Christianity and politics—United States. I. Title.
 BR526 .M345 2002
  261.7'0973—dc21
                                        2002002851

Printed in the United States of America

⊗™ The paper used in this publication meets the minimum requirements of
American National Standard for Information Sciences—Permanence of Paper for
Printed Library Materials, ANSI/NISO Z39.48-1992.

~

Contents

~

Preface

The United States is often polarized about issues of religion and politics. On the one hand, secularists treat any acknowledgment of the importance of religion to American public life as a prelude to theocracy. Mention something like supporting faith-based organizations and they hear, or pretend to hear, echoes of the Taliban, or the Inquisition cranking up its racks while intolerant armies shuffle into position for eternal religious war as America becomes like Matthew Arnold's "darkling plain where ignorant armies clash by night."

On the other hand, many Christians, though with hardly a theocrat amongst them, proceed from biblical texts to contemporary politics as if little thought were needed about how the Christian faith should come to expression in the complexities of modern life and government. Many explicitly religious people offer little evidence of any serious grappling with religious teaching about political life. On the left hand, we are offered generalizations about the need to care for the earth, about the need for community, and about the priority of concern for the poor. On the right hand we hear statements about the sanctity of human life, the importance of the family, and the moral basis of society. Probably *all* of these emphases can be defended on biblical grounds, but they provide little foundation for any political action since they say little about politics per se.

Meanwhile, other Christians lambaste politics as a worldly realm, suffused with evil and concerned only with the trivial matters of external law and behavior, rather than with the vital inner matters of the heart. They focus on the church and on changing individuals one at a time, and wait expectantly for an apocalypse that will get them out of here.

One would never guess from viewing this panoply that there are two millennia-old Christian traditions of reflection on politics that take difficult political questions seriously, and do not fall into theocracy, naïve biblicism, or withdrawal. They do not teach that we can answer a complex problem with a divinely inspired "Thus saith the Lord . . . there should be a flat tax, . . . or, no drilling for oil in Alaska." But these traditions do suggest that biblical teaching, and theological and political reflection, can shape our hearts and minds to approach politics in a way genuinely formed and informed by our faith.

As a way of responding to the positions I have described and, of course, caricatured, I try in this book to outline some of the themes of this tradition of reflection. There are other books that do this well, and I mention some in the notes, but most are aimed at specialist, especially theologically and philosophically specialist, readers. Here I have tried to address an interested general reader.

The two traditions on which I have drawn most extensively are modern Catholic political thought, and modern Calvinist political thought, particularly that associated with Abraham Kuyper. There are important differences in these traditions, but at the general level of this book, they may be regarded as saying very similar things. I also seek to relate these traditions to American constitutional thought and the principles which underlie the founding of America.[1]

This book also does not try to give definite answers to contemporary issues. Its goal is to give an *approach* to the issues before us. One reason to be careful in addressing current problems is that, while political principles are vital to politics, they are never themselves sufficient to provide answers to practical problems. Practical politics needs detailed knowledge of immediate situations, and to be shaped by political judgment and practical experience. This book points to the need for expertise and prudence, as well as for theory, but it cannot, in the nature of the case, provide them.

I have also tried, not always successfully I'm sure, to resist the academic's temptation to show how complicated things really are, or to make them even more complex. This has meant resisting the desire to keep adding another "on the other hand," and required moving several of my disputes with others to the notes. Those with more professional interests may want to peruse these to see how what I am saying relates to others' views on these matters.

This work has gained from many conversations over many years. Among those I would like to thank are Alan and Elaine Storkey, Oliver and Joan O'Donovan, Nigel Biggar, Robert Song, Byong-Yong Hong, Wesley Wentworth, Tom Wright, Jay Budziszewski, Dave Koyzis, Justin Cooper, Brian

Stiller, Bruce Clemenger, Julius Taniguchi, Robert George, Charles Glenn, Carl Esbeck, Corwin Smidt, Steve Monsma, Bill Harper, Dave Coolidge, Doug Bandow, Ron Sider, Jim Wallis, George Weigel, Robert Royal, Mike Uhlmann, Christopher Catherwood, Daniel Philpott, Allen D. Hertzke, Jean Bethke Elshtain, Luis Lugo, Ken Grasso, Russell Hittinger, James Davison Hunter, Os Guiness, Richard Mouw, Mark Noll, Bernard Lewis, Sander Griffioen, Henk Woldring, Bob Goudzwaard, Jerry Herbert, Richard Russell, Al Wolters, Cal Seerveld, and especially, my late professor, Bernard Zylstra.

The Civitas programme, run by the Center for Public Justice, hosted by the Brookings Institution and the American Enterprise Institute, and funded by the Pew Charitable Trusts, kindly arranged for a one-day conference on the manuscript, wherein over a dozen excellent doctoral students chewed it over, much to my discomfort and enlightenment. I would like to thank Heather McMillen, Diane Whitmore, Pamela Van Zwaluwenburg, Dan Young, Brian Newman, Kevin Den Dulk, Joshua Yates, Mark Mitchell, Michael Rodriguez, Zachary Calo, David Bobb, Eric Gregory, Kenneth Alexo, Lynn Robinson, Nisha Botchwey, and Scott Flipse for doing this. Ruth Melkonian Hoover and Paul Brink took part and also followed up with excellent written critical comments and suggestions. Mike Cromartie and Nancy Pearcey also added wise comments, and the Civitas and CPJ staff, especially Steve Lazarus, John Carlson, Stanley Carlson-Thies, Keith Pavlischek, and Jim Skillen, also helped on this and many other occasions.

My employer, the Center for Religious Freedom at Freedom House, gave me a leave to write this book, and I am most grateful to it and, especially, to its Director, Nina Shea. The final rewrite was done in Turkey and I would like to thank some of my fellow travelers, including Tom Oden, Diane and Ed Knippers, and Steve Ferguson for their comments, and Murat, Mehmet, and the crew of the "Wicked Felina" for helping me to survive it. Howard and Roberta Ahmanson provided gracious hospitality and sharp comments during its writing.

My very special thanks go to the Claremont Institute and its staff for supporting and funding the project, and for providing a home while it was written. Previous President Larry Arnn, previous Vice President Mike Warder, and President Tom Silver have been encouraging throughout. The staff, including Mary Schmall, Dorothy Hoffberg, Judy Day, Penny McWhorter, and Nancy Padilla, were unfailingly helpful. Nazalee Topalian pushed the project toward publication with zeal. Michael Finch, Daniel Palm, Christopher Flannery, Glenn Ellmers, Tom Krannawitter, Ben Boychuk, Brian Kennedy, Charles Kesler, and Harry Jaffa have offered good advice and criticism.

Lela Gilbert vastly improved earlier versions of this work, Denyse O'Leary provided the index, and Jane Pratt and Glenda Burton processed my illegible manuscript corrections with care and speed.

Needless to say, none of these are responsible for any errors that exist, and many disagree with much of what is said here. But they have assured me that they wish to see it published, if only so they can give their criticisms to a wider audience. I am grateful to them all.

Notes

1. John Bolt's, *A Free Church, A Holy Nation: Abraham Kuyper's American Public Theology* (Grand Rapids, Mich.: Eerdmans, 2001) attempts to explore these links in Kuyper's work.

CHAPTER ONE

~

Attacks on Religion in Public Life

Ignoring Religion

In many circles in America a book attempting to outline a Christian approach to government is likely to be regarded as anachronistic or dangerous, or both. It may be regarded as anachronistic since much of the modern academy, sheltered as it is, simply assumes that religious patterns of thought are passé. As Richard Neuhaus puts it:

> [S]everal generations of Americans have been taught, from grade school through graduate school, that ours is a secular society, or is rapidly becoming such. . . . [T]he textbooks are replete with generic statements such as: "In earlier times, people sought answers to these questions in religion, but in our secular society. . . ." The student is invited to fill in the blank or, more commonly, to accept the answer provided by the writer of the textbook who simply knows, as everybody supposedly knows, that "traditional belief" and morality are no longer relevant.[1]

Common as such attitudes are, they reflect either wishful thinking or parochialism induced by the shelter of a university town. In fact, church attendance and profession of religious beliefs have persistently increased throughout U.S. history, and are now at some of their highest levels ever. Nor is this growth confined to rural backwaters where the lame and the foolish go to hear ignorant rant. Religions, including Christianity, thrive most in the heart of bustling, pluralistic cities.[2] As Peter Berger writes:

> What has in fact occurred is that, by and large, religious communities have survived and even flourished to the degree that they have *not* tried to adapt themselves to the alleged requirements of a secularized world. To put it sim-ply, experiments with secularized religion have generally failed: religious movements with beliefs and practices dripping with reactionary supernatu-ralism (the kind utterly beyond the pale at self-respecting faculty parties) have widely succeeded.[3]

Nor is this phenomenon confined to the United States. It is worldwide in scope. Christianity, Islam, Hinduism, Buddhism, and other religions are re-asserting themselves as major cultural influences. Islam and Christianity are both growing rapidly, the latter at a faster pace than at any point in its his-tory. It is often said that the United States is unusual—exceptional amongst industrial nations—in the extent of religious belief among the population. However, the United States is actually typical (if there can be such a thing) of countries worldwide, including industrial ones. It is Europe or, more pre-cisely, Western Europe, which is unusual and, even here, the reports of the death of religion have been greatly exaggerated.[4]

Nor are these religions shorn of genuine intellectual content. They are not mere emotional, reactionary, so-called "fundamentalist" movements: they have developed bodies of theology, philosophy, and law, including in the United States. Contra Michael Weisskopf's famous *Washington Post* claim, they, including the so-called "Religious Right," are not "largely poor, uneducated, and easy to command."[5]

Why, in the face of burgeoning religion and religious thought, do many U.S. academics persist in the idea that this stuff is all so passé, and that we are, or should be, entering the brave new secular world long heralded by their version of "Enlightenment?"[6] There seem to be two reasons, sometimes in-terconnected: antipathy and ignorance. In the 1920s, the journalist, hu-morist, and caricaturist H. L. Mencken, with great loquacity but less accu-racy, described evangelicals and fundamentalists as "halfwits," "yokels," "rustic ignoramuses," "anthropoid rabble," and "gaping primates of the up-land valleys."[7] Subsequent years have brought forth waning rhetorical power but little change in the attitudes themselves, so that the modern combina-tion is somewhat worse. This can produce bigoted tirades, such as Weis-skopf's. These, too, occur in the academy. Charles Taylor, the accomplished political theorist, suggested in his *Sources of the Self: The Making of the Mod-*

ern Identity that his somewhat unorthodox Catholic views help form his theory of what a human being is. In a review, Quentin Skinner, often regarded as a leading historian of political thought, described Taylor as basically, well, mad. Skinner claimed, "Theism must certainly be false . . . it must be grossly irrational to believe otherwise. To say, however, that a belief is grossly irrational is to say that anyone who continues to affirm it must be suffering from some serious form of psychological blockage or self-deceit."[8]

This diatribe cannot be merely another attack on the Religious Right, since Taylor is a social democrat, and a Canadian to boot. It is instead part of a widespread, deep inability to understand something of the world beyond the confines of a cramped, secular mind. Taylor's reply is to the point:

> I think that it probably shows up a striking blind-spot of the contemporary academy, that unbelievers can propound such crudities about the sources of belief, of a level which any educated believer would be excoriated for applying, say, to members of another confession. The paradox is that the last members of the educated community in the West who have to learn some lesson of ecumenical humility are (some) unbelievers. When these come to talk about religion, they have all the breadth of comprehension and sympathy of a Jerry Falwell and significantly less even than Cardinal Ratzinger. The really astonishing thing is that they even seem proud of it.[9]

Much of this hostility stems from ignorance, though of course one can be ignorant without necessarily being hostile: there may be only suspicion, and sometimes not even that. In any case, it remains true that, in Berger's oft-used phrase: "America is a nation of Indians ruled by Swedes." It is a country full of fervent, multihued faiths overseen, overlooked, and overflown by self-styled, cool rationalists. To take one example from Berger:

> A few years ago the first volume coming out of the so-called Fundamentalism Project landed on my desk. The Fundamentalism Project was very generously funded by the MacArthur Foundation. . . . A number of very reputable scholars took part in it, and the published results are of generally excellent quality. But . . . *I asked myself, why would the MacArthur Foundation shell out several million dollars to support an international study of religious fundamentalists?* . . . [It seems that] . . . Fundamentalism is considered a strange, hard-to-understand phenomenon; the purpose of the Project was to delve into this alien world and make it more understandable. But to whom? *Who* find this world strange? Well, the answer to *that* question was easy: people to whom the officials of the MacArthur Foundation normally talk, such as professors at elite American universities. . . . The concern that must have led to this Project was based on

an upside-down perception of the world, according to which "fundamentalism" (which, when all is said and done, usually refers to any sort of passionate religious movement) is a rare, hard-to-explain thing. But a look either at history or at the contemporary world reveals that what is rare is not the phenomenon itself but knowledge of it. The difficult-to-understand phenomenon is not Iranian mullahs but American university professors—it might be worth a multi-million-dollar project to try to explain that!¹⁰

Strategic theorist Edward Luttwak remarks that recent currents in international relations "prohibited any sustained intellectual interest in religion itself. . . . As for religious motivations in secular affairs, they were disregarded or dismissed as mere pretense, and because this could not be done in the case of the entire history of Byzantium, the quandary was resolved by simply abandoning its study."¹¹ Political history and political theory suffer from similar problems. Textbooks on the history of Western political thought often leap from the theorists of Greece and Rome to the Renaissance, pausing only for Augustine and Thomas Aquinas, who seem to be treated as honorary Greek theorists. The influence of specifically Christian, Jewish, and Islamic elements in western thought and in Western politics is often passed over entirely.

Meanwhile, in contemporary political reflection, religion is often dogmatically excluded. As Luttwak notes, analysts who are ready to

> [I]nterpret economic causality, who are apt to dissect social differentiations more finely, and who will minutely categorize political affiliations, are still in the habit of disregarding the role of religion, religious institutions, and religious motivations in explaining politics and conflict, and even in reporting their concrete modalities. Equally, the role of religious leaders, religious institutions, and religiously motivated lay figures in conflict resolution has also been disregarded—or treated as a marginal phenomenon hardly worth noting.

This does not necessarily reflect someone's "personal attitudes toward religion," but rather "a learned repugnance to contend intellectually with all that is religion or belongs to it—a complex inhibition compounded out of the peculiar embarrassment that many feel when faced by explicit manifestations of serious religious sentiment."¹²

This attitude has persisted despite the fact that on September 11, 2001, the United States was attacked by a historically rooted, theoretically astute, and explicitly and clearly religiously based enemy. Most commentary has sought to make Osama bin Laden and his cadres theoretically domesticated by reducing their motivations to concern over poverty or globalization, to objections to

U.S. foreign policy, to sexual frustration, to just about anything except the terrorists' repeated, deep, prayerful desire to restore an Islamic Caliphate.

Deriding Religion

When religion is not dismissed as irrelevant, it may be derided as irrational, divisive, and a catalyst for oppression and war, with radical Islam cast as Exhibit A. As Allan Bloom portrayed it, there is an all too common opinion that "The true believer is the real danger. The study of history and of culture teaches that all the world was mad in the past: men always thought they were right, and that led to wars, persecutions, slavery, xenophobia, racism and chauvinism."[13]

One consequence of this opinion is a tendency to regard devoted religious believers as weird, even insane. As Stephen Carter noted: "Our culture seems to take the position that believing deeply in the tenets of one's faith represents a kind of mystical irrationality."[14] Philosopher Richard Rorty proposes to "josh" believers (and others), and thus dehumanize them as some sort of garrulous but senile relatives. The term "fundamentalist" is often used in the same way: it functions as secular shorthand for lunatic, someone to be clinically observed rather than engaged and listened to.[15] Noted philosopher John Rawls argued that "[to] subordinate all our aims to one end . . . still strikes us as irrational, or more likely as mad."[16] This attitude also involves a type of cultural imperialism, as is shown in Rawls' claims about "us" finding fervent believers insane. Who is this "us"? He seems to imply that it is "us Americans," but his view is a parochial one. It is more likely that "us" refers to the opinions of the faculty club or press room. It is also not altogether clear why Rawls and others claim to speak for America. Polls consistently show that more Americans believe that, for example, the Bible sheds light on American politics than accept views of Rawls' type.[17] Rawls has revised his views considerably in recent years, but the basic pattern still remains.[18]

A more prosaic version of secular prejudice is the widely held view that religion in politics is inherently divisive, and that most wars and oppressions are, or have been, caused by religion or religious intolerance. This prejudice erupted after the terrorist attacks on America on September 11. Not content to castigate bin Laden's travesty of religion, many commentators vented their animosity to religion of all kinds, implying or claiming that committed religion, especially monotheistic religion, is the root of terrorism, violence, and oppression. With the peculiar blindness of modern secularists, they interspersed their denunciation of others' religious beliefs with calls not to denounce others' religious beliefs, as well as with remarks trumpeting their own open-mindedness. They never seem to notice the contradiction, much less be troubled by it (see the discussion of toleration in chapter 6).

Oxford zoologist Richard Dawkins opined that "[t]o fill a world with religion, or religions of the Abrahamic kind, is like littering the streets with loaded guns. Do not be surprised if they are used." *New York Times* columnist Thomas L. Friedman wrote that "World War II and the Cold War were fought to defeat secular totalitarianism—Nazism and Communism—and World War III is a battle against religious totalitarianism, a view of the world that my faith must remain supreme and can be affirmed and held passionately only if all others are negated. That's bin Ladenism." Michael Lind fulminated that the "Moral Majority and Christian Coalition have given aid and comfort to the enemy. . . . Their fundamentalist ideology is essentially identical to that of the Muslim extremists. . . . [They] are promoting a theocratic crusade of a 'Judeo-Christian America' against an equally theocratic enemy." Noted author Salman Rushdie commented on India's violence between Hindus and Muslims that "What happened in India has happened in God's name. The problem's name is God." Andrew Sullivan worried that "[i]t seems almost as if there is something inherent in religious monotheism that lends itself to this kind of terrorist temptation."[19]

These views suffer from several glaring problems. One is that in their use of history they employ a rhetorical sleight of hand to disguise the fact that they are asserting little more than that most wars have occurred in the past and that most people were religious in the past. Both assertions are true, but totally unilluminating. It would be more accurate to say that people fight about things they care about, whether that is land or oil. Part of this pattern is that people fight about beliefs they care about, whether communism, feminism, or individual rights. And part of this pattern is that people fight about religious beliefs that they care about, whether that is Hinduism or the nature of the Trinity. Usually, religion per se adds nothing specific to the mix; it is merely one instance of a general phenomenon of human brutality—that people fight about things on which they differ. The only solution to this, if such were possible, would be not that people no longer care about religion, but that they no longer care about anything whatsoever. Even Rorty does not say this.

Another problem is that, by trying to reject any fervent belief per se, they suggest that our problems would be solved if everyone in the world became mild, vague, and relativist. But this is like claiming that if we were all nice, or all loved each other, then there wouldn't be any more war. It might be true, but so what? We aren't nice and we don't all love each other, and we won't anytime soon.

There is the additional question of what to do if people with strong beliefs, like bin Laden, attack us militarily. Who will fight against him? Surely it will be men and women, like those in the armed forces, who believe that freedom is worth fighting and dying for. We are unlikely to be defended well if the Marine Corps is composed of disciples of Richard Rorty.

While recognizing that, as we have experienced all too painfully, explicitly religious views have been, are, can be, and will be the source of atrocities (just like all else in human life), there are indications that a divorce of genuine religion from public life will likely lead to worse atrocities. For example, Miroslav Volf, a skilled theologian with personal experiences of the Balkan conflicts, has pointed out that what is most likely to lead to conflict is *not* robust, believing religion, but rather weak religion which is used as a political identifier.[20] In places such as Northern Ireland, the former Yugoslavia, and India, those engaged in religious violence are usually *not* notably pious or religiously observant. Indeed, they are often explicitly denounced by their claimed religious leaders. Even the radical Islamic terrorists who attacked the United States were, though willing to die, not notably pious Muslims, and spent a fair amount of their time in the United States in strip clubs drinking vodka. In these situations, it may not be true that the less believing religion there is in politics, the more likely there is to be peace. Indeed the opposite may be true.

Furthermore, self-professed antireligious views have been the source of the largest and worst atrocities of the twentieth century, and of history. Both Communism and Nazism opposed the traditional religions of Europe, and then produced programs of genocide on a scale and of an intensity not seen before in the world. As Veit Bader points out, "most of the atrocities, genocides and ethnic cleansings in our century have been legitimized by secularist ideologies."[21] Other self-professed secular regimes, such as in Turkey and Mexico, do not have a record as bad as Germany, Russia, Cambodia, or China, but they still have produced brutal, authoritarian governments.[22]

To overcome the awkward fact that it is secular regimes that have produced the greatest mass murders in history, some commentators, like Sullivan and *New York Times* columnist Anthony Lewis, redefine committed religion to include some secular ideologies. There is good reason to use an expanded definition of religion; this book does. But these pundits expand their definition very selectively, exempting their own views from their critique and hence redefining committed religion to include only those beliefs that they do not like. The result is that they treat committed religion as repressive simply by definition.

Another problem with this view of religion is that there are many examples of deep religious beliefs that do not produce the results the authors lament. We could take many instances, the most obvious being the United States, where most of these writers peacefully live and write, and one of the most monotheistic societies on the face of the earth. The American Declaration of Independence is explicitly monotheist (see chapter 4), as is the overwhelming majority of the population. Despite its many problems, the country lives in peace and religious freedom, largely as an expression of its monotheism.

Perhaps most embarrassing for those who try to recast the war on terrorism as a war on fervent religion is that they must assiduously avoid noticing the beliefs of those who lead, fight for, and rescue Americans. There are, of course, people of many beliefs, including atheists, in America's armed forces and police and fire departments, and I have no information about the religious composition of any of these institutions. But it seems commonly agreed that America's soldiery, fire departments, and police forces, as well as the current Federal Cabinet, are on average more committedly religious than, say, the average newspaper columnist. Hence we have a perverse parade of pundits blaming the war on those who fight on their behalf. Those claiming that the United States is at war with committed religion are left making the strange assertion that America is actually engaged in a worldwide struggle against people like, well, President George W. Bush.

Consequently, we can say that, while religious beliefs can often produce murderous and repressive regimes, empirical evidence suggests that secular regimes are *very likely* to do so. Further, the modern prejudice that religion itself is particularly prone to create conflicts and wars is just that—a prejudice. In the West, it seems to be produced by inattention to history combined with a fixation on the European wars of religion in the sixteenth and seventeenth centuries.[23] Bader's observation on this is apt: "[L]iberal philosophers' preoccupation with religions as a threat to political stability . . . [may be] understandable in the . . . sixteenth and seventeenth centuries, [but] is now myopic and outdated."[24]

Marginalizing Religion

One result of this antipathy is attempts to exclude religious beliefs and discourse from public life. R. H. Tawney, an English economic historian and socialist, correctly said that "What is distinctive of our own [time] is . . . its assumption that the habitual conduct and organization of society is a matter to which religion is merely irrelevant."²⁵ This has nothing to do with the meaning of the First Amendment to the U.S. Constitution. It is emphatically not the same as fighting against an "establishment of religion" or struggling for "the separation of church and state." Rather, it is an attempt to exclude the ideas of a whole body of people from the public realm, which would thus prevent them from exercising free and effective citizenship.

Echoes of this occurred throughout the 2000 American elections. Rather than passing peacefully into that good night, Americans' overt religion, and politicians' overt religiosity, became one of the major campaign themes.²⁶ Various columnists began griping after George W. Bush declared in one of the presidential debates that Jesus was his favorite political philosopher, less because of the strange claim that he was a political philosopher than because Bush mentioned Jesus at all. Meanwhile, Al Gore said he "believe[d] in serving God and trying to understand and obey God's will for our lives," and began quoting noted English Christian author C. S. Lewis. Indeed, Bill Bradley, former Fellowship of Christian Athletes star, was the only one of the major candidates not to make frequent noises about faith. Barry Lynn, executive director of Americans United for the Separation of Church and State (AUSCC), grasped for a sound bite by declaring that the "candidates and their cronies have turned this race into a holy war. . . ." With his customary sense of proportion, he had already said in February 2000 that the campaign was "the ugliest exploitation of religion for partisan purposes in modern political history," one apparently worse than Slobodan Milosevic's massacres in Bosnia or Sudan's current genocide.²⁷

Things livened up even more when Al Gore picked Joe Lieberman, an Orthodox Jew, as his vice presidential running mate. Lieberman promptly began talking both about his own faith and about the importance of religion in America. The Anti-Defamation League (ADL) wrote to him suggesting that his language "risks alienating the American people" and might make "atheistic Americans. . . feel outside of the electoral or political process."²⁸ Why someone would be "outside" the electoral or political process simply because somebody in a campaign said something that they disagreed with was never explained by the ADL. And if they were not outside, but only *thought* they were outside of the process when in fact they were in it, why didn't the ADL write not to Lieberman but instead an open letter to atheists to tell them they were confused? The ADL might also want to consider criticizing George Washington who, in his Farewell Address, said that "reason and experience both forbid us to expect that national morality can prevail in exclusion of religious principle."

As it was, Americans of all religious beliefs managed to stay calm, and steadfastly refused to gear up for a holy war or rush into battle with any supposed infidels. Instead, they sensibly continued to ignore the campaign until after Labor Day. Meanwhile, *Newsweek* polls showed that a large majority of Americans, equally sensibly, were "not at all concerned" that Lieberman's religion would "interfere" with his work.[29] Indeed, the most striking feature of these events was the temperance of the candidates and the American people, in striking contrast to the intolerance and intemperance of their critics.

A similar contretemps arose when Bush picked John Ashcroft, a devout Pentecostal, to be his new attorney general.[30] The ADL pronounced itself "troubled" that Ashcroft had quoted the American Revolutionary slogan that "we have no King but Jesus" (which was of course defending a republican view of government), and went on to say, "We question whether his religious views will have an impact on his role as Attorney General." It called on him to "assure the American people that his personal religious beliefs will not dictate how he will carry out his duties as attorney general, if confirmed."[31] Lynn also thought that quoting the religious sentiments of the American Revolution disqualified Ashcroft from being attorney general and showed "little or no appreciation for the constitutional separation of church and state."[32]

The pot kept bubbling when, early in his administration, Bush created a "White House Office of Faith-Based Initiatives" whose goals were, according to former director John DiIulio (a Democrat and self-described "born-again Catholic"), "to augment charitable giving, to end discrimination against religious providers of social services, and to mobilize support for grassroots groups, both religious and secular, to tackle our toughest social problems, through public/private partnership."[33] Lieberman, and previously Gore, had made comments supportive of the initiative.

A similar provision already existed in the 1996 Welfare Reform Act, which has a "charitable choice" provision allowing religious groups, as well as secular ones, to use federal funds without losing their religious identities. However, many states and agencies had not followed through on this provision, and one of Bush's goals was to push them to do so. The program was meant to give no special benefit to religious groups: exactly the same criteria applied to secular groups. The criterion was whether the group had a successful program, or a promising proposal, to deliver social services. Similar criteria have already been applied in Medicare and Medicaid funds, which can also go to explicitly religious hospitals, or in vouchers for childcare, or loans for colleges.

Lynn declared that this removal of discrimination against religious groups "would essentially merge church and state into a single bureaucracy."[34] He called the proposal "constitutional quicksand," "misguided," "dangerous," "blatant bigotry," "a constitutional nightmare," and a "[r]adical assault" on the separation of church and state.[35] His colleague Joseph Conn predicted an "all-out battle" over "one of the biggest violations of church-state separation that we've seen in American history."[36]

These confused attacks on Bush, Gore, Lieberman, Ashcroft, and faith-based policy claimed that religion or faith is simply personal or, more likely, private. The ADL maintains that "Faith is a deeply personal matter. . . ." [37] Americans United complained that Lieberman kept introducing his "personal faith."[38] They also stretched the First Amendment to cover not only the activities of government but any activities or utterances of a politician. The ADL's National Director, Abraham H. Foxman, said: "We do not think that religion belongs in the political campaign and the political arena."[39] *The New York Times* editorialized about the "constitutionally based separation of religion from public policy."[40] Lynn complained that Lieberman was "blurring the line between the spiritual and the secular, and between the pious and the political," and that America was refusing to separate "religion and politics."[41]

In arguing for these points, these critics seem congenitally incapable of understanding that they are in fact offering, and trying to impose, their own views of the nature of religion, which are, of course, necessarily religious views themselves. The notion of "separation of church and state" is, amongst other things, a religious view. These critics have the deep, and very personal, religious belief that religion is, or should be, exclusively personal, that piety has little to do with politics, that religion is separate from the basic issues of life (or that politics is), and then they demand that *these* religious beliefs should shape public policy and discourse. In effect, they demand that other Americans stop talking in public about other religious views and instead be pressured into believing, or at least saying they believe, the Anti-Defamation League/*New York Times*/Americans United for Separation of Church and State view. And then these groups have the gall to say that it is *other* people who are pushing their religious beliefs.

Every religion has views that shape public policy, whether the Baha'i stress on the equality of men and women, or recent Catholic opposition to the death penalty. Religion nearly always shapes policy, not usually by forcing adherence to a particular religion, but by shaping people's views on the major issues of life. As Lieberman's Communications Director, Dan Gerstein, said, the Senator's "faith is the source of his values. It shapes who he is and informs his view of the world."[42] Lieberman said, "It helps me answer those questions 'Who am I, and what am I doing here.'"[43] One striking current example of this influence is how the Catholic notion of "subsidiarity" (see page 61) has shaped some of President Bush's commitment to faith-based social policy, whether Bush knows it or not.[44] To this we might add Ashcroft's claim that "it is against my religion to impose my religion."[45]

Columnist Charles Krauthammer wrote that, to the anti-Ashcroft coalition, the Christian Right "is some kind of weird fringe group to whom bones are thrown by otherwise responsible Republicans to induce them to return to their caves. Politically, they are a foreign body to be ignored, bought off, or suppressed. . . ."[46] He went on to say that the attacks on Ashcroft had dashed his hopes that the "nomination of Lieberman to the second highest office in the country by the country's liberal political party would once and for all abolish the last remaining religious prejudice in this country—the notion that highly religious people are unfit for high office because they confuse theology with politics."[47]

Divorcing Religion and Politics

The attempted exclusion of religion from public life found in some secular circles has a counterpart in some explicitly religious circles, especially conservative Christian ones. I do not refer to any, almost nonexistent, attempts by conservative Christians to exclude secular ideas from discussion in American politics. I mean recent calls by Christians themselves to forsake or downplay politics.

For example, in 1999, long-time Christian Right political activist and cofounder of the Moral Majority, Paul Weyrich, stunned a goodly portion of both the Christian and conservative worlds by writing an open letter describing American culture as "an ever-wider sewer," claiming that "the United States is very close to a state totally dominated by an alien ideology," and that "we have probably lost the culture." He maintained: "I no longer believe that there is a moral majority. I do not believe that a majority of Americans actually share our values." Because of this, Weyrich concluded that "politics itself has failed" and that America's "collapse (is) so great that it simply overwhelms politics." In a mood of seeming despair, he called on Christians "to separate [themselves]. . . ."[48] While Weyrich insisted in his letter and in his follow-up articles that he most certainly was not calling on Christians to withdraw from politics, there is no mistaking the sense of despair that pervaded his gloomy prognostications about the possibilities of political life.

At about the same time, columnist Cal Thomas and pastor Ed Dobson proclaimed a similar message in their book *Blinded by Might: Can the Religious Right Save America?*[49] "It is time to assess the impact and future of the greatest political-religious movement since Prohibition. After spending millions of conservative Christian dollars, after a White House dominated for twelve years by Ronald Reagan and George Bush and a Congress run by Republicans since 1995, are we better off today than we were twenty years ago?" They concluded that a "fair-minded person would have to answer no. . . ." They thought that this failure was "not because the [R]eligious [R]ight was wrong on the issues but because the strategy for implementing our agenda was flawed." They called for "a different strategy articulated by a different king who presides over a different kingdom, which he said is 'not of this world.'"

Like Weyrich, they emphasized repeatedly that they were "not calling for withdrawal of religious conservatives from political life" but, again, there is no mistaking their tone of withdrawal. The closing words of their column announcing the book were ". . . the political road will lead to frustration and defeat."[50] Despite all the authors' caveats, cautions, and conditions, their litany of political hopelessness led most observers to conclude that theirs was an admission of defeat and a token of surrender. It caused bewilderment and anger amongst many Christians, cries of "I told you so!" from fundamentalists who had always thought of politics as worldly, and glee amongst secularists that the field would now probably be left open for them, and who felt vindicated in their claim that all attempts to "impose" religious morality on America must and should fail.

This apparent call to preemptive surrender seemed doubly strange since it came at a time not when the political hopes of religious conservatives (or the New Christian Right or the Religious Right or whatever phrase is now in vogue) were failing, but at a time when they were apparently successful. Weyrich, Thomas, and Dobson all gave an unremittingly negative portrayal of the state and direction of American culture as a whole, as a "sewer" which no amount of political reform could cleanse. But, while they were proclaiming the utter corruption of culture, the number of divorces and the number of abortions was down, the number of teenage pregnancies was down, and the number of sexually active teenagers was down. In fact, the moral opinions of current college students are the most conservative in decades. Americans are also now wealthier than they have been before, the number of poor has decreased, and welfare reform is apparently working. The water is cleaner, the air is purer, and the roads are safer. During 1998, evangelicals for the first time acted explicitly on foreign policy issues as churches became aware of the issue of religious persecution. Most statistical indicators of concern to the Religious Right are going in the right direction. At this seeming moment of success, why do some people turn aside?

One reason was perhaps that Republican presidential candidate George W. Bush, while asserting his pro-life credentials, said that there was no hope in the near future of making major changes to abortion laws, and that his prognosis has been accepted by most conservatives. There has also been repeated failure to stop even partial birth abortions. Yet a major reason for this gloom was undoubtedly the acquittal of President Clinton in his Senate impeachment trial. Weyrich has claimed that this was not really central to his view, but his letter had announced itself as "Following the Senate Impeachment Vote."

Weyrich lamented that the Religious Right had failed because its views represented only a minority of Americans. We can add that the Religious Right, a notoriously vague term, has never really penetrated even its own apparent constituency. Most evangelicals, fundamentalists, and pentecostals have never liked it, never funded it, and never voted for its candidates, even though they shared many of its goals. After all, in 1988, even Jerry Falwell supported George Bush rather than Pat Robertson for the presidency, and, in 2000, evangelicals flocked to George W. Bush, not Gary Bauer or Alan Keyes. But, beyond this, the theologically conservative Christian world has remained largely politically passive and inert. It is not that the evangelical world has failed to shape America via the Christian Right, but that the evangelical world has never been that interested in the Christian Right. American evangelicals are still much more concerned with peacefully passing through the world than they are in changing it.[51] Most conservative Christian bestsellers are spiritual self-help books or, like the *Left Behind* series, lurid portrayals of the imminent end of the world. One book in the *Left Behind* series, *Desecration*, had an initial printing of 2.97 million for its release in November 2001.

Thomas and Dobson denounced what they see as an over-politicization by evangelicals. But evangelicals have not been and are not very political. They generally look for any and every excuse to evade and avoid politics. As Mark Noll has observed, urging evangelicals to concentrate on culture rather than politics is somewhat akin to urging junkies to take drugs. In fact, these authors' swings of sentiment can be properly understood only when they are seen against the background of the cycles of evangelical political involvement over the last century. Their call for a political withdrawal and a concentration on the Church is not the slightest bit new, or the slightest bit unusual. It is merely the repetition of the pervasive, parochial, and pathological patterns that have afflicted American evangelicalism throughout most of its history.

Announcements of the birth and death of the Christian Right are not new. Back in 1976 *Newsweek* devoted a cover story to the "Year of the Evangelical." This focused on President Jimmy Carter and came right before what many commentators came to regard as years of decline in evangelical influence. In 1989, when the Moral Majority was disbanded, many commentators took this as a sign that the movement, whatever it was, was over. Then, again, when the Christian Coalition was founded in 1990, there were announcements, to the sound of drumbeats, that the Religious Right was back again.

If we go further back the same pattern is repeated. A century ago William Jennings Bryan was seen as the epitome of evangelical politics, and of a movement that could sweep all before it. Later, the success of prohibition was seen to inaugurate a new age of conservative Christian dominance, while its subsequent repeal was assumed to have announced evangelicalism's demise. Every few decades, conservative Christians feel overwhelmed by America's moral decay and fearful of government intrusion and control of their lives. The result is often a "crusade." The troops are rallied into a movement whose dominant metaphors are military or salvific, or both. The call is for crusades, battles and victories to "save," "rescue" or "win back" America from its apostasy. The movement's political principles are usually intuitive—that is, they are not argued for, wrestled with, or thought through, but simply taken as expressions of what we all supposedly know is right, decent, and true. The campaign is invariably populist—that is, it portrays itself as the campaign of the little guy—the decent, honest, hardworking, regular American—against distant elites who manipulate the country for their own selfish and nefarious ends. And the effort is more usually focused *against* something than for something. It can be antislavery, anti-Masonic, anti-Catholic, antialcohol, antievolution, anti-banks, antisecular, anti-Communist—but it is often hard to know what it is *for*, except a general morality and decency.

The result is fervent, frenetic, and usually, unfocused political activity that may make some gains, but whose usual effect is to terrify the more paranoid secular elites into thinking, or claiming to think, that they are about to be overtaken by a theocracy. It provides a bonanza for fundraising for groups such as People for the American Way and Americans United for the Separation of Church and State, whose sole *raison d'être* seems to be fighting Pat Robertson and Jerry Falwell, and who are, thus, the latter's major publicists.

No doubt there are many reasons for these wild swings, but one important one is that evangelical views of politics are theologically and philosophically uprooted. Thomas and Dobson were deeply involved, along with James Kennedy, Charles Stanley, Tim LaHaye, and others, in helping Falwell start the Moral Majority in 1979. This organization was, in principle, professedly and explicitly *not* a religious organization. It was to, and to a degree did, include Jews, Mormons, Catholics, and nonreligious people as well as evangelical Protestants. It was also formed explicitly in *reaction* to the liberalization of abortion, the apparent exclusion of God from public schools, family breakdown, gay rights, and, most especially, the increasing attempts by the federal government to control religious bodies, especially schools.

Armed with this shopping list of what they were against, the contenders sallied forth into the battle. Thomas and Dobson themselves now parody their own earlier attitudes: "We were on our way to changing America. . . . We had the power to right every wrong and cure every ill." They believed "that [they] could make right through the manipulation of the political system." This early triumphalism, bordering on the heretical, naturally met its counterpart in later defeatism. Now, a mere twenty years later, "the moral landscape of America has become worse. . . . [Our] hopes . . . have failed."[52]

The historical pattern into which they fit is widespread religious passivity eventually prodded and provoked by fear of secular intrusion and control into a fervent crusade. The crusade usually has several years of activity until repeated frustration—and the apparent resistance of the world to reform—leads to disappointment, degenerating rapidly into cynicism. It is a type of manic-depressive religious syndrome, a bipolar political affliction. In its extreme form it creates a type of theological schizophrenia, which at one and the same time proclaims the inevitable moral decline of America and calls for campaigns to arrest that decline. Indeed it often proclaims the imminent end of the world combined with an urgent campaign to save the world.

This view refuses to take real, everyday politics seriously, as anything other than a pragmatic means to achieve some moral reform. It both overestimates and underestimates the power of government. Consequently, it rapidly degenerates into a pragmatism wherein politics and movements, principles and campaigns, are judged simply in terms of whether or not they have "worked" to achieve some particular goal. Thomas' and Dobson's calls stem, in part, from a judgment that their previous ideas have not "worked." The fact that politics is an ongoing, necessary, and inescapable feature of human life, which will always affect and be affected by people whether they like it or not, is lost in a welter of images that seem to imply that politics, or government, or the state, is like a box that you take down off the shelf or put back as you will. Such views, attitudes, and actions are so distant from sober and lifelong political work that they often have little long-term effect for good or for ill.

The Place of Politics and Religion

Against those who ignore religion, we need to say that it is a vital, important and, indeed, central feature of American and world politics. Against those who deride religion we must say that they overestimate the tendency of religion to produce conflict and underestimate the predilection of secularism to produce conflict. Against those who would marginalize religion in politics, we should say that they are the most intolerant figures in the debate, and fail to see the degree to which they wish to impose their religious beliefs on everyone else. Against those Christians that treat politics as optional or as a failure, we must say that politics is an inescapable feature of human life.

To combat secular prejudices and evangelical withdrawal, it is helpful to explore what biblical religion might say about politics. What is needed is not more calls for rectitude, cries for crusades, complaints of corruption, or claims of cynicism, but, in part, an exploration of the nature and place of politics itself in the world. It requires knowing that most politics is more like raising children than raising hell, more like gardening than grandstanding, more like work than warfare. It requires realizing that politics will not bring in a utopia, or even anything remotely like it. It will neither conquer sin nor change human nature. Nor will it create a society which will not need reform the instant after it is reformed. But politics can make a difference in whether our schools are better or worse, whether it's safer or not to walk home on a dark night, whether people are healthy or hungry, whether or not we will live more at war or more at peace. While such struggles and policies are full of victories and defeats, they have no final victory or final defeat wherein we could properly and finally say "we have won" or "we have lost." Politics is a part of ongoing life in the world to be pursued patiently and faithfully.

Notes

1. Richard Neuhaus, "Secularization in Theory and Fact," *First Things* (June/July 2000): 86–89.

2. See Roger Finke and Rodney Stark, *The Churching of America 1776–1990: Winners and Losers in Our Religious Economy* (New Brunswick, N.J.: Rutgers University Press, 1993).

3. See Peter Berger, "The Desecularization of the World: A Global Overview," in *The Desecularization of the World: Resurgent Religion and World Politics*, ed. Berger (Grand Rapids, Mich.: Eerdmans, 1999), 1–18. See also the essays in Paul Marshall, ed., *Religious Freedom in the World: A Global Survey of Freedom and Persecution* (Nashville, Tenn.: Broadman and Holman, 2000).

4. See Grace Davie, "Europe: The Exception that Proves the Rule," in *The Desecularization of the World: Resurgent Religion and World Politics*, ed. Berger (Grand Rapids, Mich.: Eerdmans, 1999), 65–84; William H. Swatas and Daniel V.A. Olson, *The Secularization Debate* (Lanham, Md.: Rowman & Littlefield, 2000).

5. Michael Weisskopf, "Energized by Pulpit or Passion, the Public is Culling," *Washington Post*, 1 February 1993. For a good argument that "Anti-fundamentalism" is the only significant form of religious prejudice in America, see L. Bolce and G. DeMaio, "Religious Outlook, Culture War Politics, and Antipathy Toward Christian Fundamentalists," *Public Opinion Quarterly*, vol. 63 (1999): 29–61.

6. Of course, many political writings do take religion seriously. See, for example, Lawrence E. Harrison and Samuel Huntington, *Culture Matters: How Values Shape Human Progress* (New York: Basic Books, 2000). See also Ronald Inglehart's *Modernization and Postmodernization: Cultural, Economic, and Political Change in 43 Societies* (Princeton, N.J.: Princeton University Press, 1997); Christian Smith, ed., *Disruptive Religion: The Force of Faith in Social Movement Activism* (New York: Routledge, 1996), especially the Introduction; the work of the "Gang of Four," Corwin Smidt, John Green, James L. Guth, and Lyman Kellstadt, on the influence of religion on U.S. politics, see, for example, Corwin Smidt, ed., *In God We Trust?: Religion and American Political Life* (Grand Rapids, Mich.: Baker, 2001); Andrew Kohut et al., *The Diminishing Divide: Religion's Changing Role in American Politics* (Washington, D.C.: Brookings, 2000). My thanks to Ruth Melkonian Hoover for drawing my attention to several of these.

7. Quoted in Michael Cromartie, "The Evangelical Kaleidoscope: A Survey of Recent Evangelical Political Engagement," in *Christians and Politics beyond the Culture Wars; An Agenda for Engagement*, ed. David P. Gushee (Grand Rapids, Mich.: Baker, 2000), 15–24.

8. Quentin Skinner, "Who Are We? Ambiguities of the Modern Self," *Inquiry* 34 (1991): 133–53, an extended review of Charles Taylor, *Sources of the Self: The Making of the Modern Identity* (Cambridge: Harvard University Press, 1989). See also Paul Marshall, "Quentin Skinner and the Secularization of Political Thought," *Studies in Political Thought* 2 (1993): 87–104.

9. Charles Taylor, "Comments and Replies," *Inquiry* 34 (1991): 237–54.

10. Berger, "The Desecularization of the World," 1–2.

11. Edward Luttwak, "The Missing Dimension," in *Religion: The Mission Dimension of Statecraft*, ed. Douglas Johnston and Cynthia Sampson, 8–19 (New York: Oxford University Press, 1994).

12. Luttwak, "The Missing Dimension," 9–10.

13. Allan Bloom, *The Closing of the American Mind* (New York: Basic Books, 1987), 26.

14. Stephen Carter, *The Culture of Disbelief: How American Law and Politics Trivialize Religious Devotion* (New York: Basic Books, 1993) 6–7. See also his *The Dissent of the Governed: A Meditation on Law, Religion and Loyalty* (Cambridge: Harvard University Press, 1998).

15. For a good discussion of these themes see Ian S. Markham, *Plurality and Christian Ethics* (Cambridge: Cambridge University Press, 1994).

16. John Rawls, *A Theory of Justice* (Cambridge: Harvard University Press, 1971) 554.

17. In a Gallup survey taken 9–12 December 1999, 67 percent of respondents said that "religion can answer all or most of today's problems," *Emerging Trends*, January 2000.

18. See chapter 6 and Jonathan Chaplin, "Beyond Liberal Restraint: Defending Religiously Based Arguments in Law and Public Policy," *University of British Columbia Law Review*, vol. 33 (2000): 617–46.

19. Richard Dawkins, *The Guardian*, September 15, 2001; Thomas L. Friedman, *New York Times*, November 27, 2001; Michael Lind, UPI, September 17, 2001; Salman Rushdie, *New York Times*, March 8, 2002; Andrew Sullivan, *New York Times Magazine*, October 7, 2001.

20. Presentation at U.S. State Department, 11 May 2000. On the common coexistence of deep religious commitment, civility, and pluralism, see Rodney Stark, *One True God: Historical Consequences of Monotheism* (Princeton, N.J.: Princeton University Press, 2001), especially chapter 5.

21. Veit Bader, "Religious Pluralism: Secularism or Priority for Democracy?" *Political Theory*, vol. 27 (1999): 597–633.

22. India is an exception to this, but its version of "secular" means something more like "plural" and is close to the view of American Founders and the view advocated here.

23. John Rawls is clear that his philosophy is shaped by a deep desire to avoid a repetition of such conflicts.

24. Bader, "Religious Pluralism," note 23, 602. See also Chaplin, "Beyond Liberal Restraint"; Stark, *One True God*.

25. R. H. Tawney, *The Acquisitive Society* (London: Collins, 1961), 185.

26. See Mark Silk, ed., *Religion and American Politics: The 2000 Election in Context* (Hartford, Conn.: Center for the Study of Religion in Public Life, Trinity College, 2000).

27. AUSCC Press Release, 24 February 2000.

28. Letter from ADL to Lieberman, 28 August 2000.

29. "Lieberman's Mix of Faith, Policy Tests Public Tolerance," *Washington Post*, 29 August 2000.

30. For a brief overview, see Mark Silk, "Faith in Justice: The Ashcroft Fight," *Religion in the News* (Spring 2001): 19–20.

31. ADL Press Release, 12 January 2001.

32. "Critics See Little in Ashcroft Speech to Derail Nomination," *New York Times*, 13 January 2001; AUSCC press release, 12 January 2001.

33. John DiIulio, "Know Us by Our Works," *Wall St. Journal*, 14 February 2001.

34. AUSCC Press Release, 19 December 2000.

35. Associated Press News Service, "Bush Ready to Fund Charities," 25 January 2001; Keith Pavlischek, "Equal Treatment, YES; Discrimination and Demagoguery, NO," *Capital Commentary*, 26 February 2001.

36. Associated Press News Service, "Religious Groups Wary of Bush Plan," 21 February 2001. Several conservatives, such as Michael Horowitz and Marvin Olasky, also voiced concern that the proposals might undermine the independence and genuinely spiritual character of groups involved. On the importance of faith-based groups being able to discriminate on religious grounds in their hiring, see Jeffrey Rosen, "Why the Catholic Church Shouldn't Have to Hire Gays," *The New Republic*, 26 February 2001.

37. "10 Frequently Asked Questions About Religion and Politics," ADL statement, 2000.

38. AUSCC Press Release, 9 August 2000. See also their "God and Election 2000," December 2000.

39. "The 2000 Campaign: The Religion Issue; Lieberman Is Asked to Stop Invoking Faith in Campaign," *New York Times*, 29 August 2000.

40. "Mr. Lieberman's Religious Words," *New York Times*, August 31, 2000.

41. AUSCC Press Releases, 24 February and 29 August 2000.

42. *Newsroom* News Service, 8 September 2000. On the variety of religious political activism in the United States, see J. R. Formicola and H. Morken, *Religious Leaders and Faith Based Politics: Ten Profiles* (Lanham, Md.: Rowman & Littlefield, 2001).

43. "Lieberman Hails Religion's Rising Role in American Public Life," *Washington Times*, 2 March 2001.

44. See Franklin Foer, "The Catholic Teachings of George W.," *The New Republic*, 5 June 2000; Stanley W. Carlson-Thies, "Policy-makers Struggle with Compassionate Conservatism," *Newsroom*, 26 March 2001.

45. "Religious Right Made Big Push to Put Ashcroft in Justice Department," *New York Times*, 21 January 2001.

46. Charles Krauthammer, "The Dem's Double Standard," Column, 21 January 2001.

47. Krauthammer, op. cit.; see also Stark, *One True God*, and, for supporting survey data, Bolce and DeMaio, "Religious Outlook."

48. Paul Weyrich, "An Open Letter to Conservatives Following the Senate Impeachment Vote," 16 February 1999; "Separate and Free," *The Washington Post*, 7 March 1999.

49. Cal Thomas and Ed Dobson, *Blinded by Might: Can the Religious Right Save America?* (Grand Rapids, Mich.: Zondervan, 1999).

50. Thomas and Dobson, *Los Angeles Times*, 24 March 1999.

51. See Joel Carpenter, *Revive Us Again: The Reawakening of American Fundamentalism* (New York: Oxford University Press, 1997), especially chapter 5.

52. Thomas and Dobson, *Blinded by Might*, 37–39.

CHAPTER TWO

~

The Church and the World

The World

To avoid the problem of making too much or too little of politics, it is useful to set it in a wider context, or contexts. One broad context is understanding the place and responsibility of human beings in the world, of which government and politics is merely one part. Without such a general understanding, politics can too easily be thought of as the center of existence or the bane of existence, or both.[1]

For example, one confusion that seems to pervade Thomas' and Dobson's writings denouncing supposed Christian over-involvement in politics is that between the particular role of preachers and the role of believers at large in political activity. In a symposium following their book, *Blinded by Might*, Thomas devoted his remarks to castigating overly political preachers:

> Should those set apart to preach the gospel . . . descend to a lower kingdom . . . of the legions now competing for political power? . . . Preachers already possess a greater power than the world offers. . . . Calvin gave an even sterner warning to clergy who seek to use the way of the world to advance a political . . . agenda. . . . Preachers have spoken. . . . Conservative ministers might. . . . Preachers should not be known. . . .[2]

If the point here intended that clergy should avoid trying to be politicians and instead stick to their own calling within a congregation, then it is wise, but hardly controversial. However, this mundane observation is coupled with

21

cautions that "we," which presumably refers to Christians at large, are too politicized and need to focus our energies elsewhere than politics, as though the claims about clergy and about Christians were the same. But, even apart from the fact that two of the prime targets of their criticism of Christian political leaders, James Dobson (no relation) and Pat Robertson, are not preachers but are, respectively, a psychologist and a lawyer/broadcaster, this seems to betray a confusion about the role of the average believer. After all, the clergy are probably somewhat less than 0.1 percent of professing Christians in North America. The important question is, what should be the political role of the other 99.9 percent?

The rapid political and theological mood swings in evangelical activism we noted earlier are created in part because Thomas and Dobson, and their predecessors, blur the roles of preachers and laity by using a series of naïve theological oppositions and counterpoints that are all but guaranteed to tie them, and political action, in knots. They call, as Dobson had already in 1988, for some kind of "public philosophy." However, their chapter on "Religion and Politics: What Does the Bible Say?" leads merely to the conclusion that we should respect, submit to, and pray for political leaders, which in turn leads to only the practical conclusion that we should not tell demeaning jokes about them.[3] This might, or might not, be true, but it is not much of a public philosophy.

Instead of such a philosophy we are offered stark contrasts between the "church" and the "world," the "earthly" and the "spiritual," the "cultural" and the "political," and confusions over the role of the clergy. Thomas and Dobson stress that Christians follow "a different king who presides over a different kingdom, which [h]e said is 'not of this world,'" and seem to assume, not argue, that this necessarily implies the downgrading of worldly concerns.[4] However, while it is certainly true that there are frequent scriptural injunctions not to love the world, there are frequent injunctions that seem to say just the opposite.[5]

The reason for this is that words translated into English as "world" have several meanings in biblical writings. One meaning refers to the way humans have wrongfully ordered the world, especially society. For example, a more accurate rendition of Rom. 12:2's admonition not to be "conformed to the world" might be "don't be conformed to this age," or "don't do what everybody else does." The Roman Christians were being advised not to follow the ways of the culture in which they lived, but instead live according to the gospel they had received. Another meaning of "world" refers to geography or territory, as in "this gospel will be preached throughout the whole world" (Matt. 24:14).[6]

A third biblical meaning of "world" is "the created order," that which God has made, and made for human beings to live in. Hence, John's gospel says Jesus came "not to condemn the world, but that the world might be saved through him" (John 3:17). That is why the Church saw no contradiction between John's saying, "Do not love the world. . . ." (I John 2:15) and recording Jesus as saying, "For God so loved the world that he gave his only Son. . . ." (John 3:16). The Church understood it to mean that God loves the world he has created and that Christians should not follow contemporary cultural patterns. In this case, a simple opposition between the Church and the world misses a sense of the world as a place God loves as much as the Church.

Thomas also stresses that "real change comes heart by heart, not election by election, because our primary problems are not economic and political but moral and spiritual."[7] But actual political words, acts, and things are invariably economic *and* spiritual, political *and* moral. They need not be merely one or the other, they are usually inextricably intertwined. For example, one of the major features of modern economics is "credit," which means a person's credibility, their believability or trustworthiness. If we trust a person, then we might give them credit because we believe they will pay their debts. No modern economy can work without trust. The words "creed" and "credit" have exactly the same source. Faith, trust, and economy necessarily go hand in hand. As the rest of this book will illustrate, politics is also a matter of the heart, and of spirituality, as well as elections and laws.

Since every human hope, dream, plan, or event can be either evil or good, we need also to be very cautious about dividing up the world into parts that are supposedly good and religious and parts that are not. Both evil and holiness can permeate every dimension of life. Everything (including worship) that is done in the wrong way can be an expression of evil. Prayer can be blasphemous, and bricklaying can be holy. Sermons may be treacherous, and jokes may be healing. The question is, who or what do the sermons and jokes serve? This is shown in the book of Genesis, which stresses that God cares for the world and emphasizes the central role of human beings it.

The Importance of Beginnings

It may seem strange to begin a discussion of politics with Genesis. However, something like this is quite common in talking about government. This is because our views of politics, whoever we are, reflect our more basic beliefs, such as our view of what human beings are. For example, if we think that human nature is relatively constant and unchanging, then we will believe that governments must accommodate and adjust to it rather than struggling, like

Karl Marx, or perhaps Jean-Jacques Rousseau, or perhaps Hillary Clinton, for a new age inhabited by new people. Alternatively, if we think that human beings change in fundamental ways depending on the situation they are in, then we will be much more open to political proposals, from Rousseau or Clinton, to reshape the social order. If we think that human duties are given to us by God, or arise through nature, then we will seek to *discover* those duties. Alternatively, if we believe that the universe outside of ourselves gives us no moral direction, then we will seek to *create* our morality rather than discover it. All political thinking is always embedded in, though not totally reducible to, our view of the world itself.[8]

Obviously, there are a myriad of potential dimensions to such basic views, and these can cover every aspect of religion and philosophy. One key dimension is questions of origins—Where did we come from? How did we begin? How did we get here? This is one reason why Genesis, whose name means the book of origins, the book of beginnings (the same root as genes, generation, and genealogy) is so important. It provides an account of the beginnings of human life and, hence, of human beings' place in the universe.

Descriptions of origins are common, even standard, in influential western political thought, particularly in the last few centuries. Some are elaborate world histories, such as in Giambattista Vico, Georg Hegel, Karl Marx, or Auguste Comte. Others are undeveloped allusions, such as in Thomas Hobbes, John Locke, or Thomas Jefferson. But all of these descriptions provide a framework for understanding more specifically political writings. One key aspect of these portrayals of the origin and development of the human race is depictions of what has gone wrong with us, attempted explanations of how it has happened that the world is full of pain, suffering, and injustice. To answer these questions, many theorists resort to their own version of something like what theologians call "the fall," an account of how human beings have gone from a previous state of nobility, morality, and justice into our present moral squalor. Some, like Augustine or Thomas Aquinas, stick close to a biblical account of the fall which we will describe. Others, like Marx or Rousseau, find the source of our problems in the development of private property, or our entry into civil society. Yet others, like Friedrich Nietzsche or Martin Heidegger, create their own elaborate, developed mythologies or cosmologies. Yet others, like the seventeenth-century English philosopher Locke, unconsciously combine elements from various traditions, including the Bible, classical accounts of a golden age, and material from reports of the seventeenth-century voyages of discovery.

Since Locke's writings have been influential in and for America, he can serve as a useful example of the importance of origins. He described a past golden age of humankind which occurred before "vain ambition, *amor sceleratus habendi* (a vain love of possessions) and evil concupiscence" had afflicted us.[9] He described people living in a "state of nature," without any political authority. He imagined that seventeenth-century America was like this, even saying that "in the beginning all the World was America."[10] But Locke also believed that life in this setting was difficult. While people may have had the moral right to defend themselves, they often lacked the power to do so. They were at the mercy of any band of marauders that came through. Hence, to overcome this lack of power, they came together and made an agreement as to what laws they would create and follow together, and who would have the authority to enforce those laws. This picture of politics as arising out of a voluntary agreement or contract of people is often called a "social contract" theory of government, and it, together with the theory of an original "state of nature," is one of the dominant underlying themes, even mythologies, of western political thought in recent centuries. It tries to give a reason why we should think of politics as arising from a voluntary agreement, and, hence, why laws should be subject to the consent of the people.

In Locke's case, it is not entirely clear whether he thought that such a contract creating political society had, in fact, literally, historically, taken place (there were analogies to it among New England Puritans, such as those who agreed to the Mayflower Compact), or whether he was using it as an interpretive model to illustrate the basic nature and deeper foundations of politics. However, in either case, he tried to justify his understanding of government by an account of its origins.[11]

Hence, beginning a discussion of politics with a story of the origin of human life in Genesis is no parochial or perverse practice. It simply parallels many other contemporary and influential accounts. To those who might object that an account of origins is one thing, but why pick a religious book like Genesis, it should be said that this book is far and away the most influential account of origins in world history. As the beginning book of Judaism, Christianity, and Islam, it lies, nominally at least, at the core of the beliefs of nearly half the human race. Any educated person must pay attention to it. To this we might add that, to believers and nonbelievers, it makes far more sense of the world than most of the competing accounts of origins in modern politics.

The Cultural Mandate

The early command, "Be fruitful and multiply, and fill the earth, and subdue it" (Gen. 1:28), spoken by God to the first man and woman, is often referred to by theologians as "the cultural mandate." It is God's injunction to human beings to develop culture and society upon the earth. Significantly, it comes as the culmination of the story of the creation of the world. This story (Gen. 1:1–2:3) forms a literary whole that is plainly meant to be understood as a unit. It opens with the declaration that God created both the heavens and the earth. The focus then shifts to the earth. Genesis describes how, through eight creative words, God produced the variety of the world out of that which was at first "without form and void."

On the first day darkness was distinguished from light, night from day. On the second day the waters above and below were separated. On the third day the lower waters were divided into dry land and sea, and then the land was filled with vegetation. On the fourth day the lights were made to appear in the heaven—the sun, the moon, and the stars. On the fifth day the air and sea were filled with birds and fishes.

This description of the first five days is not random, as if God had worked at whim. It shows a definite progression of working and shaping, gradually building a world which had been planned from the beginning. God's acts on the sixth day are, hence, not merely the last acts on the list before the seventh day of rest: rather, they are portrayed as the culmination of what God is doing. The sixth day is the day that tells us the point of the whole exercise.

On this day God created the animals, then man and woman. Having made them, their Creator said to them, as the last act in the drama of creation, that they must "be fruitful," and that they had "dominion" over the fish of the sea and over the birds of the air and over every living thing that moves upon the earth. This instruction is presented as the climax of the story of creation, and so reveals God's purpose. Human beings are to be responsible to care for the world that has been made—all of it. After the man and woman have been given their task, after they have been told what they were made for, then the work of creation has been completed. God pronounced it good and rested.

Not only the timing, but the way that the man and woman were created is significant. In all the other acts of creation we are told that God simply said, "[L]et there be. . . . [A]nd it was so." But, on the sixth day, we are told, for the first time, of God first planning the creation of humankind (Gen. 1:26), and only then carrying out the plan (Gen. 1:28). The idea of intention is introduced and we are told what the intention is. It is to make humankind "in our image" and to "have dominion." Thus human "dominion" is described as part of God's creative act; it is built into the very way that the world is made. The cultural mandate is part of a plan of world creation. Human molding of the earth is the continuation of God's creative acts.

Indeed the expression "cultural mandate" may be something of a mis-nomer. "Mandate" means command or instruction. But the emphasis here in Genesis is less on the *instructions* given to human beings and more on the *nature of their creation*. It is not as though God simply made human beings and, since they now happened to be there, decided they needed something to do and so told them what it was. It was not an instruction given after the fact. Rather, it was a plan given before human beings ever appeared.[12] Genesis says that human beings were made with a particular purpose in mind and were created expressly to fulfill that purpose; having dominion is built into human nature. We are portrayed as designer creatures, made in a particular way, with particular gifts, and with particular skills. This purpose is built into human nature itself. If humanity tries to live without responsibility for the creation, it not only defies God's command, but also subverts its created nature.

This mandate also shows something of what it means that human beings are made "in the image" of God. To be in the image of God is to be like God in some way. There are various possible expressions of this image—the New Testament mentions righteousness, holiness, and knowledge. In Genesis it seems specifically to refer to having authority over the creation. Genesis 1:26 is commonly translated "Let us make humankind in our own image, after our likeness; and let them have dominion. . . ." It is better translated, "Let us make humankind in our image . . . in order that they might have dominion." This is a theme found in the Psalms: "Thou hast given him dominion over the works of Thy hands, Thou hast put all things under his feet" (Ps. 8:5–6). One way of being like God is to obey God in having dominion over the earth, to be a steward of the creation, to be fruitful.

The works of the previous days, the command to multiply and have do-minion, the revealing of God's intent, the creation of humankind as God's image, God's resting after giving the mandate—each of these highlights the importance of the mandate that God has given. A central theme of the be-ginning of the Bible is that God made human beings to be responsible for the world.

Sin and Redemption

Of course, this description of a cultural mandate in Genesis passes over many things. The most obvious thing neglected so far is the account of the fall and of sin. After human beings had disobeyed God (Gen. 3), the un-folding of the generations is then always described as marked by sin, cor-ruption, and distortion. Evil affects everything. When Adam and Eve ate of the fruit of the tree, they were separated from God (Gen. 3:8). In turn, they were separated from each other: Adam turned against Eve and blamed her for what had happened (Gen. 3:12). Because of their disobedience he now began to dominate her (Gen. 3:16). The effects of evil even spread beyond human beings themselves. The earth itself became corrupt: "[C]ursed is the ground because of you; in toil you shall eat of it all the days of your lives; thorns and thistles it shall bring forth to you. . . ." (Gen. 3:17–18). Even the act of begetting the further generations became tainted: "[I]n pain you shall bring forth children" (Gen. 3:16). The apostle Paul, in his letter to the Romans, in what is in effect a commentary on Genesis, summarized this whole process as "death spread to all men" (Rom. 5:12), and the "reign of death" (Rom. 5:21), in which "the creation was subjected to futility" and "bondage to decay" so that "the whole creation has been groaning in travail" (Rom. 8:20–22).

This rapidly expanding circle of evil again illustrates the vast responsibility that humans had. Precisely because they were the ones who were to steward the earth, sin is portrayed as having a ripple effect throughout the earth; every relationship in the world became corrupted. Since human beings are inevitably responsible for the earth, no part of the earth can remain immune from the consequences of their actions. Hence, they are divorced from God, from one another, and from the world around them.

But, despite these catastrophic effects, the fall is never described as ending the cultural mandate. Eve still brought forth the generations, Adam still worked the ground. In fact, they could never have stopped fulfilling it, for that is how God had made them. Even though fallen, they, and we, do not cease to work, or play, or bring forth children. But, because of human sin, the drama of filling the earth and shaping life together is always filled with suffering and injustice.

Nor does God desert them. Immediately after the fall and the curse, perhaps in pity for the miserable leaf clothing they had made for themselves, "God made for Adam and for his wife garments of skins, and clothed them" (Gen. 3:21). He also gave aid to Eve to bring forth children (Gen. 4:1), and provided another child to replace the one she had lost (Gen. 4:25). He heard the cry of Abel's blood (Gen. 4:10), and even preserved Abel's murderer, Cain (Gen. 4:15).

Then Noah, who is described as having found favor with the Lord, is announced with the words, "Out of the ground which the Lord has cursed this one shall bring us relief from our work and from the toil of our hands" (Gen. 5:29). With Noah, the toil which came with sin was mitigated. The story of Noah also tells of further judgment because of the way in which people were destroying the earth and perverting their task: "God saw the earth, and behold, it was corrupt; for all flesh had corrupted their way upon the earth"

(Gen. 6:12). To end this continuing evil, God is described as deciding to flood the world but to save a remnant who would carry out their responsibility for the world, and each other, properly.

When Noah and his family and the animals had been saved from the flood, before they were dispersed over the earth, they were once more given the mandate which had been given at the dawn of creation. The mandate has not ended. Even after the fall and the flood, the saved remnant were again told to "be fruitful and multiply, bring forth abundantly on the earth and multiply in it" (Gen. 9:7). To make this task easier Noah's children were now allowed to eat meat (Gen. 9:3), whereas beforehand they had been restricted to eating plants (Gen. 1:29, 30). This is apparently one way in which the promised "relief from the toil of our hands" was brought about.

The Range of Redemption

Noah's act is remarkable. He was called to build an ark not only to save human beings but also to save animals. No doubt if he had taken fewer animals on the boat, he could have taken more people. But this isn't what he did. This fact is too little noted, either in Christian or other circles. Noah should perhaps be declared the patron saint of genuine environmentalism.[13]

With Noah, the cycle of human culture is described as beginning once more. "Noah was the first tiller of the soil" (Gen. 9:20), and from his children "the whole earth was peopled" (Gen. 9:19). Also from these children "the coastland peoples spread" (Gen. 10:5), and from them came Nimrod, "the first on earth to be a mighty man. He was a mighty hunter before the Lord" (Gen. 10:8, 9). Just as the story of the generations of Adam recounts the spreading effect of evil, the story of the generations of Noah asserts that, even after the fall, there was still the same purpose for the stewards of the earth. Human beings were given new help and a fresh start to their task. God established, or re-established, a covenant that never again would the earth be destroyed by flood, and gave the rainbow as the sign of that covenant. It is important to note that this covenant was made not only with Noah and his descendants but also "with every living creature that is with you, the birds, the cattle, and every beast of the earth with you, as many as came out of the ark" (Gen. 9:10). The covenant concerned not just the people but the entire creation.

A stress on the creation-wide range of divine concern occurs throughout the Bible. When the law was given to the people of Israel, its precepts were not devoted exclusively to what moderns might call moral or spiritual concerns. The law was designed to cover all of the dimensions of Israel's relations to God, to each other, and to the earth itself. Detailed instructions were given for their politics, something to which we shall return in later chapters. Guides were laid down for marriage and family life. There were also rules governing what sorts of food they should eat (Lev. 11), how to build safe houses (Deut. 22:8), how to care for the land (Lev. 25:1–7), how to treat animals (Deut. 22:6), how to maintain health (Lev. 12–15), even how to use the bathroom (Deut. 23:12–13). Israel's life was related not only to the commands but to the gifts of God. In the construction of the tabernacle we read: ". . . .[T]he Lord has called Bezalel . . . and he has filled him with the Spirit of God, with ability, with intelligence, with all knowledge and with all craftsmanship, to devise artistic designs, to work in gold and silver and bronze, in cutting stones for setting, and in carving wood, for work in every skilled craft. . . . He has filled [him] with ability. . . ." (Ex. 35:30–35). Artistic design is tied to the infilling of God's Spirit.

Nor is this merely an Old Testament theme which is supposedly replaced in the New Testament. It is a false view that the Old Testament deals with what is external whereas the New Testament deals with what is internal. It is wrong to say that the Old Testament focuses on works whereas the New focuses on faith, or that the former focuses on law and the latter on gospel. In both Testaments redemption is always portrayed as rooted in God's grace, never in human achievement. Equally true is the teaching, in both Testaments, that religious belief always be manifested in each and every type of human activity in the creation.[14]

This is shown in, for example, the apostle Paul's comments about work. Paul continually criticized idleness and exhorted his readers to work (cf. 2 Thess. 3:6). He made no distinctions between physical and spiritual work. In fact he used the same terms to refer both to his apostolic service, and to the manual labor by which he earned a living (1 Cor. 4:12; 15:10; 16:16; Eph. 4:28; Rom. 10:12; Gal. 4:11; Phil. 2:16; Col. 1:29; 1 Thess. 5:12). Often it is difficult to know to which he was referring, or whether he himself was interested in making any such distinction.

For Paul, all different types of work originated in faith. When he outlined the service of the "new nature . . . created after the likeness of God," he urged "doing honest work with [one's] hands." Clearly the new nature he envisioned was not some disembodied, spiritual creature, but had hands fitted for labor. The new person was to work in the world, supply the needs of others, and shape the development of human life (Eph. 4:17–32, esp. v. 28; 2 Cor. 11:9; 12:13; 1 Thess. 4:9–12; 2 Thess. 3:8; Acts 20:35). As in Genesis, this human activity in the creation is related to being in the image and likeness of God.

What Paul wrote about work contrasted sharply with many of the attitudes in the surrounding world. He did not describe religion as a spiritual activity separate from work. He regarded all aspects of life as equally religious and called on his readers to manifest the image of God explicitly through their day-to-day work. The reiteration of this view of work was one of the major features of the Reformation. In contrast to some medieval teaching and practice, which had elevated the contemplative life above all others, the Protestant Reformers emphasized that the priesthood of all believers meant that all of human service was equally divine service to God.[15] Martin Luther wrote:

> If you are a manual laborer, you find that the [B]ible has been put into your workshop, into your hand, into your heart. It teaches and preaches how you should treat your neighbor . . . just look at your tools . . . at your needle and thimble, your beer barrel, your goods, your scales or yardstick or measure . . . and you will read this statement inscribed in them. Everywhere you look, it stares at you. . . . You have as many preachers as you have transactions, goods, tools and other equipment in your house and home.[16]

One of the articles of heresy for which William Tyndale, the father of the English Bible, was convicted was that he had said, "There is no work better than another to please God: to pour water, to wash dishes, to be a souter (cobbler) or an apostle, all is one; to wash dishes and to preach is all one, as touching the deed, to please God."[17] In Luther and Tyndale, as in Paul and Genesis, religion and redemption related not just to spiritual or pious duties, but for the entire way believers live in the world.

Hence, the story of creation and the cultural mandate in Genesis is not some obscure part of scripture. It is given at the very beginning of the biblical record to announce the purpose of human life. It teaches that humanity is not a set of apprentice angels better suited to and awaiting existence on another spiritual plane (see also Heb. 2:5–9). Human beings are made for the earth and charged with the task of cultivating the world. The rainbow after the fall was a sign for "every living creature of all flesh" (Gen. 9:12, 15, 16, 17) that God would keep faith with all of the creation.

The earliest chapters of Genesis describe a pattern. Human beings are set in the world as bearers of the divine image with a task to perform. They pervert this task. But God forgives them and directs them back onto their path. Sin corrupts but it does not change the human calling. Human beings are still those called to be the stewards of the earth. Obedience to God is still to be manifested in service in all dimensions of earthly, human existence. Human history and culture still go on.

Human culture, and the world itself, also requires renewal. In the letter to the Romans, Paul wrote:

> For the creation waits with eager longing for the revelation of the sons of God; for the creation was subject to futility, not of its own will but by the will of him who subjected it in hope; because the creation itself will be set free from its bondage to decay and obtain the glorious liberty of the children of God. We know that the whole creation has been groaning in travail together until now, and not only the creation, but we ourselves, who have the first fruits of the spirit, groan inwardly as we wait for adoption as sons, the redemption of our bodies. (Rom. 8:19–23)

He wrote that the creation itself suffers because of the sin of its stewards. The creation itself waits eagerly for freedom from oppression. The creation itself will be set free just as (and because) humans are set free. Redemption is not to be limited to any one area of the creation. Not only people, but nations, kingdoms—the entire creation—will be reconciled. There will be, not the abolition of earth, but a new heaven and a new earth wherein justice dwells (Rev. 11:15; 21:1–5).

In modern English, the word "creation," apart from its occasional contrasts with "evolution," carries the connotation of "nature," the natural, as opposed to the human, world. But this is not biblical usage. Creation includes the human as well as the natural. Hence, responsibility for the creation extends far beyond the boundaries of the natural world—of earth, oceans, and sky. Human beings are also part of creation. Stewardship includes human life as well as the rest of nature. "It includes Mozart as well as mountains; parliaments as well as porpoises; friendships as well as fields and forests. What began in the Garden of Eden culminates in a city—the New Jerusalem. Creation includes culture as well as nature."[18] The scriptural teaching is that God is not concerned with rescuing people from human existence, or concerned only with the internal life of believers, or concerned only with the internal relations of the religious community itself. Redemption concerns the reconciliation of all things within the creation.[19] God is concerned about architecture, about food and furniture, about poverty and suffering, about play, art, and music, about neighborhoods and economics, about animals and trees, about sex and intimacy, and about politics.

Religion, Creation, and Politics

An understanding of God as concerned with all of human life shows that a division of religious concern between the church and the world, the spiritual and the earthly, the inner and the outer, is false. God's Kingdom is not *of*, that is, it does not conform to the pattern of the world—but it does come into this world, and to no other. Hence, the idea that politics must be inherently less important than the doings of pastors or priests is contradicted by biblical testimony. So is the idea that external laws are of no importance compared to inner change.

Cal Thomas, Ed Dobson, Paul Weyrich, and others of similar views are skeptical about what changes can actually be produced by political action. Clearly such skepticism is nearly always justified, since the possibilities of politics are so often and easily overestimated. But several of their sentiments are misplaced precisely because they are rooted in these stark contrasts between church and world, inner and outer, and divine and human. Thomas and Dobson write that "religious conservatives, no matter how well organized, can't save America, only God can." But this says nothing particular about religious conservatives or any other political group: the entire force of the sentence lies in the juxtaposition of conservatives and God, in that ultimately only God can save. But the same stark juxtaposition can be applied to anything. We might as well say that the church (or drug treatment programs, newspaper columns, books, sermons, prayers, virtue, or strong families) cannot save America, only God can. This is no doubt equally true. But such sentences say nothing, of course, about the importance of drug treatment, churches, prayers, families, politics, or anything else.

The authors also contrast the spiritual and the political: "[P]olitics and government cannot reach into the soul. That is something God reserves for himself." This, again, relies for its strength on a juxtaposition with God. But nothing else can do what God can do, including sermons, prayers, and Bible readings. However, this again tells us nothing about the relative importance of these other things. Similar comments can be made about the claim that "these wrongs require spiritual help, not merely political adjustment."[20] After all, everything requires spiritual help, but that does not mean that they don't also require political adjustment. Even political adjustment requires spiritual help.

It is true that governments and laws don't necessarily change people's hearts. But that doesn't mean that laws are useless. Sometimes just changing people's behavior, no matter what is going on inside their hearts and heads, is vitally important. There's a twenty-five-mile-per-hour speed limit on the road outside, and people generally respect it because they don't want to get a speeding ticket. Maybe most of them, in their heart of hearts, would do fifty if they could get away with it. But they can't, so they don't. And since, now, the children on the street are safer, that's a good thing in itself, even though the motorists' hearts remain as unchanged as before. Similarly, the law may not stop one person hating another, but it may stop him from murder, and that's very important, especially for the one who is hated. The law may not keep someone from lust, but it can keep him or her from rape. That too is important.

Also, while laws cannot change someone's heart directly, they do shape our behavior, and, in turn, our behaviors can become our habits, and our habits help shape our patterns of mind and heart. After a time, we may begin to think and feel differently. Parents know this from dealing with their children. We establish rules for children and, of course, know that the rules will not immediately change what is inside them. They keep the rules partly to please us, partly to escape disapproval or punishment. But we also know that if they learn to act politely, work hard, and respond forthrightly, then they are more likely to grow up as polite, diligent, and honest people. Laws and other rules can shape our inner lives, albeit slowly.[21]

These authors also describe the political world as full of compromise and conflict. This is certainly true. Politics is dirty and corrupt, or at least it can be. But this is no more reason to steer clear of politics than of anything else. Churches can be dirty and corrupt, too. There can be lying, greed, bribery, and a panoply of other sins—just as in the New Testament church. Paul's first letter to the Corinthians gives a rich catalog of the mischief that churches can get into. Or read history. Christian theologians stress something called "original sin," something on which we have already touched. This means, amongst other things, that every human being and every human activity and every human institution is affected by sin: no exceptions. The church is no exception. In fact, in the wider public mind, the expression "evangelicalism" is often synonymous with trickery. And, in any case, evil places are precisely where good people are supposed to go and bring change.

Finally, the authors say that a "trickle-down" morality is "the only process that actually works."[22] But here their image of politics remains that of their Moral Majority days, as if politics were only concerned with moral renewal in society. The actual nature and strengths of politics are ignored. The possibly beneficial effects of laws and policies are slighted. The welfare reforms of 1997 seem to have led to many people being able to support themselves, and this can change many other things in their lives. Recent changes in police practice have brought about dramatic drops in U.S. rates of murder, rape, and robbery, especially against the poor and needy. These beneficial changes can also bring changes in personal morality.

Further afield, we have just completed the bloodiest century in human history. Political ideologies have led to the deaths of hundreds of millions of people. While these ideologies certainly needed to be, and were, combated in the realm of ideas and individual morality, they also had to be opposed militarily and, hence, politically. In May of 1940, Britain almost sought a peace treaty with Hitler, which would necessarily have amounted to a virtual surrender. Hitler could have consolidated his position in Europe and perhaps defeated Russia. He could have dominated the world. The British decision hinged on debates within the Cabinet and War Cabinet from May 24 to May 28, debates in which Winston Churchill pushed furiously and successfully to resist any compromise with the Nazis.[23] The political decision to fight on de-termined the fate of the world in the last half of the twentieth century. With-out such political moves, then social renewal, "trickle-up morality," or talk of changing hearts would have effected little. Millions more would have died and millions more would have lived in slavery. Politics involves matters in the world that are vitally important, and for which there is no substitute. It is a fundamental part of creation in which we were made to live.

Notes

1. On this, see H. M. Kuitert, *Everything Is Politics but Politics Is Not Everything* (Grand Rapids, Mich.: Eerdmans, 1986).

2. Cal Thomas, "Have We Settled for Caesar?" *Christianity Today* (6 September 1999).

3. On this point, I am indebted to Keith Pavlischek's review in the *Christian Century* (May 19–26, 1999): 587.

4. Cal Thomas and Ed Dobson, "The Message Remains True, but the Method Must Change," *The Washington Post*, 24 March 1999.

5. The following sections are adapted from Paul Marshall, *Heaven Is Not My Home: Learning to Live in God's Creation* (Nashville, Tenn.: Word, 1998).

6. Revised Standard Version (RSV) Bible quoted here.

7. Thomas, "Have We Settled for Caesar?" 48.

8. This is true even if our view of the cosmos is that there is no true view of the cosmos.

9. See P. Laslett, ed., *John Locke: Two Treatises on Government* (Cambridge: Cam-bridge University Press, 1960), *Second Treatise*, paragraph 3. See also paragraphs 107, 108.

10. Laslett, *John Locke*, paragraph 49.

11. The most systematic recent attempt to dissociate a social contract type of theory from an account of origins is in John Rawls' A *Theory of Justice* (Cambridge: Harvard University Press, 1973). Rawls uses an imaginative construct of people making decisions while ignorant of what situation they will occupy in society. However, in his later writings, he has needed to stress that what he offers cannot be a general theory of politics, but only a clarification of what he thinks are the dominant American views.

12. In the same way, much law should be understood not as an external command but as an internal principle, as in the law of gravity. On this, see Al Wolters, *Creation Regained* (Grand Rapids, Mich.: Eerdmans, 1985).

13. There is a frequent accusation made in secular circles that Christianity's view of human stewardship of the creation is responsible for the ecological crisis. This view is historical nonsense. For a good critique, see Steven Bouma-Prediger, "Is Christianity Responsible for the Ecological Crisis?" *Christian Scholar's Review* (December 1995): 146–56.

14. See my "Calling, Work and Rest," in *The Best of Theology*, vol. 3, ed. J. I. Packer (Carol Stream, Ill.: Christianity Today, 1989), 193–212.

15. On the development of Protestant views of work and calling, see my A *Kind of Life Imposed on Man: Vocation and Social Order from Tyndale to Locke* (Toronto: University of Toronto Press, 1996).

16. Martin Luther, *Works*, vol. 21 (St. Louis, Mo.: Concordia, 1956), 237.

17. William Tyndale, "A Parable of the Wicked Mammon" (1527) in his *Doctrinal Treatises and Portions of Holy Scripture* (Cambridge: Parker Society, 1848), 98.

18. Marshall, *Heaven Is Not My Home*, 23.

19. In this sense sin should not be understood as a thing in its own right, but always as the corruption of a thing. It is a type of parasite. Richard Mouw correctly says that error is usually "distorted truth." See his *Distorted Truth* (Pasadena, Calif.: Fuller Seminary, 1999). I have given the biblical theme of creation more prominence than it should have vis-à-vis redemption, though of course they should not be played off against each other, since it is the creation itself that is redeemed. My strong stress on creation is intended as a small counterbalance to the general neglect of this theological theme. A more rounded view of biblical theology would have to give as much prominence to other themes.

20. Cal Thomas and Ed Dobson, *Blinded by Might: Can the Religious Right Save America?* (Grand Rapids, Mich.: Zondervan, 1999), 8, 44.

21. See Robert George, *Making Men Moral* (New York: Oxford University Press, 1995).

22. "The Message Remains True."

23. See John Lukacs, *Five Days in London* (New Haven: Yale University Press, 1999).

~

CHAPTER THREE

The Beginning of Politics and Justice

Cain and Punishment

As with the story of human responsibility for the world discussed in the previous chapter, the biblical account of the beginning of political development unfolds in the earliest chapters of Genesis. In the story of Adam and Eve's son, Cain, we find the appearance of an authority to uphold justice.[1] Cain murdered his brother Abel, and then we are told that the Lord appeared to him and said, "The voice of your brother's blood is crying to me from the ground" (Gen. 4:10). The word translated here as "crying" or "crying out" is *ze'aqah*. The same word is used frequently throughout the Old Testament to mean the cry, complaint, or appeal of one who is suffering injustice. It is the word used to describe the lament of the poor and needy which led to the destruction of Sodom and Gomorrah (Gen. 18:20; Ezek. 16:49).[2] It was the plea of Israel during their years of slavery (Exod. 2:23, 24).

"Crying out" was also a more technical legal term. It is similar to the current legal term "appeal," when a higher court is called to judge the action of a lower court. Similarly, the use of "crying" implies that if a human court does not fulfill its duty to defend the wronged, then the cry will come to God, who is the final court, judge, and guardian of all justice. Hence, the use of the term "crying out" to describe God's appearance in response to Abel's death shows that it is being described in early judicial terms. God appeared to Cain as a judge, as a governing authority.

In keeping with this role, there was a judicial verdict and sentence. God declared to Cain: "Now you are cursed from the ground . . . when you till the ground, it shall no longer yield you its strength; you shall be a fugitive and a wanderer in the earth" (Gen. 4:12). Cain then complained that this was a greater punishment than he could bear and he, mistakenly, described his punishment as twofold: "Thou hast driven me this day away from the ground [i.e., to be a wanderer]; and from thy face shall I be hidden [i.e., to be unprotected]" (Gen. 4:14).

At this point God responded, "Not so!" God was not saying that the punishment would be made easier, nor that Cain really didn't deserve the punishment, nor that Cain couldn't really bear the punishment. God said that Cain had misunderstood the second part of what the punishment actually was. Whereas Cain thought he was going to be also hidden from the face of God (as well as simply being a fugitive and a wanderer from the face of the ground), God corrected him and said this was not so. The significance of this is that, when Cain complained that he would be hidden from God's face, he was terrified that he would be denied God's judicial protection (so, "whoever finds me will kill me" [Gen. 4:14]). The implication of God "hiding his face" is that God would remove himself, would not respond to the cry of the people, that God would be silent and not come to His people's defense. This is also outlined in Psalm 27, which reads: "When evildoers assail me . . . I will inquire in his temple. . . . Hear, O Lord, when I cry aloud. . . . Thou hast said, 'Seek ye my face.' My heart says to thee, 'thy face, Lord, do I seek.' Hide not thy face from me. Turn not thy servant away in anger, thou who hast been my help. Cast me not off, forsake me not. . . ."[3]

The imagery is that, when God's face is revealed, righteousness and justice prevails. When God's face is hidden, evil prospers and the wicked triumph. Hence, Cain, as a murderer, was not afraid that he would have to keep hiding from God's face. His fear was exactly the opposite: that, against his own will, he would always be hidden from God, so that he would never have a protector, a defender. He was terrified that, in the future, no righteousness or justice would be available to him, so that people could use or abuse him as they liked without any fear of retribution. Cain was afraid that he would become a literal outlaw, one whom the law had abandoned and would not protect. This was the fate that Cain mistakenly believed was his.

It is to *this* part of Cain's complaint that God firmly replied, "Not so!" There would still be justice—even for Cain. God's face would remain upon him. When Cain said "Whoever finds me will kill me," God, following legal formula, announced a verdict that "if anyone slays Cain, vengeance shall be taken on him sevenfold." The "sevenfold" here indicates "rightly," "justly," or "completely," seven being a repeated scriptural number signifying perfection or completeness. There would always be a penalty for any attack on Cain. Contrary to what Cain had thought, he was still under God's protection, still under God's order of justice, still before God's face.

In saying this, God put a "mark" on Cain. This mark was provided in case anyone should try to kill him (Gen. 4:15). Despite popular myth, this mark of Cain was not some sort of curse—a brand that would always identify him as a murderer and an outcast. Rather, it was a mark intended to protect him, to prevent him from being killed. It was a mark testifying that God would still defend him from lawlessness and would justly avenge any attack on him. In fact, the "mark of Cain" was probably not a visual sign at all. It was more likely a verbal sign, a word, a testimony given to Cain in the same way that God's verbal assurance to Moses was a "sign" (Exod. 3:12). The sign was the very word that God spoke, the actual assurance that God's justice would be maintained.

In the story of Cain a legal order appeared. Penalties were established for Cain's murder of Abel but, in turn, Cain himself was not left to suffer anarchy. This order incorporated both Cain and anyone who would seek private revenge on him. The mark of Cain was not merely particular to Cain as an individual: it was also a sign that God had appointed an order to maintain justice. This order embraced all human beings and demanded that they treat each other as God intended.

After his judgment by God, Cain went away, married, had children, and founded a city. His generations are described briefly until the story of his great, great, great grandson, Lamech. Lamech boasted, "I have slain a man for striking me. . . . If Cain is avenged sevenfold, truly [I] (am avenged) seventy-seven fold" (Gen. 4:23, 24). Then, immediately, the narrative stops. We switch back to Adam and Eve and follow the generations of another one of their sons, Seth. To Seth was born Enoch, and, "At that time men began to call on the name of the Lord" (Gen. 4:26).

The story of a new generation was introduced, and the story of Lamech and his generations was abruptly broken off, precisely at the point at which it became clear that with Lamech the generations of Cain descended into terrible evil. Lamech refused to honor a just order. Instead of giving a proper, "sevenfold" response to an attack, he avenged a mere blow with death itself, a "seventy-seven fold" vengeance. With Lamech there was no justice, only revenge; no measure, only anger. He reacted with a barbarism that struck out at his enemy, with no concern at all for just relationships.

In Lamech, a generation abandoned its responsibility for justice. It refused to respect the mark of Cain and, instead, substituted naked force and vengeance. Hence, Genesis immediately gives up on Lamech's line and switches to another generation.

The story of Cain says that, just as plowing, hunting, city-building, and music-making appeared on the earth in the earliest generations, there also appeared an order which was to be an order of justice. It was what we would now call a legal or political order, complete with judgments distinct from primitive self-defense and anarchy. Humankind was given the responsibility to respect and follow the rules that God had decreed. As the earliest history of human beings is described in the Bible, a legal authority appeared, and this authority was to uphold justice, a "seven-fold vengeance."

Coercion and Evil

The story of Cain raises questions about the relations between sin, politics, and coercion. These questions have been a major feature of, and problem for, political theology and political philosophy for millennia. It was often thought, by Augustine, for example, that since government involves coercion, it cannot be part of the original good creation, but is something that could only come into existence because of sin, and, hence, will last only as long as evil does. However, since evil appears almost at the very beginning of Genesis, virtually every human action and institution is described in the Bible as appearing only after the fall and, consequently, as being affected by sin.

This is true of, for example, music-making—which also appeared in the generations of Cain (Gen. 4:21). But, while we may have our doubts about much of what comes over MTV these days, it is doubtful that music only came into existence because of sin. It depends on the song sung. Similarly, the use of bricks and tar is first described as part of the building of the tower of Babel, a project conceived in pride (Gen. 11:3–5). But this, presumably, does not mean that building is wrong. Many fundamental features of human life appeared only when sin already existed in the world, and took their shape partly in reaction to that existence.

Because of these and other examples, it is not necessary to conclude from the story of Cain, or from Genesis itself, that politics and law are only necessary because of evil. An answer to this question would depend on how we conceive of government, and the law and justice associated with it. Does it have only a negative task—the restraint of evil—or also a positive task, such as promoting and shaping justice between people? Such a positive task could be rooted in the way God has made the world, and would continue to be part of human responsibility even after evil had been swept away. Revelation says that kings will bring their glory—and the honor of the nations—into the New Jerusalem, suggesting that the political enterprise may have its own intrinsic merit even apart from the effects of sin (Rev. 21:24–26). The story of Cain teaches that the formation of law and politics has an intrinsic connection with justice and injustice. Law is meant to rectify wrongs, punish evil, and uphold right relations between people.

One of government's tasks is punishing people, but, of course, people usually do not want to be punished. This highlights the question of compulsion and coercion, something that hardly seems to be addressed in the Bible. Instead, it seems to be accepted throughout that, in order to perform their task, political authorities may have to compel people to follow their dictates, and that this may require the use of force. This is not so much taught, as it seems to be assumed, as a fact of life. While many particular instances of political force are condemned, the practice, in itself, is not. It seems to be accepted that, in the context of sin, if the government could not use compulsion to carry out its duties, it simply would not be able to carry out those duties at all, and so it would simply cease to exist. Consequently, the possibility of a just political order would also cease to exist.

While government itself need not necessarily be seen as existing only because of evil, it does seem that the coercive element of government only arises because of evil. It is hard to conceive of why people would need to be compelled to do something if they had done and will do no wrong. Consequently, Christians, and others, have always found it difficult to know the degree to which they may properly be involved in coercive activity. This has been a major challenge posed by groups such as Mennonites and other Anabaptists, who are often committed to nonviolence. But it is a question that goes far beyond issues of warfare or policing or prison services.

The compulsory and coercive aspects of government are not confined to military and police functions; they permeate the enterprise itself. It is hard to see how basic functions, such as collecting taxes, could continue if they were not compulsory. If we knew that there would be little or no consequence if we did not pay our taxes, then few people would pay them. If there were no penalty for evading our taxes, and if the I.R.S. merely sent out polite notes each year asking whether we would send something, then the government would likely not exist beyond next Friday. In our situation, the question of coercion in government becomes extremely difficult to separate from the question of government itself. Apparently, in a wicked world, if there is no coercion, there is no government.

Since people who had the duty to exercise coercion, such as judges, lawgivers, and kings, were frequently commended in the Bible, this suggests that compulsion is a proper human responsibility. Hence, we should accept the disciplines, including coercion, involved in government. However, at the same time, we should not lose sight of the fact that coercion is not something that God intended from the beginning. Hence, it is never something in which to rejoice, and something to be accepted easily. It must always be used with restraint. We should avoid violence and coercion whenever possible, and never be hungry for punitive actions and coercive measures, either against other countries or lawbreakers. One positive way of putting this is that the more politics reflects God's will, the less coercion there will be.

Power

The story of Cain also highlights the question of power. This notion of power can be troubling, even if it does not involve outright coercion. After all, exercising power hardly seems to show the willingness to be last and to suffer that Jesus called for. And power is easily perverted. Lord Acton famously said that "power corrupts and absolute power corrupts absolutely." The more power we have, the more evil we can do. Power is all too frequently used to exploit others. Many contemporary social theorists, especially religious ones, have called for the abolition of a "power model" of society, organizations, and hierarchical structures. They brand these as remnants of oppressive, discredited, and often, patriarchal ways. In their place they call for an ethic of sharing and equal community. Circles that stress nonviolence warn of the seductions of power politics and instead urge us to take up the role of servants.

But there is no particular virtue in being helpless, or refusing to exercise power when the world (or the Church) is engaged in oppression and injustice. We also appreciate good leaders. Anyone who has sat through an unstructured meeting with, ostensibly, no one in charge, and where no one will make a firm proposal for fear of upsetting anyone else, knows the yearning for proper structure and authority, for someone to take responsibility.

In any case, in the end we all do and will exercise power. Some do so with sneaking guilt. Others just accept power and its consequences uncritically, whether it is the coercion that lies behind much political power, or the demeaning of others that can be produced by thoughtless intellectual power in argument.[4] There are many forms of power over people, including wealth, appointed office, intelligence, access to information, charisma, skill, physical strength, and military means. There is also power over things, like cars and computers. Nor does power exist only in large-scale settings; we can speak of a powerful argument, a powerful computer, or (rarely) a powerful sermon. Anything which can accomplish a goal is a form of power.

The Bible stresses that legitimate power comes from God and belongs to God (Matt. 26:64; John 19:11). The New Testament gives explicit attention to Jesus' power and emphasizes that this is a manifestation of his kingdom (Mark 4:14; 5:17; 11:20–22). In turn, this divine power is delegated to human beings in the form of authority or office (Gen. 1:26–28; Ps. 8:5–8). These offices include those within the Church, such as bishops or elders, and also those in the world at large, such as presidents or teachers. All proper human power and authority is seen as power delegated from God, held as an office or a position of authority by human beings.

While it may be true that power corrupts, it is also true that an unwillingness to use legitimate power can and will corrupt. The Western powers' refusal to intervene meaningfully in the genocides in Rwanda and Sudan has allowed the death of millions. We must be cautious with power, even suspicious of it, and we must always judge its forms and ends. But we can never escape the responsibility to exercise power. We *will* exercise power; the only question is *how* we will.

It may also help to use a common distinction between "power" (often understood as the mere ability to achieve something) and "authority" (understood as legitimate power). This is close to the New Testament's distinction of *dunamis* (cf. 11 Cor. 8:3; Eph. 3:16) and *exousia* (Matt. 21:23–27). The late philosopher Hannah Arendt went so far as to treat these two as opposites: that people begin to use power when they have no authority. But we do not need to contrast them quite that sharply in order to benefit from the distinction.

The existence of legitimate authority includes the crucial fact that even power over people need not be exercised contrary to the will of those subject to it. Many forms of power (especially those in politics) stem from leadership which wins people over voluntarily and gladly. This is something that any good preacher or political leader exemplifies. Abraham Lincoln's words awoke, shaped, and moved the Union before and during the Civil War. Even as the leader of an empire, one of the greatest powers that Winston Churchill had was his use of words. His speeches roused and mobilized the British people to face Hitler with an immovable resolve, without which their armaments would have been mere lumps of metal. In a less elevated vein, current Federal Reserve Chairman, Alan Greenspan, can affect the U.S. economy by the authority of his utterances almost as much as his power to shape interest rates directly. A great general commands not merely by military discipline and threat, but by inspiring those who are commanded. The power to face death comes more often from inspiration than fear.

The form of power properly called authority is something which we should and must exercise. The use of this authority is in turn tied not only to official position but also to the skills we have. When we have a particular knowledge and talent, whether healing, administration, judging, preaching, or auto maintenance, we thereby already have a real, factual authority in that area because we have an ability. Knowledge and skill are always types of authority. We should, and usually do, follow good administrators in organizations, accept good medical advice in health, and learn from wise elders. In each case we are recognizing an authority, a power, which comes from skill and knowledge; at the same time, we are conferring that authority and submitting to it.

The key to using power well is not by avoiding it in a desperate search for a nowhereland where none is ever subject to another. Rather, by knowing our strengths and temptations, we can recognize and submit to knowledge and ability.[5] The power that lies at the heart of the political order can be and often is misused, but it is itself a gift to be used wisely.

Doers of Justice

After the story of Cain, the next figure to whom Genesis devotes major attention is Noah. Noah is not only a person entrusted with saving people and animals, he was also a bearer of new human political responsibilities. As with Abel, God said to Noah, "For your lifeblood I will surely require a reckoning" (Gen. 9:5). However, unlike the situation with Cain and Abel, when God had appeared directly as a judge, this "accounting" was now no longer God's sole responsibility—it was to be shared with human beings. In Genesis 9:6, after the Ark had landed, and as part of the renewal of the cultural mandate, God stressed to Noah and his family their responsibility for dealing with injustice, saying "who sheds the blood of man, *by man* shall his blood be shed, for God made man in His own image."

Many discussions of this text focus only on the issue of capital punishment. But here I want to emphasize not what the penalty was, but who was supposed to apply the penalty. With Cain, it was God who appeared and judged directly. But now, the response is "by man." Human beings were charged with the responsibility for dealing with injustice themselves. They were no longer simply to wait for God's appearance, but were to be active. A new vocation had been given. Human beings were to be not only planters and herders and artists—they were to be judges as well. As Noah and his offspring spread throughout the world, they took with them the task of maintaining a just order in human relations. Judicial responsibility had been delegated to humankind.

This new responsibility is further elaborated when, after the stories of Cain and Noah, we find the history of Abraham and his children. Here the biblical focus is now on the people chosen to be the bearers of the Messiah, the redeemer of the whole earth. God is still described occasionally as intervening directly and maintaining justice, as with Sodom and Gomorrah (Gen. 18:20; Ezek. 16:49) and with Sarah (Gen. 12:17). But, increasingly, we find growing and changing human responsibility for maintaining a just order.

Abraham, as the father of a family, which by this point has become a clan or mini-tribe, functioned as the family lawmaker and rule giver. He was the chief of the tribe as well as the priest. For Abraham, as in many tribal settings, parental and political authorities were not distinguished. When he divided the land up between himself and his nephew, Lot, he appeared to be exercising both roles at once (Gen. 13:2–12).

Later, when he rescued Lot from warring kings, he refused to take anything except what was rightfully owed him (Gen. 14:13–16, 21–24). Abraham is here portrayed as one who did not seize whatever he could get away with, or even what he could rightfully claim, but, instead, as one who maintained a just response to violence, something for which he was later praised by the "priest of God Most High," Melchizedek (Gen. 14:18–20). Abraham was introduced as one who had a concern for, and knowledge of, justice. Consequently, later, when God was contemplating destroying the cities of the plain, he said, "Shall I hide from Abraham what I am about to do? . . . No, for I have chosen him that he may charge his children and his household after him to keep the way of the Lord by doing righteousness and justice. . . ." (Gen. 18:17–19). Abraham had been chosen to maintain and to continue dispensing justice throughout the generations. He was also to teach others how to do justice. It was because of this vocation that God decided to tell him that Sodom and Gomorrah were going to be destroyed.

Abraham's response to God showed his awareness of the nature of and need for justice. He actually began to argue with God about it: "Wilt thou indeed destroy the righteous with the wicked . . . suppose there are fifty righteous? . . . Far be it from thee to do such a thing, to slay the righteous with the wicked, so that the righteous fare as the wicked! Far be that from thee! Shall not the judge of all the earth do right?" (Gen. 18:23–25). Abraham said that, since God is the judge of all the earth, then God's requirement of justice covers all humankind, including those outside the chosen people, even those in Sodom and Gomorrah. He then argued that justice means we cannot treat the righteous and the wicked in the same way, but that each must be rewarded rightly ("do right") according to their deeds. He pressed the point home: "what if there are forty-five [righteous in the city]? . . . or forty? . . . or ten?" (Gen. 18:26–32). In the end we are told that God yielded to Abraham's arguments about justice and decided not to punish the cities if there were ten righteous people left in them. Abraham questioned God on the basis of divine promise and justice itself. Abraham is presented in scripture as one who knows and dispenses justice, and who will teach this to the generations.

Changing Political Order

For a time, the types of political and parental authority embodied in Abraham remained intertwined but, by the time of Moses, there were major changes. Exodus describes God's calling out of Moses as choosing the one to answer the *ze'aqah*, the outcry for justice of Israel in Egypt (Exod. 3:7, 10). In response, Moses returned to Egypt and eventually delivered Israel from captivity. He led them through the wilderness and gave them the law for their lives—how they were to live in the promised land. Moses was no longer a father-ruler of a family tribe, a patriarch, like Abraham; he was simply a lawgiver and judge. In Moses, parental and political authority became distinct.

At Sinai, Moses received the Law which provided the order for Israel's life together as people, as families, and as a nation. Israel, in turn, covenanted to love God and to keep the commandments. Moses declared laws concerning marriage, adultery, theft, murder, manslaughter, debt, land ownership, house ownership, legal testimony, dealing with foreigners—the whole range of relations and duties which would be required in the new nation. He then called the elders of the people to witness the law and to carry out its decisions and consequences. Israel took upon itself the implementation of God's law.

This implementation showed great flexibility. For example, Moses began by being the only judge in Israel. Consequently, as might be expected, "the people were standing round him from morning till evening" (Exod. 18:13, NJB). His Midianite father-in-law, Jethro, noticed this and gave him some fatherly advice: "What you are doing is not right. You will only tire yourself out, and the people with you too, for the work is too heavy for you. You cannot do it all yourself." Jethro followed up with a few suggestions: "Your task is to represent the people to God, to lay their cases before God, and to teach them the statutes and laws. . . . [C]hoose men who are trustworthy and incorruptible, and put them in charge . . . as heads of thousands, hundreds, fifties and tens, and make them the people's permanent judges. They will re-fer all important matters to you, but all minor matters they will decide them-selves, so making things easier for you. . . ." (Exod. 18:17–22, NJB).

Jethro, an outsider, a priest of Midian, saw that Israel needed more than one judge and, so, proposed to have a number of judges with additional courts of appeal. Moses was to be the judge of final appeal, the Supreme Court of Israel, so to speak. He was also to teach the law to the people and lay the cases before God. While it was left open to see whether God approved this advice (Exod. 18:23, NJB), the whole process seems remarkably prag-matic and easygoing. A non-Israelite saw a major problem in the adminis-tration of the law, and suggested a whole scale revision of the entire way Is-rael was governed. His suggestions were then followed.

Later, when Israel had settled in the land, they did evil and, in turn, were plundered by their enemies. To deal with this, the Lord raised up more judges, who "saved them out of the power of those who plundered them" (Judg. 2:16). We also read that "the Spirit of the Lord came upon" the judges (Judg. 3:10, 6:34; 11:29; cf. Isa. 42:1, 54:21). Unlike Moses, who carried out priestly as well as legal tasks, these new judges appeared to be quite distinct from the priests. Hence, in the book of Judges we find a growing, though not complete, distinction of parental, priestly, and political authority. Since the judges now included women, such as Deborah (Judg. 4, 5), political author-ity was not paternal, patriarchal authority. There were now distinct roles of parent, priest, and judge, each having authority from, and responsibility to, God for a specific office and duty.

Later in Judges (8:27ff; 9:1ff) and in 1 Samuel 8, Israel is described as seek-ing to pervert political authority by putting a king in the place of the judges, a king who would exercise authority in place of God. Gideon resisted this call (Judg. 8:23), but Abimelech, after murdering his brothers, arranged to have himself proclaimed king. He then initiated a reign of violence and slaughter (Judg. 9) until God returned his evil upon his own head (Judg. 9:56).

During the time of Samuel, the people again called for a king. This time they had two reasons for doing so. One was that Samuel's sons were pervert-ing justice (1 Sam. 8:3). The other was that they wanted to "be like all the nations." Like Gideon, Samuel warned them of the possible dire conse-quences that could come with having a king (1 Sam. 8:11–18). Nevertheless, God instructed him to "hearken to their voice and make them a king" (1 Sam. 8:22).

Apparently Israel wanted a king, in part, for the wrong motives—in order to make war in imitation of the nations about them. But God went along with their request anyway, declaring that the king "shall save my people from the hand of the Philistines, for I have seen the affliction of my people, because their cry has come to me" (1 Sam. 9:16). Despite Israel's bad motives and their desire to put a king in God's place (1 Sam. 8:7–9, 10:19), God is still described as appointing a king as an action of restoration and justice. Israel now needed a king to defend them. Also, perhaps Samuel could not see the injustice his own sons were doing as judges, and God had to supplement the judges' role.

When the king was installed, Samuel told the people of the rights and duties of kingship, and wrote them down in a book (1 Sam. 10:25). The king was to be no absolute ruler, but was bound to follow God's law, and the people were to be educated in that law so that they could judge the king and call him to account. The first king, Saul, began his kingship by abiding by the ordinances of God (1 Sam.11:12–15), and Samuel announced: "behold, the Lord has set a king over you . . . and if both you and the king who reigns over you will follow the Lord your God, it will be well" (1 Sam.12:13, 14). The king became the anointed of the Lord (1 Sam. 26:8–12) and, later, Solomon was also known as Jedidiah, the "beloved of Yahweh" (2 Sam. 12:24, 25). A full institution of kingship arrived in Israel. Although we are told Israel desired it wrongfully, at least in part, God was seen as graciously providing it, and making it a source of blessing and justice.[6]

Later still, the prophets evolved from out of the seers (1 Sam. 9:9). The prophets took up a role of challenging the kings and priests and judges, and challenging them not to pervert justice but to uphold the laws given by Yahweh. They were seen as almost professional critics of the political authorities. The sociologist Max Weber had a valid point when he compared them to a free press—those whose task was to speak the truth and expose injustice.

This very brief overview of several centuries shows something of the evolution of political authority in Israel. There was an expansion and differentiation of roles. The offices of judge and king were not the same as the priest, nor the prophet, nor the parent, nor the father—they were a distinct authority under God. There was a gradual development and evolution of specific political offices, of people who had authority to interpret the law and to reward both the righteous and the evildoer according to their deeds.

Political Authority

The New Testament reflects this Old Testament pattern, most markedly in insisting that God is the source of political authority. Jesus stressed this theme in telling Pilate: "You would have no power over me unless it had been given you from above" (John 19:11). Paul wrote that all creation would share in the redemption of Jesus Christ, and told the Christians in Rome that government, even the pagan government of the Roman Empire, was neither a demonic thing nor a realm apart from the ordinances of God. He argued that "there is no authority except from God, and those that exist have been instituted by God." He reiterated that political authority "is God's servant for your good" (Romans 13:1, 4).

Both Testaments say that genuine political authority is authority from God, and that those who hold political office, even if they do not believe in God, do their job because God has authorized their office. Political authority was not seen as an area apart from true religion—those who wielded it carried out a divine ministry. Politics is described as a ministry just as any office in the Church. This authority was also not understood as separate from the reign of Christ, but as a manifestation of the authority of the "King of Kings" (Rev. 1:5; 17:14; 19:16), who said, "All authority in heaven and earth is given unto me" (Matt. 28:18).

Paul stressed that, in its proper role, government has an authority under and from God that individual people do not have. In his Sermon on the Mount, Jesus had told the disciples: "Do not resist one who is evil. But if anyone strikes you on the right cheek, turn to him the other also" (Matt. 5:39). He also said, "Judge not, that you be not judged" (Matt. 7:1). Paul knew something of this and restated the same themes in his letter to the Romans: "Beloved, never avenge yourselves, but leave it to the wrath of God; for it is written, 'Vengeance is mine, I will repay, says the Lord'" (Rom. 12:19–21). However, immediately after he echoed Jesus' teaching against revenge, Paul went on to describe the task of government. He wrote that governments are "instituted by God . . . [he] who is in authority is the servant of God to execute [h]is wrath on the wrongdoer" (Rom. 13:1,4).[7] We are not to seek private revenge, but to leave things to the "wrath of God," and this includes leaving things to governments, which are seen as one instrument of that "wrath." What people alone cannot do, God will do, and will do it (at least partly) through governments he has instituted.

Paul's emphasis is that it is God, not individual people, who should punish evil and reward good. No human being has any innate authority over another. But God's means of doing so or, at least, one of God's means of doing so, is through the governing authorities provided to exercise precisely this role. Leaving it to God to execute justice also means leaving it to the governing authorities to execute justice.

No individual has a personal authority over another. But, because God, in the course of human history, has given governments authority to execute justice, then those who rightfully hold government authority may and should avenge evil and reward good. (This is one reason why, as will be suggested later, just war theory stresses that only legitimate authorities can wage war. Such authorities are not understood as engaged in self-defense but as protecting the population that God instituted them to protect. They defend another, an innocent third party).

Because of Paul's distinction between individual action and authorized political action, it is wrong to oppose the Sermon on the Mount to Romans 13. It is not accurate to say that Jesus' reign is one of nonviolence and peace, as opposed to the reign of government where force may be necessary. In the body of New Testament teaching, governments are also under Jesus Christ and, under that reign, have the particular task of avenging good and evil.[8]

Paul says, in effect, that the state is what God has set up to maintain justice. Its officers are ministers of God, just as are prophets and priests. The authority of government is authority from God just as is authority in the Church. "Thrones or dominions or principalities or authorities—all things were created through him and for him . . . in him all things hold together" (Col. 1:16–17; 1 Pet. 3:22).

Because Paul described political authority as an aspect of the authority of Jesus Christ, the next thing he told the Roman Christians to do was submit to that authority. This submission was not only to avoid "wrath" but was "also for the sake of conscience" (Rom. 13:5); that is, not simply out of fear but because it was right and proper. Furthermore, "He who resists the authorities resists what God has appointed and will incur judgment"(Rom. 13:3).

Submitting to government authority was not seen by Paul as optional. Government was not a happenstance thing, something to be followed only insofar as we approve of its policies. Real government authority was seen as an aspect of God's authority. A true religious realm was not set apart from a governmental realm, since obeying true government was understood as one part of obeying God (see also Titus 3:1; I Tim. 2:1–3; Jude 8).

The Limits of Government

A central element of biblical teaching is that governments are also limited. They should not be treated of as mini-gods that can do anything, while our only individual responsibility is passively to obey. In each instance where the New Testament speaks of governing authorities (and in relevant cases in the

Old Testament), it describes them in terms of the specific task or function they have, and it speaks of what their specific authority is for. Peter wrote of "governors . . . sent by him to punish those who do wrong and to praise those who do right" (1 Pet. 2:14). Paul claimed that "rulers are not a terror to good conduct, but to bad . . . .He is the servant of God to execute his wrath on the wrongdoer" (Rom. 13:3, 4). Paul unquestionably knew that actually existing governments often were, in fact, very much a "terror" and punished those who did good—the death of Jesus was his prime example (I Cor. 2:7, 8). Paul knew that governments unjustly executed Jesus, as well as many others. Therefore, what he described was not what existing governments always or usually did, but what the proper task of governments should be, what governments were for.

Governments were not seen as having the authority to do anything they might please. Jesus famously said: "Render to Caesar the things that are Caesar's, and to God the things that are God's" (Mark 12:17; see also Acts 5:29). Clearly, then, Caesar could not claim all things—there were things which are God's and not Caesar's. In fact, as suggested, Caesar's authority could only come from God and was, in turn, defined by God. God and Caesar were not two separate realms. Caesar was under God and, hence, should be rendered only what God said should be rendered—that is, obedience and honor according to Caesar's rightful task. That is why, when Peter was summoned before the Sanhedrin and questioned as to why he disobeyed the command not to preach in the name of Jesus, he said "We must obey God rather than men." (Acts 4:29; see also Acts 4:19, and I Peter 2:13–14)[9]

Nor should we imagine that in Romans 13 Paul gave government *carte blanche* in its activities. He did not blandly accept the status quo of Roman imperialism or advocate quiescent submission to it. Although Romans 13 has often been interpreted, as it was by many Christians in Nazi Germany, as a call to total and unconditional obedience to whatever government might just have happened to get into power, the epistle shows just the opposite. Paul's statements were anything but passive. He was aware that Jesus' kingship was not like the kingdoms of this world (John 18:36).[10] He stressed that the power that Jesus brought into the world to transform it, "to bring to nothing the things that are" (1 Cor. 1:28; see also Luke 1:52), was a power that would not bow before tyranny. It would, instead, challenge and transform it. Paul himself, as a servant of Jesus, was frequently in prison and in trouble with political authorities. He was always challenging political authority. Many of the New Testament epistles are prison writings.

When Paul wrote his letter to the Church in Rome, the emperors had taken for themselves the titles of "Son of God," "Savior," and "High Priest." When a new emperor came to power, the proclamation of his enthronement was called *evangelion* (gospel). The symbol of Roman justice and law was the cross, symbolizing crucifixion—its ultimate punishment. As Paul and the Christian Church applied these titles and symbols to Jesus, they necessarily denied them to Caesar and, so, challenged his claim to ultimate authority.[11]

In Romans 13, Paul reinterpreted the then-accepted Roman political order. He rejected the self-image of the Empire, criticized its legal structure, and downgraded its claimed political authority. He said that governments were not lords, that they did not exist for themselves, that they were not the supreme authority. Writing at a time when the Emperors were setting themselves up as deities, Paul insisted that governments were *servants*, a remarkable thing to say at the time of the Roman Empire. We are used to, perhaps too much so, descriptions of governments as servants, to the language of "civil servants" and "public service," so perhaps the claim does not strike us as radical. However, it was radical. It said that government leaders were not gods, not lords, but servants.

Paul was saying that the Empire was not the only or the final sovereign. This is why he concluded his discussion of politics in Romans 13 by saying "Pay all of them their dues, taxes to whom taxes are due, revenue to whom revenue is due. . . ." (Rom. 13:7ff). Give them what they are due, and nothing more. The government is under God's just order and must give and receive only its due. It cannot claim everything; it is not the final authority.

This view of authority determines the relation of ruler and subject, and government and citizen, and delineates their place in relation to one another. We are not to surrender all to government; instead, we are to give only what is properly due and required. Paul relativized the Roman imperial order. He refused to accept the Emperor as the ultimate authority and said, instead, that the Emperor was *under* God—a servant, one with a particular task to do, one who should not stray from that task. In Paul's letters, as in Peter's, government was seen as subject to, and bound, to carry out God's laws. A government which rejected this task was called into question.

Jesus and Political Authority

As far as the Roman authorities were concerned, Jesus was crucified for doing something similar to what Paul advocated in Romans 13. When the Sanhedrin questioned him, they concentrated on his claim to be the Messiah, the Christ (Matt. 26:61–64; Mark 14:60; Luke 22:66–71). But the charge before Pilate was that he was *"forbidding us to give tribute to Caesar,* and saying that he himself is Christ *a king"* (Luke 23:2, my italics).

This is the line of questioning that Pilate pursued and, so, he asked: "Are you the King of the Jews?" (Matt. 27:11; Mark 15:2, 8, 12; Luke 23:3). Later the Roman soldiers mocked Jesus with the words "Hail, King of the Jews!" (Matt. 27:29; Luke 23:37), whereas the people gathered outside cried, "[L]et him save himself, if he is the Christ of God, his Chosen One" (Luke 23:35; but not always, see Matt. 27:41, 42). The Roman inscription on the cross was "This is the King of the Jews."

The Romans were not particularly concerned about claims of messiahship per se—they could regard this as another one of the internal, interminable, incomprehensible, Israelite religious squabbles they seemed always to face, important only if they led to civil unrest. However, the Romans would be worried if one of these Messiahs also claimed to be a king. This got their attention. The fact that Jesus' kingship was intended to be of a different type from worldly kingdoms did not mean it was unconnected to the kingships of the earth. While Jesus' kingship did not claim to derive from this world order, and while its marks were to be radically different from the then and now existing political orders (Luke 27:24–27; Acts 1:6; Romans 14:17), it had major implications for who the kings of the world were and what they might do.

The Romans were far more politically astute than many moderns, who read through the letters to the Romans or Luke's description of Jesus' passion as though they were politically irrelevant. They were representatives of a political order that claimed to be the authority, the final authority. Like most empires, they could and did accept many other authorities, including religious authorities, as long as these authorities acknowledged that they were subordinates under the Roman order. But the Romans would not accept any other allegiance that claimed to be higher than their own authority.

The Romans, from vast experience, knew all about the political meanings of religion, and knew that, when Jesus said that he was a king (Matt. 21:5; John 1:49–51), he could be a major threat to their rule. It didn't really matter to them what type of king Jesus said he was. Even though he was not about to take political power (Acts 1:6–8), the authority that he did claim would challenge any political power that claimed to be the final authority over all.

While the followers of Jesus were to obey the Roman authorities as ministers of God, they could not yield total or final allegiance to the Empire, or to any other political order. They, like their brothers, the Jews, always had another allegiance, one which could conflict with and override their duty to the Emperor. Hence, as long as they were faithful to their God, they could never be taken for granted by any ruler, for their other allegiance could be a force superior to their allegiance to the emperor. This is why, later, they were viciously persecuted by the Romans. The problem, as far as the Romans were concerned, was not what Christians did believe (the divinity of Jesus), but what they refused to believe—the divinity, and therefore final authority, of the Roman gods and, therefore, of Rome itself. Christians were persecuted as disbelievers in Rome.

Christians have usually not been easy subjects. The Church itself has often questioned, challenged, and redefined the political orders in which the Church has been placed. This allegiance to something other than and beyond the political order has been a constant source of complaint for many western political theorists, such as Niccolò Machiavelli, Thomas Hobbes, or Jean-Jacques Rousseau, who wished to make the state the undivided, all-encompassing human community. This is why communists and fascists, and anyone else who wants to make the state the final human community, currently try to repress and control the Church.[12] They cannot tolerate the existence of other authorities, or other communities, which might challenge their own claims to ultimate authority. In fact, rather than any specific Church teaching, probably it was the mere continued existence of the Church, as a body with authority distinct from the political order, which helped keep alive in the West the idea of limits on state power and, consequently, provided a later basis for the growth of modern constitutional government (see also chapter 6 on church and state).

Jesus and Paul also said much more than stating that governments are merely servants. Paul added that they are "God's servants for your good" (Rom. 13:4). Jesus said something similar: "The kings of the Gentiles exercise lordship over them. . . . But not so with you, rather let the greatest among you become as the youngest, and the leader as one who serves. . . . I am among you as one who serves" (Luke 22:25–27). One consequence of this was that political authority was understood as existing for the good of the citizenry. Political power was to be defined as servanthood. Government was called to serve those in its jurisdiction and to defend those who suffered injustice.

Justice: An Eye for an Eye

I have emphasized that justice was a central element of the biblical depiction of God's call on humankind, that the restoration of a community in terms of the covenant between God and humankind necessarily implied justice.[13]

This justice can be expressed in many ways, but one of the most fundamental ones is political authority. The Psalmist said, in the "kingly psalm," "Give the king thy justice, O God, and thy Justice to the royal son. . . . May he defend the cause of the poor of the people, give deliverance to the needy, and crush the oppressor" (Ps. 72:1–4; see also Ps. 45:4–8).

While justice is central to scriptural descriptions of politics, it, like all important words, is much easier to sense than to define. It is almost impossible to give a precise definition. However, we can give some idea of how it is used in the Bible. Psalm 72 ties justice to the defense of the poor, the needy, and the oppressed and, in turn, to the punishment of the oppressor. The same idea occurs in the New Testament, where one theme is that the political order is called to "reward" both the righteous and the evildoer. This involves paying each of them back according to their deeds: evil deeds are to bring evil consequences, good deeds are to bring good consequences.

The Genesis examples referred to earlier bring out further senses of justice. With Cain there was a "sevenfold" vengeance, which contains the sense of what is "fitting" or "complete," a full but not an overfull vengeance (Gen. 4:15). Abraham argued with God that "shall not the judge of all the earth do right (i.e., justly)" (Gen. 18:25), and that the righteous could not be slain with the wicked (Gen. 18:24). This stressed that justice required responses tied to the actual culpability of those involved.

This theme was repeated when the law was given to Israel at Sinai. God pronounced the famous *lex talionis*: "You shall give life for life, eye for eye, tooth for tooth, hand for hand, foot for foot, burn for burn, wound for wound, stripe for stripe" (Exod. 21:24, 25). This saying is often pictured as a brutal and barbaric one, replete with images of eyes being plucked out. But the *lex talionis* was nothing of the kind. Nowhere in all the laws of Israel are these types of punishment advocated. We simply do not find eye-plucking or foot chopping.

The immediate context of this saying shows what it was meant to teach about justice. The very next verse says: "When a man strikes the eye of his slave, male or female, and destroys it, he shall let the slave go free, for the eye's sake" (Exod. 21:26). If we were to interpret an eye for an eye literally, then this passage would be a complete contradiction, for the slave did not pluck out the master's eye but instead went free. However, this next verse, and the ones that follow, are not contradictions of, but were given as immediate applications of "an eye for an eye." The example of the slave is the first illustration of the principle that had just been announced.

The point of "an eye for an eye" was that it was wrong to respond to an offense by taking two eyes, or two teeth, or two lives. It was meant to stop revenge, especially ongoing family blood feuds. It was meant to eradicate raw vengeance, such as Lamech's "seven times seventy" response (Gen. 4:23, 24). The principle it gives is that the severity of the punishment must fit the severity of the crime, whether that be great or small. Smaller misdeeds deserve smaller responses, larger misdeeds deserve larger responses. In short, "an eye for an eye" is an illustration of what is now called the judicial principle of equity—treat equal cases alike and let the measure of reward or punishment be appropriate to the gravity of the deed. The law given at Sinai gave a clearer sense of what justice, the original "sevenfold vengeance" of Cain, was about. It was to be equitable, to include everybody, and to treat people according to their deeds. This broad sense is similar to the classical definitions of justice as "giving each their due."

The Range of Justice

The Hebrew words which can be translated as justice occur in various forms more than 500 times in the Old Testament. The corresponding New Testament sets of terms occur more than 200 times.[14] Many of these different instances involve subtle and complex variations on the major theme. Consequently, we can here only give a very brief summary of some important facets. Nevertheless, before such a summary, it should be noted just how much of the Bible is about justice. The word "righteousness," which we often use instead, seems to have different connotations in the modern world, and is often also used to mean individual "holiness" or "morality." However, if we substitute variations of the term "justice" wherever we read "righteousness," then the text sounds quite different. Justice is stressed again and again in reference to God, to Jesus, to kings, judges, priests, prophets, the poor, and the rich.

The term "justice" refers, first of all, not to particular persons or acts, but to the fact that there can be a just ordering of things in the world according to God's will—that God maintains a just order in the world. We are to conform our actions and institutions to this order, and to judge all things and all actions according to it. When we say that something is just or unjust, we are judging it in terms of an order of justice given in the world by God.

This just order should be upheld by all; if humankind does not act justly, then God will still uphold justice in the world, and will judge in a right way. One aspect of this is showing no partiality; God is not a "respecter of persons." This means that all people are judged equally (John 5:3, 7:24; Acts 17:31; Rom. 2:11; Eph. 6:9; 1 Pet. 1:17, 2:23; Rev. 16:7, 19:2).

Everybody is required to be just in the sense that each must act fairly in relation to others. Being just, in this sense, means that people must refrain from idolatry, adultery, robbery, and violence. But it requires not only abstaining from negative things, but also actively pursuing positive things. The just person should care for those who are hungry, defend the poor, and judge fairly between others (cf. Ezek. 18:5–9). The unjust are the ones who do not do these things (Matt. 5:45; Luke 1:6, 15:7, 23, 50; Acts 24:15).

In court cases people could be judged as "just" or "unjust." In a legal conflict between two people, the judge would pronounce one of them as the "just" one. This did not mean that this person was without any fault, but that in this particular case this person was in the right. In a conflict over land between two people, the judge would decide who was "in the right" in the case. This person was then called "just" and given the right to the land.

In turn, judges must themselves be just. An unjust judge is one who does not judge rightly, who takes bribes or shows partiality to one party, or kowtows to the rich and does not defend the poor (Deut. 16:18ff; Deut. 25:1).[15] In this respect judges are to be imitators of God, showing no partiality, but judging rightly, just as God shows no partiality and judges rightly. Like God, a judge is to be no respecter of persons. This is part of what it means that judges take up a divine task—in the matter of judgment they must do what God would do. This is one reason why governments were described as ministers of God.

The Bible also relates justice and the poor. The "poor" included those who were poor in a number of ways—they were coupled with the hungry, the homeless, the stranger, the widow, the orphan, the sick, the meek, the oppressed, the prisoners, the blind, and those who were bowed down (Psalms 10, 146). It is certainly true that orphans or widows are often in dire financial straits, but they can also suffer from loneliness, isolation, and lack of stability—things not related solely to financial conditions. The poor were those who lacked the social, economic, or political resources to fulfill their life's responsibilities. The command to care for the poor was a command to care for all who were suffering and sorrowing.

In the law, God was depicted as one who continually told Israel to care for the fatherless, the widow, and the sojourner (Exod. 22:21–24; Lev. 19:15; Deut. 1:7, 10:17–18). It was God who had brought Israel itself out of bondage and who always defended the poor and needy (Exod. 6:5–7, 20:2; Deut. 5:6, 10:17–18, 26:5–8). These commands were also the continual refrain of the prophets. Isaiah called Israel to seek justice and righteousness—specifically in caring for the fatherless, the widow, and the poor (Isa. 1:21–26). The psalmist praised God "Who executes justice for the oppressed; who gives food to the hungry. The Lord sets the prisoners free; the Lord opens the eyes of the blind." They also condemned those who oppressed the poor, including those who did not aid them. Amos denounced those "who oppress the poor, who crush the needy" (Amos 4:1), while Isaiah condemned those who "turn aside the needy from justice" (Isa. 10:1–4; see also Mark 12:40).

Jesus announced his own ministry quoting the words of Isaiah 61:1–2. "The Spirit of the Lord is upon me, because he has anointed me to preach good news to the poor. He has sent me to proclaim release to the captives and recovering of sight to the blind, to set at liberty those who are oppressed" (Luke 4:18–19). These words were not only spiritual, since Jesus was described as healing the physically sick, and the blind, feeding the hungry, and saying, "I was hungry and you gave me food, I was thirsty and you gave me to drink. . . . I was naked and you clothed me. . . . Truly, I say to you, as you did it to one of the least of these my brethren, you did it to me" (Matt. 25:35–40).

It was not that the poor were regarded as personally righteous, as some sort of inherently honest salt-of-the-earth, but rather that righteousness required justice for the poor. Also, these texts do not mean, as has been claimed by some theologians, that God is biased toward the poor or "on the side of" the poor. God was seen not as having a "side," but a standard, a law. God required equitable treatment for *all* people: "You shall have one law for the sojourner and for the native; for I am the Lord your God. . . . You shall not be partial to the poor or defer to the great, but in righteousness shall you judge your neighbor" (Lev. 19:15, 26:22).[16] The stress on the poor is simply because they are usually weak, and therefore, almost by definition, the ones denied justice.

This understanding of justice raises the question of what is due to people. There are various answers offered in modern society—that people should get what they worked for, or else the same amount as everybody else, or else the same opportunity as everybody else, or else whatever people need. Even with a focus on "need," we face the question of "need in order to do what?"

An answer to the question of what is "due" can be addressed in terms of a just order, of the place of things in the world. Everyone is responsible in particular ways. Each has tasks to do and responsibilities to take up. Everyone has a "calling" or "callings" to fulfill—to try to be faithful husbands and wives, loving parents, industrious workers, caring neighbors, responsible citizens, steadfast friends. Due to each is what is needed in order to discharge their life's responsibilities. To put this loosely in more modern language, we can say that everyone has a right to be able to fulfill the responsibilities that God has given. Hence, justice means that each should have the possibility of what is needed relative to others in terms of the place and the callings of everything and of everyone in God's world. Emil Brunner's summary is useful:

The Christian conception of justice . . . is determined by the conception of God's order of creation. What corresponds to the Creator's ordinance is just—to that ordinance which bestows on every creature [i.e., created thing] with its being, the law of its being, and its relationship to other creatures. The "primal order" to which everyone refers in using the words "just" or "unjust," the "due" which is rendered to each, is the order of creation, which is the will of the creator made manifest."[17]

Justice relates to the world, to creation. Being just requires giving something its right, its created place in the world. Political authorities are given authority and power to judge, impartially and without favor, the relations of things in the world in terms of justice and injustice. They are to correct injustice by restoring things to their right relation. This restoration implies, and is itself, a rewarding of those who are just and a punishing (or negative rewarding) of those who are on the unjust side of the relation.

The Limits of Government

Governments are to do justice, but it is not their job to try to correct and control every relationship; after all, everyone else is also supposed to do justice. Hence, a key question is *when* governments should, and should not, use their authority and power. Governments do not have the authority to do anything that they might feel like. It is vital that they be kept in their proper place since, in the Scriptures as elsewhere, there is a repeated refrain concerning the dangers of over-powerful and overreaching government authority. The litany of injustices and disasters that Samuel told Israel would follow from their having created a king (I Sam. 8:11–18) was amply fulfilled by the actions of most of the kings that they actually had. When the book of Revelation pictures the coming together of the forces of evil in the world, it does so in terms of a beast portrayed like a political authority: "Who is like the beast, and who can fight against it? . . . And authority was given it over every tribe and people and tongue and nation" (Rev. 13:4, 7).

The Bible portrays governments as both potentially and actually dangerous, and as easily perverted. Governments wield tremendous power, the power to force and coerce. We must be doubly careful to ensure that this servant remains a servant and does not become a lord or a tyrant. We must know not only what governments are supposed to do but also what they are *not* supposed to do. Our politics should not be merely a listing of human ills coupled with a demand for political action; rather, we need to know what actions properly fall within the government's ability and jurisdiction, and what do not.

As we will discuss in chapter 7, we cannot just draw up our list of problems, whether they be divorce, pornography, and homosexuality, or else environmental degradation, sexual inequality, and low wages, and necessarily expect that there can, will, or should be political solutions to our problems, hopes, and wishes. Instead we need to understand the specific task of government. In turn, accepting the limits of politics and governmental authority does not mean that we are accepting evil; rather, it means that we are careful about our means of combating evil.

Apart from judgment, the Scriptures also emphasize patience. They stress that God will judge, and also repeatedly stress that the major part of that judgment will take place in the future so that, for now, we need to wait. If even God is patient with those who do evil, how much more should human beings be willing to live alongside others? Some evils we simply have to endure rather than calling on government power.

A key question for government is not merely whether people are doing evil, it is whether or not it is the type of evil that the government has the authority, which includes the ability, to stop. Everybody is responsible in distinct ways. There is no one body or person on earth who represents all authority. Responsibility and authority are not channeled exclusively through any single institution. Neither an Emperor, nor an apostle, nor a teacher, nor a parent, nor a husband or wife can claim to be the only or the ultimate authority. None can override another in the other's proper sphere of authority. Each and all have the responsibility, and therefore the authority that goes with it, to do a particular task within the world.

This diversity of responsibility reemphasizes that we should not think of politics as everything, or even as the most important thing. We must not make it the center of life. It has only a particular responsibility for particular things, and it should not go beyond those bounds. We can delineate part of government's role simply by realizing that there are other authorities such as churches, parents, or individuals, that have an authority, a right, not derived from government, and are therefore not disposable at government fiat. The authority of government ends where the authorities of others begin. In fact, unlike a family or a church, the government is not given a particular community within which it is to act. Yet, at the same time, it is charged with the responsibility for maintaining an overall order of justice in a territory. In the light of these two things, taken together, we can say that the governing authority is justly to interrelate the authorities—the areas of responsibility—of others. It is not to supplant other authorities in their roles, but it is to make sure that external relations between them, such as those between person and person, between church and church, or church and state, are ones which conform to a just order.

This theme of the limits of the government's task is reflected in nearly all western theology and permeates Christian political teaching.[18] Catholic views have emphasized the theme of subsidiarity—that the purpose of the state is to aid other bodies as they try to accomplish their own task. One essential aspect of subsidiarity is that the state should not take over the functions of other authorities, but help them fulfill their own responsibility. The state should focus on what it alone can do.

Calvinist views have emphasized sphere sovereignty—that human life includes diverse offices with diverse responsibilities that possess their own respective authorities. Society has many sovereignties, not just state sovereignty. Since these authorities do not stem from the state but from God, the state has no legitimate authority to override them. A church, family, university, or company has its own intrinsic authority that must be recognized and respected by government. Other Christian traditions have less developed theories, but we can also point to Lutheran two-realm theory, which limits government by stressing the distinct roles of law and gospel in church and state. The Anabaptist contrast between the church and the world has the same intended function.

These themes have come to the fore in recent American politics in George W. Bush's calls for "compassionate conservatism." This notion has been attacked on the right for introducing the mushy notion of "compassion" into what should be the realist world of politics. It has been attacked on the left as a cover for traditional republicanism. But it is not a mere blend of conservatism and liberalism. It is, whether Bush knows it or not, an attempt at subsidiarity—using the power of government not to usurp others but to help them in their own work, as, for example, in a stress on faith-based organizations. It is an attempt to address questions of community and poverty while recognizing the proper limits of government.[19]

Notes

1. This discussion of Cain and Lamech is derived from Meredith G. Kline, "Oracular Origin of the State," in *Biblical and Near Eastern Studies*, ed. G. Tuttle (Grand Rapids, Mich.: Eerdmans, 1978), 132–41.

2. Cf. G. von Rad, *Genesis: A Commentary* (London: SCM, 1961), 102. See also C.J.H. Wright, *Human Rights: A Study in Biblical Themes* (Bramcote, U.K.: Grove Books, 1979), 9f.

3. See also Psalms 10:11, 13:2, 22:25, 27:2, 4, 7, 8, 9, 30:8, 44:25, 69:18, 88:15, 102:3, 143:7; Job 13:2; Deut. 31:17, 18; 32:20, 35–36, 41ff; Isa. 8:17; Jer. 16:17; Mic. 3:4.

4. This ambiguity is reflected in the "theology of the powers" associated especially with Walter Wink. This view says that power formations were originally a good gift from God, but that now they have fallen and so must be treated in a dialectical way. Hence, we must now work with them but remain continually aloof to their seductions. See Walter Wink, Naming the Powers, Unmasking the Powers, Engaging the Powers (Philadelphia: Fortress Press, 1984, 1986, 1992).

5. See Peter Schouls, Insight, Authority and Power (Toronto: Wedge, 1972).

6. H. J. Boeker, Law and the Administration of Justice in the Old Testament and Near East, trans. J. Moiser (London: S.P.C.K., 1981), 40ff. The Israelites themselves were probably clearer on this matter, for there was a "book of the kingdom"; Psalm 72 may be a reflection of this "book." It is not entirely clear what the king's full duties were. He was certainly to lead in battle, but beyond that things are confused. He did not make laws, for Israel's laws had already been given at Sinai. He may also have sometimes acted as a judge, but the elders and judges still carried out that task.

7. John Howard Yoder writes that "it is inconceivable that these two verses [12:19 and 13:4] using such similar language should be meant to be read independently of one another." The Politics of Jesus (Grand Rapids, Mich.: Eerdmans, 1972), 199. I think this is true. However, Yoder then draws the conclusion from these verses that, as a Christian cannot take vengeance, "the function exercised by government is not the function to be exercised by Christians." Yoder does not allow the distinction between, on the one hand, people acting individually and, on the other hand, people carrying out a God-given authority of political office. I think that, unless this distinction is maintained, then any idea of a political order at all would be lost. We would be left only with an assertion of personal will and power. This does not necessarily invalidate action by individual citizens if they are understood to be exercising legal authority. A citizen's arrest would be one such example, while current U.S. federal law, in 10 U.S. Code 311 says: "The militia of the United States consists of all able-bodied males at least seventeen years of age. . . ."

8. Nor would it be correct to say that, while it may indeed be true that governments derive their authority from God, they do so only under a separate dispensation, such as "God's order of preservation," distinct from "God's order of redemption," which is supposedly manifested only in the church.

9. See Luis Lugo, "Caesar's Coin and the Politics of the Kingdom," in Caesar's Coin Revisited: Christians and the Limits of Government, ed. Michael Cromartie (Grand Rapids, Mich.: Eerdmans, 1996), 1–22.

10. John 18:36 should not be read as saying "not of this world" as though Jesus' kingdom were present only in another world. It is better translated as "not from this world order," that Jesus' power does not derive from the established world order but comes into it and transforms it.

11. See my Their Blood Cries Out (Nashville: Word, 1997), chapter 1.

12. See David Novak, *Covenant Rights* (Princeton: Princeton University Press, 2000).

13. N. T. Wright, "Christ and Caesar in the First and Twenty-First Century" (lecture at Ethics and Public Policy Center, Washington, D.C., 19 November 2001).

14. Cf. Boeker, *Law and the Administration of Justice*.

15. The judges' impartiality in the Old Testament also extended to judgments between those who were Israelites and those who were not, between those in the covenant and those who were not. Justice extended to all people, cf. Deut. 23:7; Ezek. 16:49; Amos 1, 2, 9:7.

16. For this reason it can be misleading to talk about "an option for the poor" or a "bias for the poor." Such expressions imply supporting one side in a conflict, and imply that the rich are beyond considerations of justice. In the Scriptures there is not a side but a standard—justice—by which conflicts are judged, and which points to what relations should be like. In terms of this standard we seek to rectify injustice, and such rectifying will, of course, mean the defending of the poor.

17. Emil Brunner, *Justice and the Social Order* (London: Lutterworth, 1945), 89. See also my *Human Rights Theories in Christian Perspective* (Toronto: Institute for Christian Studies, 1983), 17–23. It has often been claimed, especially by Karl Barth and Walter Brueggemann, that creation theology is inherently conservative and subservient to the status quo. While, obviously, it can be used that way, there is no reason it need or should be. For an excellent analysis of this, see J. Richard Middleton, "Is Creation Theology Inherently Conservative? A Dialogue with Walter Brueggemann," *Harvard Theological Review*, vol. 87 (1994): 257–77. The recent resurgence of natural law theory is stressing the same theme; see Robert George, ed., *In Defense of National Law* (New York: Oxford University Press, 1999); David F. Forte, ed., *Natural Law and Contemporary Public Policy* (Washington, D.C.: Georgetown University Press, 1999). The status of natural law is still a source of difference between many Catholics and Protestants; see Michael Comartie, ed., *A Preserving Grace: Protestants, Catholics and Natural Law* (Grand Rapids, Mich.: Eerdmans, 1999).

18. A good survey of these approaches to the nature of state authority is given in James Skillen and Rockne M. McCarthy, eds., *Political Order and the Plural Structure of Society* (Atlanta, Ga.: Scholars Press, 1991). On "subsidiarity" see Kenneth L. Grasso, Gerard V. Bradley, and Robert Hunt, eds., *Catholicism, Liberalism and Communitarianism: The Catholic Intellectual Tradition and the Moral Foundations of Democracy* (Lanham, Md.: Rowman & Littlefield, 1995); Jon Chaplin, "Subsidiarity as a Political Norm," in *Political Theory and Christian Vision*, ed. Jonathan Chaplin and Paul Marshall (Lanham, Md.: University Press of America, 1994), 81–100. See also Cromartie, *Caesar's Coin Revisited*. For a good overview of contemporary American views, see Jim Skillen, *The Scattered Voice: Christians at Odds in the Public Square* (Grand Rapids, Mich.: Zondervan, 1990).

19. Franklin Foer, "The Catholic Teachings of George W.," *The New Republic*, 5 June 2000; Stanley W. Carlson-Thies, "Policy-Makers Struggle with Compassionate Conservatism," *Newsroom*, 26 March 2001.

~

CHAPTER FOUR

Democracy and Rights

Confusion about Theocracy

Whenever the influence of religion on politics is discussed, someone is likely to raise the bogeyman of "theocracy," a term as ill-used as it is ill-defined. In its common usage, the word is well-nigh meaningless. For example, there is a widespread and mistaken view, common inside churches and outside them, that Old Testament government was a type of theocracy, in which, supposedly, either priests ruled or else God ruled directly. This mistake is one consequence of the fact that often little attention is paid to actual political structures in the Bible. In fact, neither theocratic structures, nor even the term "theocracy," which literally means rule by God, is found there. The term itself was apparently coined by Josephus, a first-century Jewish historian, to describe patterns in ancient Israel. He used it to emphasize what he saw as God's direct involvement in Israelite affairs, principally in giving the law at Sinai.

Josephus' use of the term was confused, as have been most subsequent uses, since he not only described God, but also Moses, as Israel's "law-giver." This elides the question of whether "theocracy" describes a situation where God is the ultimate source of authority or only when God is also thought to directly wield that authority. This confusion between God as a source of authority and God as a direct wielder of authority has plagued the term ever since, with the result that even mild natural law views have been pilloried by their more overheated opponents as theocratic.

If "theocracy" is used to refer to God's direct rule in human life, then it would seem to require God's continual appearance—perhaps as a type of oracle, or else a human being who is divine (or claiming to be one who provides unmediated divine authority). Examples of the first could perhaps be attributed to the Old Testament before the time of Noah (ending perhaps at Gen. 9:6). Examples of the second might include the claims of pharaonic Egypt, imperial Rome, or imperial Japan.

Since, in Christian theology, Jesus is both human and divine, the Church could perhaps be described as an internal theocracy while he was on earth, though Jesus himself apparently never sought to exercise any organizational role. It could perhaps also be used of a case when the Holy Spirit is thought to lead directly. But it is difficult to see how any of these instances might be easily relevant for our own politics, and furthermore, few people, including charismatics who emphasize the role of the Holy Spirit, believe that these should be the only or correct form of rule. Most Christians—indeed, most human beings—accept the need for some official mediation of the divine will for the political order. In short, if "theocracy" is used to signify only God's direct rule, then the Christian faith does not seem to lead us to want theocracy in the present age, and few people believe in it or desire it.

On the other hand, there are many societies where the ultimate source of political authority is believed to be God, or divine standards, or divine law. And these societies include far, far more than those usually depicted, or slandered, as theocratic. Divine authority can be expressed or exercised by priests and kings, but it can also be expressed or exercised by judges, prime ministers, elected legislators, or by the population itself. Many theories of democracy, especially in the United States, explicitly maintain that the people exercise political authority, but, at the same time, they also maintain that this authority is given to the people by God. This argument is, in fact, the source of many of the more powerful contemporary theories of human rights—those that emphasize that rights are given to human beings by God (see section on "Rights" below).[1]

Similarly, and another way of saying a similar thing, many Western constitutional democracies maintain that their laws reflect a higher divine or natural law. Perhaps most notably, the American Declaration of Independence bases its authority (rights) on "Nature's God." It also says not only that people are equal, but that they are equal because they are *created* equal. One cannot be created without a Creator. In fact, the Declaration of Independence contains four distinct references to God: He is the author of the "laws of . . . God"; the "Creator" who "endowed us with our inalienable rights"; the

"Supreme Judge of the World"; and "Divine Providence."[2] In the Declaration, the divine origin of authority is seen as a fundamental guarantor of rights and democracy. If rights come from God, not the state, then the state has no authority to take them away or override them. Similarly, the Canadian constitution speaks of itself as founded on principles that recognize the "Supremacy of God." References to the divine origin of political authority (and rights) are abundant in the Western world, and they have nothing in common with what is popularly called "theocracy." In fact, they form the bulwark of a robust theory of democracy and an antidote to certain types of theocracy.

Hence, if we speak of God as the ultimate source of authority, it is perfectly possible for a country to be at one and the same time both a representative democracy and a so-called theocracy. Believing that God is the ultimate source of political authority is perfectly compatible with what is generally called "democracy."[3] The key questions are whom God gives authority to, what that authority is, and what it is for. As Harry Jaffa says, the "men who founded our system of government were not moral or political relativists, as those terms are understood today. In affirming that all men are created equal, they expressed their conviction that human freedom depends upon the recognition of an order that man himself does not create."[4] Indeed, the 1786 Virginia Act for Religious Freedom opens by saying that religious freedom is necessary precisely because "Almighty God hath created the mind free. . . ." Freedom of religion depended on a divine act.

In short, if the term "theocracy" means direct rule by God, then few want or expect it today. However, recognition of a divine source for political authority can be compatible with, conducive to, and may be necessary for, genuine democracy.

Covenant and Authority

Clearly the Bible does not directly address modern conceptions such as democracy, elections, or representative government. But we can gain some understanding of these terms by reference to the things the Bible does talk about. For example, we find conceptions of servanthood, office, responsibility, and covenant, and these are matters which are relevant to understanding the relation of governments and populations.

Jesus famously taught that the first is the last and that, hence, authority is not meant for lording it over one another but is intended to be a form of servanthood (Matt. 20:8, 27; Mark 9:35). This theme is reiterated throughout the New Testament: authority is servanthood. Having authority from God is understood, even for governments, to mean having the right and responsibility to serve others in a particular way (Rom. 1:14, 13:4; 1 Cor 3:15, 9:19; 1 Pet. 1:12, 2:16). This conception of servanthood implies that governments are called not to be absolute, but to be subordinate. They are not called to be self-centered powers, but rather to center their activities on the good of the people.

In the biblical account of Israel, we find people who can be regarded, in a broad way, as political representatives. This history is replete with references to the role of elders, who are also described variously as "princes," "foremen," "heads," and "leaders" (Exod. 5:6, 15, 19; Exod. 19:7; Num. 1:16; 1 Chron. 29:6; Hos. 5:10). Clearly, these leaders derived their authority from God. Yet they were often also appointed by judges such as Moses or Samuel, and, at the same time, they were also chosen by the people of Israel as their representatives (cf. Deut. 1:9; Num. 1:16; 1 Chron. 29:6; Hos. 5:10). This structure of authority is, like most, complex. Authority is described as coming from God, from leaders, and from the people. Similarly, when Moses announced God's covenant—the fundamental and abiding relation between God and Israel—the people responded, both directly and also through their elders, that they would hear and obey. The law had both a divine mandate and a human response (Exod. 3:16ff; 19:7ff). These dimensions were not seen as fundamentally contradictory, but as inherently complementary. Authority comes from God, is mediated by leaders, and is mediated by the people. Together these find their expression, including their legal expression, as a covenant between the people and God, with leaders as mediators.

When Israel called for a king to rule them, a similar interplay is described. Even though Israel was described as wanting a king for the wrong motives, we are told that God nevertheless still told Samuel to go along with what they asked (1 Sam. 8–10). Samuel laid out the rights and duties of the king, and finally Saul, whom we are told God had already appointed through Samuel, was chosen from among the people by lot. Lots were often thought of as an ancient form of democracy, since everybody, no matter what their rank, had an equal chance to be the ruler. These themes appeared not only in the life of Saul, but also in the story of David. The elders came to David and told him that the Lord had appointed him to be the prince over Israel. They then entered into a covenant with him and anointed him as the king (2 Sam. 5:3).

The picture we get from these actions is not like some modern versions of popular sovereignty, wherein the people give authority to a ruler solely by virtue of their own will. Throughout the Scriptures ultimate political authority stems not from the people but from God. But political authority in Israel was not simply a theocracy or dictatorship. The people shared in the responsibility and authority of political office by choosing elders and then, through these elders, kings. They then covenanted to obey and honor these leaders. Hence, the king was chosen through theocratic, aristocratic, and democratic means.

The notion of a covenant is central to the Bible, and is key to understanding political responsibility and office. Each party to a covenant agrees to the conditions of their covenanted relationship and promises to uphold them. So, for example, the Lord promised to bless Israel and Israel, in turn, promised to love God and keep the commandments. This covenant should not be reduced to the modern notion of contract, which is a conditional legal relation established for the benefit of both parties. A covenant was not simply a deal, a quid pro quo. After all, God even had covenants with birds and cattle (Gen. 9:8–17). A covenant, at least in a biblical sense, is a relation of mutual promise, commitment, and responsibility, a permanent relation that sets the pattern for the rest of life. Such covenants took place between God and Israel's kings and leaders (Ps. 132; 1 Kings 9:4, 5). As part of these commitments, there were also to be covenants between the kings, the elders, and the people (2 Sam. 5:3; Deut. 27).[5]

In these covenants, which were understood as partial expressions of God's overriding covenant with Israel, the people, as a body, took it upon themselves to uphold the law. And, as part of this promise, Israel, as a community, agreed to take responsibility for what we might now call their political affairs. Consequently, all the people of Israel were responsible to see that justice was done among them. They were not to leave this responsibility exclusively to their leaders. While the Israelites were not seen as the source of the fundamental laws under which they lived, they were to choose their leaders and ensure that they followed these laws. The Israelites, along with their leaders, held political authority from God.

Within this overall authority there were a variety of particular offices—specific roles with defined duties and authority. Those who filled the offices of priest, elder, judge, or king necessarily had particular duties and the authority to carry out those duties. These authorities were distinct from those of the people at large, and the office holders were to answer to God and their fellow Israelites in the context of the mutual responsibility of the covenant. They, together with all the people, had a covenant with God and with each other to do justice by upholding God's laws.

In summary, in the government of Israel by the time of the kings, and in the teaching on leadership and servanthood in the New Testament, we find that political authority is delegated to leaders and to the people as a whole. Leaders and people were responsible to one another, and together responsible to God. While this is not a model for a modern state, it has implications for how we might view the relation between government and population in our own day.

The land of Israel was not a modern, religiously and organizationally diverse society. It was a compact, intimately interwoven community of religious, political, economic, and social relations. We, on the other hand, live in a society where these aspects of life are much more diverse. This is to be expected, in view of the increasing diversity of offices which, as we saw in the previous chapter, grew throughout Israel's own history. Now a variety of different tasks are carried out through distinct institutions such as corporations, schools, churches, and governments. It is also true that Israel was much more homogeneous in terms of its beliefs, culture, and understanding of life than are most of the societies of modern states. But, despite these differences, we can still suggest that the political order is intended to be a body of people with diverse offices and responsibilities called to implement justice within their territory.

This pattern of responsibility is not just an external moral demand, but is also an empirical and abiding feature of political orders. It manifests itself in different ways in different political structures through history, but, even in those situations where emperors or dictators or tyrants have ruled with little concern for the welfare of the populace, they have still almost always at least *pretended* that what they were doing reflected some common or overall good; that in some way they, as leaders, represented the whole political order. This representation has been variously described as a divine or a historical mandate to govern, or that the ruler was somehow typical of the people, or else was an outstanding example of the people, and therefore properly spoke on behalf of those who were ruled.

Whatever the rationale, few of even the worst rulers have tried to rule without at least pretending that they had some reason for representing the population, as well as the gods, in doing so. This reflects the fact that the political order lends itself to a representative pattern. Abraham Lincoln was right to speak of government "of the people, by the people." Political authority is called to be an act of self-government. It is to be a recognition of a just order given for the world, and a challenge to implement this justice in the changing circumstances of life.

Democracy

The term "democracy" has a multitude of meanings, and there is now an unfortunate tendency to use it to refer to almost anything thought to be good in the political order. Americans are particularly prone to describe any supposed defect in politics, from large campaign donations to Supreme Court decisions, as "undemocratic." Even countries like the former Soviet Union, or present states such as China or Cuba, like to refer to themselves as "peoples' democracies" in order to acquire some of the legitimacy that the halo of democracy gives. Hence, we need to be careful with the term.

Clearly, many of the things which are called "democracy" should be applauded. But there are also uses of the term about which we should be much more cautious. For example, if by democracy we mean simply that the government should always do the will of the people, or should always obey the majority of the people, or should simply be elected by the majority of the people, then all sorts of hideous things can follow.

To take the starkest example, Adolph Hitler did not come to power in Germany at the head of an advancing army or by means of a coup. He was elected by the population at large. Of course, the Nazi party intimidated its opponents and manipulated elections, but, at least in the middle stages of his career, Hitler enjoyed the popular support of the German people and grew in power because most people supported him.

In this very crude sense, Nazi Germany was a democracy. It was popularly supported. It had an elected government under a constitutional order. It broke no German laws. Yet it was a regime which brought the greatest horror of the modern age—the Holocaust—into the world. It exterminated millions and led the world into a bloodbath. This was done not by a king or a military junta, but by a democratically elected government. If democracy means simply having the electoral support of a majority of the voting population, then it can be compatible with genocide and totalitarianism.[6]

This is one reason the U.S. Declaration of Independence says that governments derive not their powers but their *"just* powers" from the consent of the people. Even popular consent cannot give a power that is inherently unjust—that is, one that undercuts the rights of those who consent. Similarly, Locke emphasized that, because people did not own themselves, but were made and owned by God, they could not, in a social contract, give a ruler the power to destroy them, since this would violate God's right over them. Such a ruler would be destroying God's property. The restrictions on the power of the ruler depended on prior restrictions on the will of the people because God had made them.[7]

Evil, even political evil, is not confined to dictators and generals. It is something that affects all people. Sin is universal. There is no absolute guarantee that the people at large will not desire to do evil and choose a government to do it on their behalf. We should not romanticize "the people," the common people, the little man. We are as capable of evil as anybody. Problems with government do not only occur if it is out of touch with the popular will. Governments can do evil with the support of the people or without it. Therefore, we cannot simply be democrats in the sense of believing that popular support alone legitimizes government actions.

However, there are other meanings of democracy which emphasize not mere popular support, or that popular will is the ultimate source of political authority, but that the government represents the people and governs on their behalf. In this sense everybody, whether a president, member of Congress, member of the city council, or a voting citizen, bears political responsibility and political office. A citizen holds a political office, one part of which is choosing the people who will carry out other offices. This parallels biblical themes mentioned earlier. We together exercise authority and responsibility for how we are governed. In turn, government leaders are held accountable for what they do by the population at large.

Hence, while even popular governments can do evil, representative government reflects a truer conception of the nature of human responsibility and authority. This manifests itself practically in the fact that, usually, governments are much better if they are restrained by the need to win popular support for their actions. When a government is held accountable by the whole population in frequent elections, it is less likely or able to do great evil. While some monarchs in countries as diverse as Spain and Thailand have been exemplary in recent years, governments which derive their authority through popular elections have a much better record than those that occupy their position by force of arms or inheritance. Hence, democracy, in the sense that a government should exercise authority when it is chosen by and is held accountable by the people at large, should be understood as a standard in the modern age.[8]

So far I have suggested two things about government responsibility. First, that government is responsible for doing what is right and just, and should not do unjust things even if most of the population wants them. Second, that governments should be responsible to the population for what they do. These two responsibilities are not inherently contradictory—they are simply two, among many, standards of government conduct. However, they can be in tension with one another, and neither can be neglected. This means that governments should try to do both things simultaneously: they should do what is right and seek to do so with the support of the population. These two elements will also be intertwined since, with representative government, the population at large is involved in the decision about what is right.

On the one hand, a government which only seeks to do what the senior office holders alone deem right, regardless of what the population wants, will find itself treated with derision and cynicism. It will erode the necessary bond of trust which is vital if governments are to function with genuine democratic authority rather than naked power. If it continues in this path, it can degenerate into a dictatorship, benevolent or otherwise. It is far too simple merely to say that politicians should do what they believe is the right thing. On the other hand, a government that does only what the majority of the population wants at any given time can, as we have seen, also end up doing great evil. Popular support per se does not justify any action. Hence, neither normative direction nor popular support can be neglected.

Consequently, if we want to do what we believe to be right, and this is against the wishes of many in the population, then we should try to lead by seeking to win over the population to our views. This requires publicity, education, and debate to try to gather the support needed. This is a major function of elections, although it also needs to go on apart from elections. If and when we win such support, we can go ahead. If we fail to win such support, the action may need to be deferred to a later date, or else the government must do something which most of the population does not want. This can be necessary, as we do not want governments that are mere bellwethers of political opinion, driven by the results of the latest opinion poll. However, no democratic government can consistently ignore popular will in its decisions, or else its ability even to lead will be undercut.

This interplay of leadership and support is never a simple, isolated, or automatic process, since no government deals with only one issue at a time. Some actions are more popular than others. A government won't have majority support for every one of its actions. But it must consistently seek to create and maintain such support and be accountable for its overall program. It governs by consistent interaction with those it represents. The greatest example of this was Lincoln's approach to slavery in the United States. He opposed slavery, but believed, as a genuine democrat, and a genuine republican, that he could only act with the consent of the people and in accord with the U.S. Constitution. He struggled to win over the American people, and follow American law, in a fight against a monstrous injustice. And he succeeded.[9]

Political Parties

At a time when there was discussion whether there should be a paperback version of Salman Rushdie's *The Satanic Verses*, a book condemned by some Islamic authorities, and whose author had been declared an apostate worthy of death, civil libertarians on a TV program defended an almost absolute right to publish freely. They thought that this was no reason to censor free expression. They demanded that the government remove all barriers to the book's free publication and wide circulation. They said this was their political position.

The second segment of the show involved relatives and friends of hostages then being held in Lebanon. They felt that the government was not doing enough to secure the hostages' release—too afraid of losing face and of giving up too much. Why had the French been able to make better headway with their hostages? The relatives felt that the governments should not stand on pride or abstract principle, but should be willing to negotiate to obtain the captives' release. They called this their political position.

The producer had a rare brainwave, or perhaps an insight into what is really involved in politics. The third segment of the show brought both groups—civil libertarians and hostage supporters—together in the same discussion. The interviewer then asked the hard question—that is, the real political question: "If the terms for the release of some hostages was the suppression of a paperback version of *The Satanic Verses*, would you do it?" (This was not a far-fetched suggestion; such a demand was made.) "What if the hostages would be killed if the book were not withdrawn?"

This question produced a rare, for television, silence. The civil libertarians then waffled. No one was willing to accept the death of a known person in order to further their cause, especially if that someone's wife were sitting opposite him, or, at least, none were open to say that they were willing to, especially on television. The relatives and friends were more direct. "Absolutely yes!" they said, "If that's the condition, meet it. Withdraw the book, and let us free real flesh and blood human beings, not printed pages."

The discussion continued, but now in a wayward fashion. The diamond-hard moment had come and gone. Briefly, the question had been no longer some abstract demand but a real life question, a genuine political question. It was no longer a debate about one single ideal, one single demand, one single good, or one single assertion. It was not even about two ideals, demands, goods, or assertions. It now addressed many ideals, many goods, many demands, many assertions together. And the different demands of different people were inherently not all achievable at the same time.

This confrontation illuminates one of the central facts of politics. It is the difference between governing and interest group pressure. It is the difference between governing and ideals. It is the difference between governing and demands. An interest group can simply push for one thing, regardless of how it affects other issues and people, and without ever having to face the demands that other people raise. An interest group is not held accountable by or responsible to those whose policies it may hurt. It can be held practically responsible only by those who support it, and nobody else gets a say. Idealists do not have to deal with the people who oppose them; they only have to claim that their ideal is right. The fact that 50 percent or 90 percent of the population may radically disagree with them is irrelevant as far as they are concerned.

But governing a country, or a state, or a school board necessarily requires dealing with many demands and ideals at the same time. This is true not only of short-sighted, selfish demands, but even of legitimate, proper demands. A genuinely democratic politics means that decisions should, in principle and in practice, be accountable to all the population: Greenpeacers and forestry workers, New Yorkers and Californians, Christians, Jews, Muslims, and atheists. In a democracy, all policies will be judged and held accountable by *all* the people, including the people opposed to them.

This is why, for all their aspirations and pretensions, groups like Greenpeace, the U.S. Chamber of Commerce, the AFL/CIO, the National Organization of Women, Concerned Women of America, the Episcopal Church, the National Association of Evangelicals, and others are, in the political arena, functioning as interest groups and not really as political groups, in the sense just described. I do not mean they are necessarily self-interest groups, looking out only for themselves—they may well have a far wider interest. But they are still interest groups. They do not face the requirement to deal with many legitimate interests at the same time and they cannot be held accountable by the whole population.

There is absolutely nothing wrong with being an interest group, as long as the interest is a legitimate one. A large and complex society cannot function without interest groups. But interest groups necessarily deal with only a partial picture. They should not be confused with, and can never substitute for, genuine political organizations, such as political parties.

This is also why novelists, painters, professors, labor leaders, Hollywood stars, business executives, rap artists, or, especially, preachers and network news anchors should not think they necessarily have any political insight. A few cautions are necessary here. All such people have as much of a duty and right as anybody else to enter politics or to offer their views. If government policy affects something in which they are involved then they ought to say something. But what they should not do is use the platform and authority they have within their own profession or organization as a substitute for developing a genuinely political platform. For then they would be, in the most literal sense, irresponsible, because they are being held accountable for one task, one profession, one office, one talent, while advancing another for which they have no political accountability.

Real estate developer Donald Trump or movie person Warren Beatty can be held accountable only by his investors or fans. Nobody else gets any say regarding what they do. And, mostly, they are held accountable not for their political positions but for their skill at building or directing. They cannot be held practically accountable by those who disagree with their politics, or by those whom their suggestions will hurt. Whether or not the population agrees or disagrees with them is something they can safely ignore. They do not have to have such support.

The views of interest groups or famous people can be crucial input into government and politics. But they cannot substitute for politics, nor pretend to provide real political answers. Maybe our politicians sometimes don't deserve too much. But one thing they do deserve is that others who offer outspoken political positions should be willing to be held accountable in the open forum of an election by *all* those whom their policies will affect. This means that people should enter the political arena. They should not simply pontificate from a safe haven in another area of life.

A worthwhile political party proposes, according to its principles, to deal with all the legitimate interests in the country together. It also intends to seek support from and be accountable to the population at large. In doing so, it can be in a position to be accountable, and therefore has the moral authority to make political decisions.[10] This is one reason why political activists complain that governing parties have gone soft and compromise too much—the party now has a new constituency, one sometimes not shared by activists.

The standard for such political decisions—justice—is not an ideal, a blueprint, or an ultimate solution, but a standard for dealing honestly and fairly with complex issues. Justice must always deal with many things at the same time. In politics, it can, in principle at least, be practiced by a political party or a government. But, by its very nature, it cannot be practiced by a group that is supported by and addresses only one side of an issue.

Campaigns

Politics requires acting justly, and, at the same time, being involved with the population at large in deciding what is just. It involves the need to do what is right and also the responsibility to win popular support for what is right. If either is lacking, it can degenerate into either populism or authoritarianism. But there is always the problem that the people are usually divided in their views. Some will agree and some will not, and many will have no firmly established opinion. Hence, building support for politics means being open to the whole chaos and drama of what is also colloquially called "politics"—repeated, often fervent attempts to persuade people that what the government is doing is either right or wrong, and to gather popular and party support for some policy or course of action. Since this takes place in an arena of hundreds of thousands, or millions, of people with very different views, it requires principled attempts to build support by making deals, building coalitions, sharing power, trading off, giving everyone a place, and trying to get half a loaf rather than none. It involves political campaigns, donations, speeches, debates, television ads, and the whole plethora of modern political communication. Doubtless much of this is shallow or manipulative; but, even so, it is indispensable. A healthy democratic society is not one where there is bland agreement; it is one where there are endless, nonviolent conflicts and arguments about what to do.[11]

Many people are uncomfortable with such rambunctious politics.[12] It seems unprincipled, and many would much prefer some clear and direct implementation of some true principle. However, messy as it may seem, the only alternative to politics as vote-gathering and opinion-shaping is an authoritarianism where genuine public opinion and opposition can be consistently ignored or suppressed. The sprawl of elections and politics is typically the way all democratic societies have to be run. It is indispensable to shaping policy with a divided, active, opinionated, and boisterous population. As Churchill said, democracy is the worst form of government, except for all the others. If we take the divine responsibility of all human beings seriously, we must accept and take this type of politics seriously.

Often, the compromising nature of politics is summarized in the true cliché that politics is, like all human action, the art of the possible. An expansion of this was given by French President Jacques Chirac: "[P]olitics is not the art of the possible, but the art of making possible what is necessary." Perhaps we should change this to "politics is the art of gaining support for and making possible that which is right."[13]

Constitutions

I have suggested that power and authority do not stem from the simple will of the people, but ultimately from God. As noted, this sounds worrisome, even frightening, to modern ears, and is usually misdescribed and pilloried as some medieval or theocratic hangover. But it is neither. The fact the political authority stems not merely from popular will shows that neither the government nor the people have some inherent right to do whatever they want.

This view is a key element of constitutional democracies. A constitution, written or unwritten, is a set of basic laws according to which a country is governed, and to which all other laws are subordinate. It binds even public will. Even if a majority of the population wants to do something, then, if that something is not constitutional, it cannot be followed.

This is part of the basic structure of the U.S. Constitution. The Constitution sets out the powers of government, the division of powers between different government levels and officials, and the limits of government power. It sets up a Bill of Rights to protect people from government—even if that government has majority support. Hence, it places limits not only on government but also on the people themselves. These limits reflect, in turn, the fact that the Founding Fathers believed that human rights were not something that people gave themselves, but that were given by their Creator, who created them equal. Since these rights were not human creations, they could not be taken away by governments or by other people. Hence, the Constitution, in part, outlines standards, especially rights, which are given to rather than made by the people. The fact that they are given to us and not created by us is the source of their political strength. If human beings have not made rights, then human beings cannot take them away: rights are inalienable.

These restrictions on the people are not absolute. Constitutions can be changed. But, usually, constitutional amendments can be made only by a large and permanent shift in public opinion and with great deliberation. Constitutions are properly shielded from fleeting changes. This too is a recognition of the fact that we need to take account of a larger order to which government and people themselves should conform.

In fact, it is rare for any country to try to declare itself a pure democracy in the sense that the only guide for government action is the will of the population. Before long, the population would will (as it usually does) two contradictory things. Suppose it seeks, for example, many more government services combined with vastly lower taxes, a demand which the government is, as a matter of democratic principle, forced to follow. At this point, the structure immediately breaks down.

Such pure democracy can also deteriorate into the persecution of a minority by a majority. This persecution is, as we have noted, often through despotic leaders who still maintain great popular support—Adolf Hitler and Benito Mussolini were prime examples. This is why constitutions usually contain bills of rights to protect people even from a majority. It is also another reason why we should emphasize the importance of proper restraint not only on governments but also on citizens.

At times, of course, even constitutional limits may not be sufficient. Great injustice can still be done while following constitutional rules. This was the case with Hitler, who was able to get the support of huge majorities of Germans. These majorities were large enough to legally effect changes in the German constitution so that the Nazis could gradually and legally remake the German political structure in their own image. The Führer could constitutionally assume almost absolute power, and then legally disenfranchise and slaughter millions of people.

When trials of the Japanese and Nazi leaders took place at the end of the Second World War, there was no actual basis in positive law—that is, law actually passed by governments—for trying them. They had broken no human law, constitutional or otherwise. In fact, if one held to the truncated democratic idea that laws are only human-made things, and that justice is only agreement among citizens, then there was no basis for trying them at all.

But it was clear that German, Japanese, and other war criminals were in violation of something fundamental. Their rank brutality cried out for a just retribution. In order to recognize this, they were tried by the Allies on the basis of "crimes against humanity." This was a rather ambiguous category, which seems to have been coined in order to express the idea that there really are fundamental and given rules for human conduct, while still trying to hold on to the modern notion that humankind is free to make up its own rules as it goes along. (This was especially an act of hypocrisy on the part of the Russian judges at the tribunal, who represented a state which claimed that there could be no order for human conduct beyond a naked struggle for power between classes. In addition, Joseph Stalin had a rather impressive list of crimes against humanity of his own).[14] Nonetheless, the trials at Tokyo and Nuremberg reveal that justice transcends the will of majorities and even the constitutional laws of states. This is a vital element in the preservation of real human freedom. The extremes of political life show that there must be an order beyond that of popular will, sometimes even if that will has been embodied in a constitution.

Rights

In the modern age, issues as diverse as democracy, torture, international trade, the environment, homosexuality, and relations between the sexes are repeatedly discussed in terms of rights. They pervade not only the language of the academy, but also the legislature and the shopping mall. Despite this overwhelming emphasis, even obsession, with rights, there is no clarity about what we are talking about when we talk about them. Arguments over the meaning of rights are a major part of our political disputes. People from all parts of the political spectrum have a love/hate relationship with "rights," depending on exactly what right, or supposed right, is on offer.

People use human rights as a rallying cry to criticize brutal regimes such as China or Iraq. But the same people can often feel decidedly uneasy at the fact that so many domestic American issues are also addressed in terms of rights, with little attention to responsibilities. Typically, people who stress property rights reject notions of gay rights. Some people who make strong demands for rights of religious freedom can be nervous about claims for free speech when obscenity and pornography come to the fore.

For many others, the whole idea of human rights is troubling. It smacks an assertion of human pride and self-will. A clamor for rights seems to violate any belief in sacrifice and servanthood, that we should assert not our own interests but first of all serve others. The demand for rights seems to neglect the fact that, for example, the Bible pictures human beings as clay and God as the potter who shapes our lives as he wills. In this sense, rights seem to run counter to the example of Jesus' life, and to violate Paul's admonition to the Philippians: "Let each of you look not only to his own interests, but also to the interests of others. Have this mind among yourselves, which is yours in Christ Jesus, who, though he was in the form of God, did not count equality with God a thing to be grasped, but emptied himself, taking the form of a servant" (Phil. 2:4–7).

It is certainly true that the notion of rights is overstretched and misused—nowhere more so than in North America, where every call for moderation and restraint seems to be met by the claim that "I have a right." But the misuse of something need not invalidate its proper use. Instead, we need to understand rights, and their limits, properly.

Human will, or self-assertion, is not the only possible basis of rights. Rights can be gifts, endowments. This is the understanding reflected in the Declaration of Independence, where rights are described as "endowed" by God, something given to human beings that is appropriate for their nature. In thinking of rights, we can stress that people are created by God. This too finds its place in America's founding documents, which speak of human beings not merely as equal, but as "*created* equal." We should base our view of rights not on what we might decide at some point but on what we are and what is given to us.[15]

Human beings have rights because God has given them rights. We are given a place in the world in which we can make decisions and live our lives. Whether we are aware of it or not, and whether we acknowledge it or not, we are given the responsibility, and therefore the right, to fulfill the tasks that have been given to us. In short, we necessarily have the right to do what we are properly called to do. Our rights relate to and stem from our duties and responsibilities. This is why the political order should be understood as one in which men and women can freely express themselves as people made in the image of God.

Hence we can speak of the rights of parents to raise and educate their children. We can also speak of rights to marriage and family life. Because we are responsible for the politics of this world, we can speak of the rights of citizens to exercise responsibility and authority for the direction of governments. Rights should be understood as gifts, as correlates of human responsibility, and as expressions of human authority.

Economic Rights?

The question of whether economic rights, such as a right to welfare or housing or education, should really be regarded as fundamental human rights is debated fiercely throughout the world and is the cause of major arguments in international relations. Countries such as China, Iran, and Malaysia have maintained heatedly that human rights should come to very different expression in different countries. In fact, there are increasing claims by several Asian and Muslim countries that many currently recognized international civil and political rights do not have a universal character at all, but are simply Western inventions and impositions. They claim that these "rights" simply reflect Western individualism and should properly be subordinated to their own Confucian or Islamic traditions, or to communist power. Meanwhile, United Nations gatherings such as the Cairo Population Conference or the Beijing Women's Conference have continued with promiscuous abandon to advocate new, wider, and wilder rights, such as to abortion or to a clean and sustainable environment. Many seem never to have met a right they didn't like.

In this setting, the need to clarify the meaning of and justification for human rights is not a sterile academic exercise. It is, rather, a vital condition for clarifying some of the major cultural, social, and political problems we face, both domestically and internationally. In particular we need to address the question of "social" or "economic" rights. I will argue that these should not be regarded as rights, or, at least, that they would be rights of a very different kind from civil and political ones.

The question of economic rights is also tied intimately to the vexed question of the universality of rights, whether they apply to all people at all times. The problem with treating economic provisions as if they were rights is that there are often legitimate reasons why a particular government would not be able to fulfill such rights in a given historical situation. Even a well-meaning government may not be able to guarantee income, or housing, or health care, or even food. Many African countries simply do not have the resources to do so. Consequently, if we were to treat economic guarantees as rights, then we would be forced to accept that rights cannot and need not be met immediately. They would be things to be *aimed for* rather than *guaranteed*. The result is that we end up diluting rights so that they become mere goals—good things to work for in the long term.

In fact, several countries have tried to use the nonimmediate character of economic rights as an excuse to reduce all rights simply to long-term goals which governments should pursue, rather than stringent limits to which governments should always adhere. China stresses that economic rights are its long-term aspiration, and then slides into treating the eradication of torture or the need for press freedom also as long-term goals rather than as immediate demands. In the name of rights, stopping the jailing, beating, torture, and murder of peaceful opponents is put off into the long-term future.

There are also claims that economic rights are more important than political rights. This argument usually takes the form of saying something like "a hungry man or woman wants food more than elections." Doubtless, if someone is actually starving to death in a famine, this is true; but, still, the whole argument is spurious. Even when people are poor and needy, with generally not enough to eat, they may and do care very much about political freedom. Poor people throughout the world cry out for relief from repressive governments. Just because people are hungry, this is no reason to repress them as well: this is sadism of a high order.

Nor is there any reason to imagine that there is a contradiction or competition between political freedom and economic well-being, as though countries should put off freedom until they are wealthy. The results of a half century of international experience are in, and the meaning is clear. The countries with open societies are precisely the ones whose citizens have become the best housed and fed, and have the best medical care.[16] It is the countries with authoritarian governments where people usually languish in poverty, often to the point of starvation. While some Asian countries have managed for a while to combine economic growth with authoritarian government, they are a distinct minority. They also face increasing pressure for democratization.

Similarly, as Indian Nobel Prize winner Amartya Sen has argued, countries with a free press no longer have famines, since the publicity given to people's suffering ignites action for relief, and there is no shortage of relief supplies if agencies are allowed to deliver them.[17] It is only in authoritarian settings where the government has the power to repress reports of what is happening that people can be hidden, ignored, or forgotten as they starve. Modern famines are the result of political action by corrupt governments such as those found in Sudan and North Korea. Consequently, there are no grounds for rejecting political rights such as freedom of the press in pursuit of supposed economic security. The opposite is true.

Genuine universal human rights must, by definition, actually be capable of being fulfilled universally. What are currently called economic rights can make no such claim, since poverty-stricken countries can legitimately assert that they have no short-term possibility of honestly furnishing such guarantees. Even such political rights as regular elections or the provision of legal counsel can sometimes suffer from the same defect, since money and other resources may not be available. This suggests that, if we want to understand what genuine, universal human rights are, then we should focus not on what governments should do but on what they should not do.[18]

If a government is actually capable of exercising authority over its territory—that is, as long as it actually is a functioning government—then it can refrain from torturing, killing, or arbitrarily imprisoning its citizens. These restrictions do not require an especially powerful or wealthy country or government, but only a functioning government. They do not require wealth, for they do not ask a government to spend something or do something, but they ask it *not* to do something. Therefore they can be universal in the sense that they can be met by *any* functioning government.

Hence, if rights are universal, as they must be if they are human rights—the rights of all human beings—they will lie in those areas of human life where governments should refrain from acting. This is not as peculiar as it might at first sound. It is in fact the structure of most American Constitutional rights. The very first words of the Bill of Rights are: "Congress shall make *no law*. . . ." In fact, the basic structure of the first, second, third, fourth, fifth, seventh, eighth, ninth, and tenth amendments (and perhaps the sixth) is to say what the government *cannot* do. They reiterate: "no law . . . not be infringed . . . no soldier . . . no person . . . no fact . . . not required . . . not be construed . . . not delegated . . ." The third, fifth, eighth, and tenth amendments do not even use the term "rights"; they simply tell the government what it does not have the authority to do, which has the same effect. Genuine, universal human rights are limits on government; they place areas of human life off-limits to government.

The Practice of Rights

Practical legal rights need to be far more than mere moral goals and nice ideas. They must be strong and enforceable political and legal guarantees. Moreover, with human rights, we are dealing not with all the myriad injustices and responsibilities that affect our lives, but expressly with the fundamental conditions of free human life. Rights should not be squandered or diluted by reducing them to every human desire, goal, or whim, no matter how good. They should be reserved for those things without which free human life is not possible. And, of course, these are the areas that are most subject to political conflict and governmental intrusion.

Consequently, human rights laws need to able to direct and constrain governments in such a way that rights cannot easily be disregarded. This is a major reason why it is good to place guarantees of rights within a constitution—constitutional laws are not simply rules made by the legislature, which can be changed by the legislature, but they are meant to direct the government and people. Hence, the protection of rights often and properly finds its expression in constitutional bills of rights, such as that in the U.S. Constitution.

However, while bills of rights are vitally important, they are not the only form of human rights protection. Another important way of protecting human rights is democracy itself, since, if a government is genuinely answerable to the population, then it will be far more reluctant to threaten or abuse them. Other political structures, such as federalism and the separation of political power into judicial, legislative, and executive branches, are means to prevent the overconcentration of political power, and therefore they also function as protections against violations of human rights. This is one reason why the protections in the Bill of Rights were added only as amendments to the Constitution and were not part of the original document. Several authors of the Constitution believed that the restrictions that they had already put on the power of government would be sufficient to protect the people's rights. It was only subsequent pressure in order to get the Constitution ratified that led to additional guarantees in order to satisfy those demanding more assurance of protection.

Another form of protection developed in recent decades has been international human rights law. In such law, states make treaties with one another to protect rights. Because the treaties exist between states, then governments can be held accountable by others when they abuse their own populations. They cannot claim that such abuse is simply an internal matter since it is already part of a treaty, an agreement that they have made with other countries. If human rights are codified in this way, and if it is the task of governments to work for justice even beyond their own boundaries, then the protection of human rights is not only important internally in the United States, but also should be a part of foreign policy.

Civil Disobedience and Rebellion

That constitutional limits may not be sufficient controls on government leads to questions of civil disobedience and rebellion against a government.[19] Civil disobedience means breaking the law nonviolently for conscientious reasons. The term is recent, but the practice, or something like it, is old. It was present in ancient Greek drama, in the life of the prophet Daniel, and, arguably, in Israel's exodus from Egypt. More recent noteworthy examples include the campaigns against slavery and the slave trade, the fight for women's suffrage, Gandhi's campaigns against the British in South Africa and India, and Martin Luther King's campaigns for civil rights in the United States. Its tactics can include sit-ins, illegal marches, tax boycotts, and blockades.

Such disobedience is different from full-scale rebellion, revolution, or any other attempt to overthrow a government, a regime, or a political order unconstitutionally and violently. Civil disobedience is not an attempt to overthrow an order, but to dissent from it in some way, and to show that dissent in actions rather than simply words. In some cases, such as blocking a logging road or an abortion clinic, it is an attempt actually to impose an outcome by nonviolent means. It is then not merely a symbol or a statement, though it will usually have these overtones as well, but is an active attempt to stop something from happening, or to start something.

In other cases it may simply be an individual or collective act of conscientious refusal of a tax, a law, or an order, because some people believe that they cannot morally carry out a particular directive from a government. They may have no wish to start a political movement and are not necessarily convinced that their act will alter government policy. They simply will not violate their conscience.

Disobedience can be carried out against an entire regime, against a particular law, or against a particular government action. If against a particular law or action, typically acts of disobedience accept the overall legitimacy of the government as such. People who protest abortion or certain types of logging do not (usually) deny all legitimacy to government or deny the validity of other laws. They grant a basic legitimacy, but nevertheless believe that, in one or more instances, government has overstepped its bounds. Civil disobedience always contains this combination of rejection and acceptance. This is why, though disobedient, it is also called *civil.*

This combination has commended civil disobedience to many ethicists. It seems to respect the apostle Paul's stricture that the powers that be are God's ministers (Rom. 13:1–8) as well as Peter's claim that "we must obey God rather than men" (Acts 5:29. See also 1 Pet. 2:13–14). These can be combined in Jesus' admonition to give to God the things which are God's and to Caesar the things which are Caesar's (Mark 12:13–17). This is why civil disobedience has won the support of people in many different Christian communions, although of course they often disagree on when it is appropriate. It is practiced by groups as divergent as Operation Rescue on abortion, and Sojourners on refugees. Even religious groups who do not think of themselves as engaging in illegal acts, or even as politically active, engage in widespread acts of civil disobedience, such as taking Bibles into closed countries, or making contacts with underground believers in countries such as China or Saudi Arabia, or conducting evangelism in areas where it is forbidden. All these are also acts of civil disobedience.

In more extreme situations, people may go beyond civil disobedience and reject the legitimacy of the regime as such. This situation occurs when people believe a government has become so corrupt and tyrannical that they must disobey not only some of its laws but the regime itself. This is rebellion against a government. While they have always emphasized caution on the matter, most Protestant and Catholic, and some Orthodox, theologians and philosophers have said that such rebellion and resistance may be at times be required.

This position is usually based not so much on the idea that we are rebelling against authority, but that a tyrannical government has itself rebelled against proper authority. If the government is violating basic justice, or even its own laws, it would then be illegitimate to obey it. For instance, we would be quite justified in disobeying a policeman who tried to tell us who we should marry. We are not rebelling against proper authority if we disobey, since the policeman has no proper authority over such things. He has exceeded his authority and need not be followed. He is the one that is rebelling, while we are following constituted authority. In the same way, several consistent views of such rebellion portray it not as a rejection of legitimate authority, but as obedience to legitimate authority. This is one reason many theologians, including John Calvin, have held that rebellion should spring not from the population at large, but only from those people holding subordinate authority—the "lesser magistrates."[20]

We should be extremely cautious about opposing governments by unconstitutional means. For the reasons mentioned above, most classical theologians emphasize not so much a right of disobedience as a duty of disobedience. It is not a matter of personal discretion but a matter of responsibility. This, in turn, necessarily raises not only the vexed question of the legitimacy of a ruler, but the complex question of the legitimacy of an opponent of a government. Who properly has the authority to say that the government is wrong and that a law should be disobeyed? The anarchic idea that any individual person (or congregation) can and should just decide simply to "obey God rather than man" is a manifestation more of extreme Western individualism than biblical insight. What is necessary is some form of legitimate alternate means of exercising authority. Within the Christian community, the Catholic Church and the Orthodox can address this, but it is something that Protestants, especially, are loath to face.

It is useful to apply the criteria of just war to civil disobedience or rebellion (see the discussion of just war in chapter 8). In particular, we need to ask whether our acts are a last resort, whether all legal avenues have been exhausted, whether the actions are appropriate to the cause and their effects are proportionate to the outcomes, and whether they have a specific and achievable end.

What we have loosely called democracy—the growth of representative and constitutional government, the division of political power, and the legitimizing of legal opposition—raises these questions to a higher pitch. If a government has been constitutionally elected by the population, then who can claim the authority to challenge its laws, and why? The growth of democracy also means that there is a very wide variety of legal means available to oppose particular bad laws, or even a corrupt government as a whole. There are elections, lobbying, media, and party organizations. Too often people, especially younger ones, find civil disobedience more attractive because it can be easier and more glamorous than the tedious, boring, day-to-day work of politics. But if we have not yet campaigned, organized, voted, and lobbied long and strenuously, and found it utterly futile, then we should not too quickly leap to civil disobedience. It can be a lazy cop-out, and also, by alienating people, can be more of a hindrance than a help.

We are to take up the legal avenues that have been given to us to pursue a political calling. We are not usually called to crusades but to ongoing work. In order to do this fruitfully, we need to understand something about the world in which we are living. We will take a closer look at this in the pages that follow.

Notes

1. Paul Marshall, *Human Rights Theories in Christian Perspective* (Toronto: ICS, 1983); Michael J. Perry, *The Idea of Human Rights: Four Inquiries* (New York: Oxford University Press, 1998).

2. Thomas A. West, "Religious Liberty: The View from the Founding," in *On Faith and Free Government*, ed. Daniel C. Palm (Lanham, Md.: Rowman & Littlefield, 1997), 3–28. My point here is not that leaders such as Washington, Madison, Jefferson, or, later, Lincoln were all orthodox in their theology. It is that their thinking was shaped in fundamental ways by Christian beliefs. In the case of Lincoln, a man "visibly influenced" by a faith he did not share, see Allen Guelzo, *Abraham Lincoln: Redeemer President* (Grand Rapids, Mich.: Eerdmans, 1999). See also James H. Hutson, ed., *Religion and the New Republic: Faith in the Founding of America* (Lanham, Md.: Rowman & Littlefield, 2000); Michael Novak, *God's Country: Taking the Declaration Seriously* (Washington, D.C.: American Enterprise Institute, 2000).

3. From my article "Theocracy" in the *New Dictionary of Christian Ethics and Pastoral Theology*, ed. David J. Atkinson and David H. Fields (Downer's Grove, Ill.: InterVarsity Press, 1995).

4. Harry Jaffa, "On the Nature of Civil and Religious Liberty," in *Equality and Liberty* (Claremont, Calif.: The Claremont Institute, 1999), 177–78. Originally published by Oxford University Press, 1965.

5. See Daniel J. Elazer, *The Covenant Tradition of Politics*, 4 vols. (Rutgers, N.J.: Transaction, 1995–98); David Novak, *Covenantal Rights* (Princeton, N.J.: Princeton University Press, 2000).

6. Cf. J. L. Talmon, *The Rise of Totalitarian Democracy* (New York: Praeger, 1960).

7. This is why Locke's *Second Treatise on Government* opens with a discussion of the wrongfulness of suicide, since this would violate God's property rights.

8. On Christian views of democracy, see Jonathan Chaplin, "Christian Theories of Democracy," in *Contemporary Political Studies 1998*, vol. 2, ed. Andrew Dobson and Jeffrey Stanyer (Nottingham: Political Studies Association, 1998), 988–1003; Greg Maddox, *Religion and the Rise of Democracy* (London: Routledge, 1996).

9. See Harry Jaffa, *A New Birth of Freedom: Abraham Lincoln and the Coming of the Civil War* (Lanham, Md.: Rowman & Littlefield, 2000).

10. See Edmund Burke's comments in his *Reflections on the Revolution in France* (Indianapolis, Ind.: Bobbs-Merrill, 1955), 221.

11. Bernard Crick, *In Defense of Politics* (Chicago: University of Chicago Press, 1993); Ralf Dahrendorf, *Class and Class Conflict in Industrial Society* (Palo Alto, Calif.: Stanford University Press, 1959).

12. And not only Christians. See E. J. Dionne, *Why Americans Hate Politics* (New York: Simon and Schuster, 1991).

13. This section is based upon my article, "Politics," in *The Dictionary of Everyday Life*, ed. Robert Banks and R. Paul Stevens (Downer's Grove, Ill.: InterVarsity Press, 1996).

14. The trials of accused war criminals in Rwanda and the former Yugoslavia may be in a different category since there is now a greater basis for their prosecution under international law.

15. See Marshall, *Human Rights Theories*.

16. See Adrian Karatnycky, ed., *Freedom in the World: The Annual Survey of Political Rights and Civil Liberties, 1999–2000* (New York: Freedom House, 2000).

17. Amartya Sen, *Development as Freedom* (New York: Knopf, 1999).

18. See my "On the Universality of Human Rights," in *International Morality in the Post Cold War Era*, ed. Luis Lugo (Lanham, Md.: Rowman & Littlefield, 1998).

19. Drawn from my article, "Civil Disobedience," in *The Dictionary of Everyday Life*.

20. John Calvin, *Institutes of the Christian Religion*, all editions, Book 4, Chapter 20, Section 31.

CHAPTER FIVE

~

Understanding the Modern World

Human Freedom

Politics deals with relations that we ourselves shape. Of course, political institutions do not reflect only human choice; they are not infinitely malleable, but already reflect something about how the world is made. However, they also always reflect real human choices and, so, they properly change over time.

This change means that some common ways of trying to interpret the Bible leave people poorly equipped to deal with politics. On the one hand, some biblical conservatives seem to assume that everything must be done in the same way as in biblical times. However, in our very different world, this, apart from its other problems, appears to be a futile quest. On the other hand, many think that, because our situation is now so very different, it is equally futile to expect the Bible to speak to it or anything like it.

Both of these views are wrong, simply because one essential feature in the Bible itself is the importance of change—of history, of real human responsibility, of human freedom. This responsibility means that an essential part of being committed to acting properly is being free to work out what that means in our own times. Previous chapters described briefly an ongoing development of human life and society throughout biblical history. Part of this development was in political structure and authority. As biblical history moves from Cain to Abraham to Moses to Samuel to David, there are new political forms and offices, including judges, kings, and prophets, who appear as new circumstances develop. There is no reason to expect that this, or any other process of political development, would stop at the end of the biblical period. Indeed, the stress on human responsibility for culture at the beginning of Genesis shows that historical change and development are understood as part of God's intentions for human life. Human beings are called to create, to develop, and to adapt what is about us. The core of being human, of being made in the image of God, is that humanity is given responsibility for the earth and all that is in and on it.

This pattern of human responsibility occurs in biblical discussions of law. Perhaps the starkest example was when Jesus was faced with questions of divorce. The Pharisees asked him: "Is it lawful to divorce one's wife for any cause?" Jesus answered that God had made and intended man and woman to be one from the beginning of creation so that "What therefore God has joined together let no man put asunder." His questioners then asked, referring to Deuteronomy 24:4, "Why then did Moses command one to give a certificate of divorce, and to put her away?" Jesus replied, "For your hardness of heart Moses allowed you to divorce your wives, but from the beginning it was not so" (Matt. 19:3–9).

Admittedly it was Jesus who said this, and one could argue that Jesus might do things in relation to the law that others could not. However, he is described as giving an example of how properly to read the law. In doing so, he argued that God had, from the creation itself, put men and women together permanently and so they should not be separated. This is what God wants. But he then suggested that, because people, being hard of heart, could not manage to live with this complete restriction, Moses allowed them to divorce in order to avoid even worse problems. In reading the law Jesus focused on its basic intent ("from the beginning this was not so") and he read the particular law given through Moses as one way of expressing this intent in a particular circumstance ("Moses allowed you"). He said that Moses' practical lawgiving had to take the sinful situation into account. In commenting on this point, Calvin, often misrepresented as some sort of Old Testament fundamentalist and tyrant, took the argument further:

> "[T]he statement of some, that the law of God given through Moses is dishonored when it is abrogated and new laws preferred to it, is utterly vain. . . . For the Lord through the hand of Moses did not give that law to be proclaimed among all nations and to be in force everywhere. . . ."

Instead, Calvin suggested that we make diverse laws "with regard to the condition of times, place, and nation. . . ." And commented, "[h]ow malicious and hateful toward public welfare would a man be who is offended by such diversity. . . ?"[1] Calvin says that we should do what Moses did: honor God's basic intention in "the condition of times, place and nation" in which we live.

This example suggests one way to understand the law, and to give it expression in differing circumstances. Indeed, as Gordon Wenham has pointed out, the Mosaic law contains internal examples of its own application in particular situations.[2] This law is not only comprised of basic principles which we may then apply to our particular circumstances. Most of the writings in the books of the law are, in fact, already the working out of such principles in the various circumstances of Israelite life. In the Torah, the Ten Commandments are central. Much of the rest of the legal material contained in, say, Deuteronomy, is a type of "case law"—law that draws on what is central and applies it in particular cases.[3] In this sense, even biblical law is developed in terms of concrete circumstance.

This is not to say that God's fundamental intent changes, but rather that this intent must always be expressed in such a way that its purpose is fulfilled. The implementation of the law is always the implementation of an abiding order of and for justice within the concrete and variable situations of human life.[4]

The Jubilee

An illustration of the difficulties and dimensions of this implementation is given in the biblical year of Jubilee. Every fiftieth year was to be a Jubilee. This year had major rules to alleviate poverty in Israel. Land which had been previously sold was to be freely returned to the seller (Lev. 25). As the land was meant to have been equitably distributed among the Israelites when they had first entered the promised land, this redivision meant that no one should irreversibly be separated from their land, their means of livelihood. Hence, the major economic resources would continue to be spread among the population (Lev. 25:6).

At the turn of the last millennium, many groups, including the World Bank, the Vatican, and other churches, called for a type of Jubilee which would forgive the debts owed by poor Third World countries to rich Western institutions. There is much to be said for this proposal, if carefully carried out. However, it would be a mistake to interpret the Jubilee, or anything else in the Bible, apart from the covenantal relations in which it was embedded. Failure to do this could lead to a wooden means of biblical exegesis, leading to bad economic and political decisions.

The Jubilee laws not only focus on redistribution of wealth, but also anchor this redistribution in the centrality of God's redemption. This is why the year of Jubilee was to be proclaimed on the Day of Atonement. On this day, Israel commemorated the fact that they themselves were once poor, oppressed, and aliens in Egypt, and that they had been delivered by the grace of God. The Jubilee year was a memorial of this deliverance. The fiftieth year, as well as the seventh, sabbatical years, were times particularly to remember, proclaim, and reenact that deliverance. These were years that "proclaimed the Lord's release" (Deut. 15:2; Lev. 25:9–10). The redistribution of land was almost part of a liturgy, a religious ceremony, carried out by Israel. It was no more a simple redistribution than Christian communion is intended to be a simple meal, or the Muslim hadj—the pilgrimage to Mecca— is intended to be tourism. The sense here is that the Israelites were called, as God's covenant partners, in remembrance to act toward one another as God had already acted toward them: "You shall remember that you were a slave in the land of Egypt, and the Lord your God redeemed you; therefore I command you this today" (Deut. 15:15).

This is what Jesus alluded to in the Lord's prayer when he said, "Forgive us our debts, as we also have forgiven our debtors" (Matt. 6:12). Do to each other what God has done for you. It is in terms of this picture of forgiveness and redemption that Jesus first announced his own ministry. At Nazareth, perhaps his first public event, he introduced himself in Isaiah's words as the one who will "proclaim the acceptable year of the Lord" (Luke 4:19). Isaiah's words were in turn a reference to the proclamation of Jubilee (Lev. 25:10). Jesus introduced himself as the one who would fulfill the year of Jubilee, the year of release, the year of the forgiveness of debts.

The picture given by the Jubilee and the sabbath laws is one of redemption and atonement expressed in the concrete realities of human life. Debts were forgiven, that which had been lost was redeemed, the slate was wiped clean. The poor were to begin again—we are not stretching the point if we say to be born again—economically.

The foundation of the Jubilee was to be trust in and gratitude to God. It was not a simple economic act, but was also an act of faith; it called for trust in God.[5] In the Jubilee, Israel was also to let the land rest and the animals rest, which meant they should not plant crops. The previous year, the fortyninth year, would also have been a sabbath year (which occurred every seventh year), wherein the land and the animals were also to rest. This meant that for two consecutive years Israel had to leave the land fallow.

This was a dangerous thing to contemplate for any agricultural people— no planting for two years. What if there was a drought in the third year?

What if any of the number of blights which afflict human life, especially agricultural life, came upon them? They would starve or find themselves forced, like Jacob's children, once more to give themselves up to others in exchange for food. God anticipated the fear that Israel would experience if it followed the Jubilee and said, "[I]n case you should ask: 'what shall we eat in the seventh year if we do not sow or harvest the produce?' I have ordered my blessing to be on you every sixth year which will therefore provide for you for three years" (Lev. 25:20 –21). Here God said, if you do it, I will provide. Carrying out the Jubilee called for trust in God, a realization that Israel's life was always in God's hands. It meant relying on God's promise of food, and then refraining from caring for themselves for two long years.

Given this faithful and liturgical reality, then simply trying to transfer the Jubilee year to a modern situation when there is no longer the faith on which it was founded would be to invite disaster. The application of Jubilee must be complex. This is not to deny the modern call for forgiveness of debts. But it is to say that modern economic policy should not be pursued by transplanting biblical practice.

The modern implementation of justice is and will always be difficult, simply because of the inescapable complexity of unraveling the many dimensions of a biblical commandment from its expression in a particular age. Nevertheless, this difficulty, too, is an ongoing aspect of human responsibility.

Understanding the World

We don't know how to act without some standards provided by laws and principles. They provide the backbone and structure for how we live. Without them, we would be left in a situation simply of infinite variability. But, while we can never act properly without them, neither can we act properly if principles are *all* we have. No principles can themselves be sufficient to give full human guidance. Apart from principles and universals, we always need to know about the particulars and concrete situations of life.

If we want to drive properly, we don't need to know just about what cars are like, we need to know about the particular car that we have. We don't just need to know about highways, we also need to know about this highway, the one we are to drive on. Similarly if we want to train our dog, we don't just need to know about what dogs in general are like, we also need to know what this, our dog, is like. If we want to knit a sweater, we don't just need to know what shape most people are, we also need to know what shape this particular person is. Similarly, if we are to help govern a country, we don't just need to know about countries as such, we need to know about our particular country. If we want to make a law, we need not only to know about laws in general, even divine laws, but we also need to know about these citizens, this legislature, this president, this constitution, these laws.

If principles and universal truths were by themselves sufficient to make laws or to run governments (or churches), we would no longer need personal judgment. But we know that we need people who have the skills to, among other things, make an accurate judgment about a particular person, city, office, or offense. These decisions require us to know and make judgments about the infinite variabilities and idiosyncrasies of human life.[6]

We should understand not only the biblical Word but the world. We cannot, nor should anyone want to, try to find all the answers to all our questions in the Bible or any other book. While one can certainly repair a car in a responsible way, and while the Bible certainly says things relevant to auto repair (the use of technical gifts in service to our neighbor), yet none of us would want a mechanic who knows nothing but Bible texts. Good mechanics must always know the structure of car engines. They must know what a car is and how it works, and they need to know about this particular car. There is no substitute for this.

The scriptures are not intended to be some divinely inspired Encyclopedia Americana wherein all human knowledge is found in godly form. They are not given to tell us everything, but to show us the foundation of everything. They are focused on the central dimension of life—on showing who God is, who we are, how we came into being, what we live for, how and why we do evil and know suffering, and especially how we might be redeemed.

The psalmist described God's word as a lamp unto his feet, a light on his path (Ps. 119:105). A lamp is not provided so that it can be stared at for itself, but instead it is used to illuminate something else. It is to help us understand the "something else," the world in which we live. In this metaphor, the Word is also meant to shine ahead of us on the path we walk. It illuminates the path we take. It is a guide in discovering the world, to understanding it correctly.

The neglect of this fact has caused many problems in the Christian Church today. The decline in the influence of Christian social teaching parallels the development of the industrial revolution. This influence declined in large part because it was not able to give guidance in a new and rapidly changing situation. The examples of social and economic life in the Old and New Testaments are largely in agricultural settings. They refer to rents, land boundaries, gleaning fields, tending animals, and so forth. Hence, their relevance was more easily seen when a country was largely rural.

But now, unless we are able to use these same examples and discern their meaning in a world of capital, factories, division of labor, large corporations, unions, and mass production, then they will appear to be totally irrelevant. This irrelevance quickly became obvious to most economists at the time of the industrial revolution, and it gave them a greater excuse to declare their science to be free from any moral concerns.

Political action requires understanding *the world*, uncovering new things, learning new facts, responding to new situations, and devising new plans. But, this world is not something that just happens somehow to be here: it is something that, as Genesis says, has been *made* with humankind explicitly in mind. Since God created the world good, the way the world is made is meant to speak of the will of its maker. Even though twisted by sin, the creation has not lost its character as the expression of God's will.

Clearly, most of the things that exist in modern politics (elections, civil service, policies, legislatures, parties) did not occur in biblical times. Hence, we cannot determine a political policy solely by some simple process of biblical exegesis. We cannot proof-test a solution to welfare or foreign policy. We must always know the situation itself. What we can do, however, is approach such questions, as much as we can, guided by what is given in biblical revelation. We can try to understand what is required now, in this modern age, as responsible stewards of the world.

Perhaps another way of illustrating this fact loosely is to say that we are given us the basic rules of the game—what the conditions are and what the goals are. Obviously, we cannot play any game at all, be it chess, golf or basketball, without knowing the rules. However, simply knowing rules is never enough to play any game at all. Tiger Woods is not a great golfer merely and simply because he keeps the rules. He is a great player because he has learned what the millions of possibilities are within the rules, and he has the skills and intelligence to act out those possibilities. Merely knowing the rules does not teach us how to drive, chip, or putt. Rules tell us what we are trying to win, and what we cannot do. They give normative direction. But we still have to learn to play, to know what the myriads of possibilities are within the rules.

In similar terms, political action can never be reduced to following divine rules. It is not an exercise whose answers and strategies are already known before we begin. Our end is not predetermined (except in the final sense of the judgment and renewal of all things). Politics always involves knowing the world, and very real questioning, probing, trying, learning, and revising as we struggle to act well in our historical situation. What follows in this chapter are attempts to develop some criteria for such knowing and questioning.

Biblically Shaped Analysis

It is wrong to think that religion provides us only with values, and that then we must somehow plug in the facts in order to get strategies. The content of Christian (or Jewish or Muslim or other) faith is not just some moral norms or values which can be applied to a situation. It is also a way of seeing and understanding that situation itself. Consequently, it would be strange to take certain purported values, such as love or justice, and then try to work them out in international relations via either a quasi-Marxist analysis of world trade, a systems theory of international interaction, a Keynesian theory of political economy, or a behaviorist or functionalist theory of the state. Rather, we should seek, as much as we can, to ensure that the concepts and categories with which we analyze and interpret our situation are consistent with our basic beliefs.[7] If we fail to do this, then we may find that any attempt we make to understand the world will be shaped more by the analysis we pick up and little by our beliefs themselves.

One example, in nonpolitical settings, occurs among many religious psychologists, who often uncritically construct their framework for counseling from various, often secular, ideas. They may pick and choose from an assortment of concepts drawn from theorists such as Sigmund Freud and Carl Jung, Frederic Skinner and Lawrence Klein, and Erik Erikson and William Glasser, even though few of the selected theories have analytical room for the fact that human beings are, as a matter of fact, created in the image of God. Indeed, several of these theorists regard religious faith itself as a possible sign of insanity or infantilism. In the process of applying this synthesis of ideas to their patients, such therapists may attempt to include some particular Christian insights on the nature of guilt, hope, and change, and, in doing so, they may try to add some truer spiritual dimension to their analyses. However, the result may not be counseling that reflects a biblically attuned view of a human being. It can be the latest psychological trend plus some add-on biblical texts.

A similar example of the uncomfortable marriage of strange ideological bedfellows can be found in liberation theology. This theology is ostensibly an interpretation of the Christian faith, shaped in response to decades of suffering in, primarily, Latin America.[8] Theologians and priests, many of them from Europe, found themselves among people in deep poverty and misery. These societies had vast disparities of wealth, and political regimes which existed to maintain this situation rather than to seek any genuine justice.

Suppose you are a priest working with a family in a city in Peru where the husband was picked up by the police a month ago. You try to find out where he is, or even if he is alive. It happens not once but again and again, until you realize that you face not only an individual pastoral problem but an organized repression. You conclude that this pattern must be resisted. You work with peasants who are hungry and seeking land, of which they have none. Then, after a time, you realize that the lands are tied up in *latifundias* (landed estates) which produce nonfood crops such as coffee and sugar for export to rich countries. Your training seems totally foreign to this situation. Theological discussions in the rich lands where you studied now appear to be sterile academic affairs, far removed from your own calling in oppressed countries. Politics seems to dominate the situation, and when, and if, you enter politics in opposition to what you believe is oppression, Marxists and other revolutionaries are already there, and what they say appears to fit the situation.

Liberation theology claimed to emerge out of these attitudes and concerns. It was intended to be a theology oriented not to abstract theories of God but to concrete action, to commitment to the poor, to practical politics, to liberation from oppression, and to justice as a central element of the gospel. Such theology has been prominent among the Sandinistas in Nicaragua, the Zapatistas in Mexico, and in opposition to General Augusto Pinochet in Chile. Later on, variants appeared in Africa, notably South Africa under apartheid, and in Asia, with a particular Korean variant. It became widespread in the industrialized West, especially in foundations and theologically liberal seminaries. Generally it now survives only amongst such theologians and other academics.

One of the principal tenets of this theology was that it grew from experience and that anyone who did not share this experience could not properly speak to it. Its practitioners could be impatient with more discursive critiques of their work from more comfortable lands. However, it was also true that most liberation theologians were well qualified academically, were proficient in German, Hebrew, and Greek, could write dense dialectical prose and, in general, gave evidence of owing a very large debt to more radically inclined European intellectuals. It would be extremely naïve, then, to see liberation theology as emerging full blown only from Latin American experience. It had clear, well-established roots in the longstanding traditions of Western philosophical radicalism.

In their desire to escape from what they saw as theological sterility, liberation theologians preached that abstract talk of justice would not do—theology had to be supplemented by social, political, and economic analysis in order to relate it to the concrete world. They spoke of Christian values which needed social analysis in order to get at the facts of human life. However, just any social analysis wouldn't do for Christian action. The so-called value-free social sciences, dominant especially in Western Europe and North America, were rejected, seen as the tools and self-images of an increasingly controlling and manipulative capitalist society. A different social analysis was sought, one which would highlight the system of oppression. The analysis that was chosen was usually a form of Marxist theory, though often not crude Marxism-Leninism.

There are diverging views as to why this type of analysis was selected. Some suggested that such tools of analysis were really a science, value-free and objective; hence they could be used by Christians as instruments whose use was independent of their, or any, faith. Another view was that Marxist-style analysis was certainly committed and value-laden, as is all science. However, this view maintained that, since Marxism had an ethos or outlook similar to that of Christianity—a search for justice—then its analysis was one admirably suitable as a tool for Christian concerns. Due to either set of reasons, such theologians usually ended up with supposed Christian values, supplemented by supposed Marxist analysis.

The argument ran and runs like this: theology is good only if it stands with the poor and expresses their interests. But, to know what these interests really are, one must have a social analysis. The most suitable social analysis is a type of Marxism, a theory which is addressed to oppression. However, in such a scheme, it is manifestly the social analysis which actually tells us about the purported real, structural situation of the poor, out of which we should then act. Social analysis is at the core of action. All the emphasis on theology arising out of experience and on learning from the poor should not obscure this fundamental fact.

Hence, if the poor felt their real interest might be in supporting a military junta to preserve stability, or in working hard simply to get 10 percent more money next year, or starting a small business, or in being left alone to hope for heaven (all very common options), then this view was not adopted by theologians of liberation. These theologians believed that not the immediately expressed views of the poor, but their own social analysis, revealed the real roots of poverty—exploitation—and showed the only way out—political and class struggle. Hence, members of the poor eventually needed to be brought round to the theologians' views. This process could be called education, consciousness raising, conscientisation, empowerment, or what you will, but liberation theologians usually had at least some strategy shaped by their analysis beyond which they would not go, and to which the poor would need to agree.

The resulting process then went (and goes) like this: the chosen tools of analysis determine the perceived situation of the poor, which then determines the theology of liberation. However, in such a scheme, the theology can have no real critical input into the analysis that ultimately determines its content. The element provided by the Christian faith is only some "commitment," a value, that might provide the dynamic but not the content of the process and the politics.[9] The content of the strategy is determined by the analysis chosen. Indeed Hugo Assman described theology as the "second word" which only follows the "first word" of the social sciences.

However, social science tools of analysis do not fall fully formed from the sky, but are always the expression of trends in social theory, which in turn reflect a whole view of the nature of humankind, the world, history, justice, wealth, work, destiny, and salvation. If the analysis shapes the theology, and if that analysis is indebted to Marxism, or any other theory, then the Marxist tail will inevitably wag the Christian dog. The Christian faith does not add anything distinctive to the scheme; it merely tells us to do good while other factors will tell us what actually is the good to be done.[10]

I use the example of liberation theology because it most clearly illustrates the crucial nature of the relation between faith and social analysis. But the tendency to borrow from and, in turn, to be shaped by analyses with roots far from and even antithetical to faith goes far beyond liberation theology. A few further examples might help.

The great French, Christian sociologist, Jacques Ellul, has certainly contributed his own distinct and valuable elements to sociology, especially in his trenchant analyses of technology; yet the influence of Marx on his thought is deep. He was a professing Marxist for only a short period of time in his youth but, even after clearly abandoning it, the influence still remained with him. Much later Ellul himself referred to his "twofold intellectual origin in Marx and [Swiss theologian Karl] Barth," particularly with respect to his own view of dialectics as the basic structuring principle of society, history, and indeed, the creation itself.[11] In turn, Barth and Ellul became two of the dominant influences on one of the most persuasive of North American Anabaptist theologians, John Howard Yoder. These three have in turn become some of the major influences (apart from several biblical and ancient ones) on much of the Anabaptist revival associated with magazines such as *Sojourners*, and with many current stresses on Christian nonviolent action and antimilitarism.

Alternatively, Falwell, when leader of the Moral Majority in the United States, like many conservative Christians, borrowed most of his views of the economic duties of governments from free-enterprise economists. His favorite was the Nobel Prize winner Milton Friedman, a leader of the conservative economic school at the University of Chicago. Indeed, for a fundamentalist, Falwell was markedly reluctant to make any consistent reference to or study of the Bible on economic matters.[12]

My point is that, in borrowing such forms of analysis, many Christians and others already determine much of the content of the proposals they will offer as policies "stemming from the gospel." In fact, anyone reading a Christian book on politics or economics, and wanting to get a quick handle on the author's perspective, can usually look in the first place not at what parts of theology or the Bible they use, but what sorts of social theory, and what sorts of social study, they borrow from. For example, Jim Wallis of *Sojourners* has frequently used Richard Barnet's work as his means of understanding world trade and corporations, and Barnet gives a very negative view of the effects of capitalism. In contrast, the Christian Coalition's *Contract with the American Family* leaned heavily on the Heritage Foundation, a conservative think tank. Ralph Reed, a major figure in conservative Christian politics in the 1990's, has borrowed from more conservative analysts, but has usually concentrated mostly on outlining the problems he sees and then tends simply to affirm that conservative responses are the way to deal with these problems.[13]

This is not to suggest that any or all of these analyses are totally or mostly wrong. However, it does suggest that such social analyses fundamentally shape our politics, and, so, we must have clear grounds for why we adopt any particular means of interpreting what is happening in the world. Furthermore, we must try to work with ways and means of understanding society which themselves reflect our most basic beliefs.

The next sections will attempt to give some beginning suggestions for understanding societies. Developing a richer analysis more firmly rooted in biblical insight remains a task crucial to any enduring politics. No doubt readers will be able to discern foreign and un-Christian elements and assumptions in what is written here, and elsewhere. But only as we continue to critique these elements in one another can we move beyond them.

Religion and Idolatry

Suggested earlier was the idea that all human action in the world can and should be seen as a service to God and our neighbors. This means that there is, therefore, no specific area of life which we can call religious, as though other areas of life were not equally religious. To put it briefly, we may say that life is religion—that our religion is what we believe, think, say, and do each and every moment of our lives.[14] As one friend remarked "I can tell more about your faith from reading your checkbook than your prayer book." Everything we do is religion in the sense that it is done in faithfulness, or in unfaithfulness, to our fundamental beliefs.

This is true not only for Christians, but also for Jews and Hindus, and for each and every other person. All people are made in the image of God. That image, though stained and twisted by sin, still distinguishes each and every human person. All people participate in the cultural mandate, either in obedience or disobedience to God, and usually both. If this were not so, then no human life would be possible, for human life is itself called to be the imaging of God within the creation. This means that we should never consider a person, corporation, book, or government as nonreligious; they are always religious, at least in the sense that they reflect in their activities either a turning toward or away from God's will for human life. Of course they may not know that, and they may even deny it, but it still remains true. As a popular Bob Dylan lyric points out, "You gotta serve somebody." Everybody serves somebody. If we do not serve God, then we will necessarily serve something else. The somethings else that people serve are what the Bible usually calls idols.[15]

The history of Israel is full of references to "idols," "graven images," and "high places." Israel's sin is usually portrayed as turning away from God and turning to idols. We might even say that idolatry is seen not just as another sin alongside the rest, but is used as a particular way of speaking about all sin. All sin is described as a particular expression of the basic sin of idolatry, of putting something else in the rightful place of God. This is one reason why idolatry is the very first theme that opens the Ten Commandments—"You shall have no other gods besides me. You shall not make for yourselves a graven image. . . ." (Ex. 20:3, 4).

In the Scriptures no one is described as an atheist; rather, if someone does not worship and serve the one true God, then he or she is expected, inevitably, to worship and serve another god. These other gods are things within the creation, either already given there or else made by human hands. They become things that we worship and serve, things that we fear, things that we trust in, things that we rely on to save us. (In these terms a real atheist would be a person who ostensibly trusts nothing at all, but such people are practically nonexistent).

Habbakuk said, "What profit is an idol when its maker has shaped it, a metal image, a teacher of lies? For the workman trusts in his own creation when he makes dumb idols" (Hab. 2:18). Paul described idols as "a representation by the art and the imagination of man" (Acts 17:29), and he condemned "worshipping the creature rather than the creator" (Rom. 1:24). Idolatry here means putting any created thing in the place of the Creator, often a created thing we have made.

The worship of idols is never portrayed as a purely formal or liturgical matter, like having a little shrine in the living room. Such worship is seen, like all worship (Rom. 12:1; James 1:27), as an act of one's entire life. Idolatry is portrayed as putting our final trust in anything within the creation. Whatever, apart from God, we might hold to be the fundamental core or key to our problems, is an idol.

Idolatry can be manifested in many ways. When the prophets spoke of it, they often put it together in a list of acts of pride and oppression. Isaiah said

> For thou hast rejected thy people, the house of Jacob, because they are full of diviners from the east and soothsayers like the Philistines, and they strike hands with foreigners. Their land is filled with silver and gold, and there is no end to their treasures; their land is filled with horses, and there is no end to their chariots. Their land is filled with idols; they bow down to the works of their hands, to what their fingers have made. (Isa. 2:6–8)

The list of sins which Isaiah cites is a list of many different ways of turning away from God. The house of Jacob gave heed to the guidance of false gods (through diviners and soothsayers). It relied on foreign treaties rather than God (striking hands with foreigners). It sought security through wealth (gold and silver) rather than trust in God. It relied on military might rather than God (chariots—the means of attack, the means of aggressive, not defensive warfare). All of this was then summarized in Isaiah's final saying that the land is filled with idols. Idolatry was not listed as another additional sin: it was the summary, the description, of all the preceding sins. It was the summary of Israel's sin.

Just as Habakkuk condemned the workman "trusting in his own creation," so Isaiah condemned "trust in chariots" (Isa. 31:1). A chariot—military power—could be an idol as potent as, or as useless as, Baal, Moloch, or Ashtaroth. The worship of money, the act of relying on money for peace or health, is quite simply mammon-worship. And Jesus said, "No man can worship two masters" (Matt. 6:24). Idolatry is manifested, inter alia, as concrete human behavior and trust.

In this supposedly secular and rational world are people and governments believing, trusting deep down in their hearts, putting their lives on the line in hope that mere military power will itself bring peace, or that mere wealth will necessarily bring happiness, or that mere education will inevitably bring tolerance, or that the laws of history will finally bring a new society. This brings to mind Paul's cry to those he thought of as philosophical idolaters at Athens: "I perceive that in every way you are very religious" (Acts 17:22). We, too, live in a very religious age.

It is not that legitimate defense, or money, or learning, or change, are wrong. All things are good and are meant to be used rightly. All of these are elsewhere commended in the Bible. But the key is that none of them should be the final cause of hope, or the foundation of peace, or the source of love. None can be trusted in, or relied upon, as the ultimate source of salvation. All are to find their proper place when approached in a more basic reliance upon God's faithfulness, justice, and mercy.

Biblically, idols ancient and modern always have an effect upon those that worship them. The psalmist described this effect: "The idols of the nations are silver and gold, the work of men's hands. They have mouths but they speak not, they have ears but they hear not, they have eyes but they see not, nor is there any breath in their mouths. Those that trust in them are like them! Yea, everyone who trusts in them" (Ps. 135:15–18). People become like their idols. We create them, but then we, in turn, become transformed into their image. We become like whatever we worship. And, as we are the molders of history and the shapers of society, we will in turn shape our society into the pattern of the idols, the gods that we worship. In what we build and create, we give expression to the beliefs, intentions, and hopes of our hearts. Ralph Waldo Emerson expressed this well: "The Gods we worship write their names on our faces; be sure of that. And a man will worship something—have no doubts about that, either. He may think that his tribute is paid in secret in the dark recesses of his heart—but it will out. That which dominates will determine his life and character. Therefore, it behooves us to be careful what we worship, for what we are worshipping we are becoming."[16]

From his own consideration of idolatry, economist Bob Goudzwaard formulated three general rules to explain the connection between the relation of God, or gods, and theoretical and practical pursuits. They are:

1. Everyone serves god(s) with their lives
2. Everyone is transformed into an image of their god.
3. Humankind creates and forms a structure of society in its own image and, hence, into the image of its idols.[17]

One example is cities. Cities come, of course, in all shapes, sizes, rhythms, and predicaments. But their structure is not wholly haphazard. People usually put what they most value at the center of their lives. The most valuable buildings are usually put on the most valuable real estate. And, in cities, the most valuable real estate has usually been in the center. Therefore, as a rule of thumb, we will usually find what a culture values most highly embodied in the buildings at the heart of its major cities. As literary critic Northrop Frye has pointed out, "In what our culture produces, whether it is art, philosophy, military strategy, or political and economic development, there are no accidents: everything a culture produces is equally a symbol of that culture."[18] Cities don't just reflect the goals of city planners and the conscious wills of those who live in them; they also reflect the deeper structure of what we think is important in life, what our beliefs are, and what our idols are.

If we consider ancient cities in the Middle East, the Far East, or Central America, we find at their heart a palace or a temple. Often these two are the same thing, since it was a feature of many ancient civilizations to treat their ruler as divine. The ruler's palace is the divine temple. If we look at the heart of medieval European cities we will find in them great cathedrals and churches symbolizing the fact that God, or the church, was at the center of human life. If we look at Western cities developed in the seventeenth, eighteenth, and nineteenth centuries we will find political structures, palaces, legislatures, and parliaments, since this was the period when modern political authority began its ascendancy. If we look at the heart of our modern cities, we usually find glass towers owned by banks or major corporations. These buildings also symbolize what lies close to the heart of our cities and life: commerce.

Clearly, cities are much too complex to be reduced to a single, simple scheme. They have grown up over many ages when successive forces hold sway. Hence, they always have many layers, including spiritual layers, embedded and built within them. Nevertheless, beyond this variation, the structures of our cities, towns, and villages symbolize the deepest commitments of life. These commitments structure our very living places. Obviously, not all human commitments are idolatrous, obsessed with one goal or attribute. We can and do judge in a nonabsolute way what things are now more important than others. But, if these commitments *are* idolatrous, then these idols will operate not merely in some small corner of human life, but will mold our society itself, even in the most concrete instances.

The nature of idolatry can also help clarify drugs and addiction. Before we first try a drug, whether a cigarette or cocaine, it has no power over us. We can usually easily decide whether or not we are going to try it. Even if we begin, in the early stages the power of the drug is weak. It is relatively easy to break away from it. But, if we give ourselves to a drug, whether heroin, nicotine, or alcohol, there is a gradual transfer of power from us to it. After a period of months or years it becomes almost impossible to break away, to break the hold it has on our lives. Breaking away can turn everything in our life upside down. It can even bring us near death.

What is the source of this power? A drug such as nicotine or cocaine is harmless if it merely lies on the table. It cannot reach out to us and grab us and hold us. The power it exercises is a power that comes only from us when we give ourselves to it. It *then* becomes a source of power in our lives. This is the structure of idolatry: when some lifeless thing without power in itself becomes the obsessive focus of human commitment, it then begins to exercise power over us. Idols draw their power from our belief and trust. The non-gods begin to function like gods.

Idolatry and Creation

I have stressed that Christianity (and Judaism, Islam, and, perhaps, other religions) emphasizes that God has made the world good, that all things in creation can and should be used to love God and our neighbors. Human beings are to shape and build the world, and be parents, administer justice, grow crops, and pray. But, because of sin, human beings have turned away from the Creator and tried to put something else, be it strength, security, sex, status, science, solidarity, or whatever, in the ultimate place. We begin to shape our world around this new false god. We put other things into the service of this god and, consequently, produce corruption and oppression.

Any interpretation of society must then seek to understand at least two things:

1. the good things given in the world, which endure despite human sin, and
2. the turning of these good things into idols, which people worship, and which cause destruction and pain.

These can help us understand the role of law, the nature of economics, the function of democracy, the goals of foreign policy, and political parties. Parties have at least a twofold character. One side, related to their fundamental commitment, is a vision of the nature and purpose of human life. The other side, related to the fact that they, like all of us, live not in a haphazard world but in God's world, is a real recognition of problems and a program to combat those problems.

On the side of fundamental commitment, political parties are usually not groupings of people who claim only to have some ideas about what may be best for the country. They also express a basic view of what is important in life, what the root of evil is, and what the purpose of politics is. Parties reveal a vision of life, either in the service of God or of an idol, or, most often in a divided world, an uneasy combination of these. Certainly, Paul's description in his letter to the Romans of his own divided heart can also be applied to parties, or economics, or churches, or anything in society (Rom. 7).

This is most clearly shown by revolutionary parties. Such parties are never simply oriented to combating injustice, though this may be a part of their goal. Invariably, they also maintain that they possess some key which will create a new man and/or a new woman, and hence a new society in which the problems of the past will be definitively overcome. They rely on some god, whether that be evolution, nature, progress, society, reason, history, equality, freedom, the individual, or whatever.[19] As a rule of thumb, if what they rely on has a capital letter, it brings problems. For example, the French Revolution was thoroughly religious in character. This was perhaps most clearly revealed when a prostitute was dressed up as the goddess Reason, put on the altar in the Cathedral of Notre Dame in Paris, and worshipped by the surrounding crowd. The same impulses came to the fore in the Russian and Chinese revolutions, and in the development of fascism and nazism. They were present in the Sandinistas in Nicaragua and the Khmer Rouge of Cambodia. Such movements never ultimately defined themselves only in terms of concrete political goals such as land reform, regular elections, or literacy programs, but also in terms of an overarching vision of a new society and a new world. The French and the Khmer Rouge even attempted to restart the calendar, with their own revolution as the new date for the beginning point of counting the years, and hence of history itself. Hence, if we try to interpret revolutionary movements simply as responses to injustice, we will fail utterly to understand them at all.

What is true of right- and left-wing revolutionary movements is also true of more mundane conservative, liberal, and middle-of-the-road parties. The difference (apart from the actual content of the program itself) is that revolutionaries have clear radical convictions, whereas those in the middle are more pragmatic and tend to waffle. Nevertheless, their programs and speeches reveal at least some partial vision of what human life is about. There is scarcely a political manifesto available, and hardly a major political speech given, that does not call explicitly for faith in some principle or program, and which does not claim to be the foundation for a new order of things. In the United States, presidential state-of-the-union speeches are invariably explicit calls to faith in something or other. They reveal, wittingly or not, the core beliefs of the president. This shows that our religion is revealed in our politics, and especially in our core, our visionary speeches.

But, at the same time, politics, like each and every human activity, can never be defined completely by the fundamental commitments of its members. All human activity takes place in the world and is always shaped and limited by the nature of that world. We may try to pretend that we are gods, but we will never be able actually to act as gods because we always remain human beings in God's world. In the same way, human political activity never completely loses its fundamental nature as a search for a just ordering of society. Political programs always deal with the world that we all share. The French and Russian revolutions were, despite their idolatrous commitment to the state, also outcries at the suffering of the poor, and revolts against the oppression they suffered. The Sandinistas in Nicaragua, along with their destructive ideology, did face a real tyrant—Somoza. Current politics on left and right are also, despite their distortions, genuine attempts to formulate practical solutions to real problems.

Consequently, we can support what political parties, movements, and ideologies genuinely recognize, while not idolizing it or them. While we should never be socialists—that is, people for whom some purported "social whole" is the center of politics—we should emphasize the importance of the social dimension of political life. While we should never be complete conservatives—in the sense of believing that what has gone before is without fault, or that we can never change what we have inherited—we should always want to conserve in our politics. We must respect the continuity of human life through the generations. While we should never be committed to liberalism—in the sense of believing that the enhancement of individual human freedom is the goal and center of politics—we should always treasure individual freedom as one of God's greatest gifts.

It is good to be social, to be liberal, to conserve. These are great things to be. The problem with political ideologies in our modern age is *not* that they value these things; they are right to value them. The problem is going beyond rightly valuing them to making them the core, the center, the foundation, the central organizing project of politics and human life itself. In doing this, they flirt with idolatry.

An analysis of existing political parties should reflect the dual character of a religious commitment combined with a genuine search for justice. For example, it is possible that we might think, along with the Democrats, that the government needs to be more active in combating unemployment or in providing for the needy. But we should never believe that a stress on human equality, or on the primacy of society over the individual, is itself the key to human happiness. Similarly, we might believe with the Republicans that government control is too all-pervasive, and hence needs, in most instances, to be restricted. But we should never believe that reliance on individual initiative is, in itself—apart from any other human consideration—the key to human happiness.

The question is not whether we think human freedom and human tradition are valuable. Of course they are valuable. Who in their right mind would not value human freedom or the importance of what we have inherited? But we must always treat them as good, not as absolute or divine. Consequently, our attitudes toward political parties may be critically supportive, but should always retain a level of detachment. If we are serious about idolatry, then we must have the courage to insist that nothing within the creation itself can be the ultimate key to politics.

Notes

1. John Calvin, *Institutes of the Christian Religion*, 2 vols., ed. John T. McNeill (Philadelphia: Westminster Press, 1960) Book 4, Chapter 20, Section 16. See also Book 40, Chapter 20, Section 3.

2. Gordon Wenham, "Law and the Legal System in the Old Testament," in *Law, Morality and the Bible*, ed. Bruce Kaye and G. Wenham (Leicester, U.K.: UCCF Press, 1978), 24–52.

3. The problem with what is often called theonomy or reconstructionism is not that it emphasizes the validity of Old Testament law; this is a good thing to do. Its problem is that it does not consider the difference of function and situation of "law" in the Old Testament and in a modern state. For examples of theonomy, see Greg Bahnsen, *Theonomy in Christian Ethics*, 2nd edition (Phillipsburg, Pa.: Presbyterian and Reformed, 1984), and R. J. Rushdoony, *Institutes of Biblical Law* (Nutley, N.J.: Craig Press, 1973).

4. These types of concerns have often been addressed by Western Christian and Aristotolian political thought under the heading of "prudence." This is discussed briefly in chapter 9.

5. See my "Calling, Work and Rest," in *The Best of Theology*, vol. III, ed. J. I. Packer (Carol Stream, Ill.: Christianity Today, 1989), 193–211, and my *Heaven Is Not My Home: Learning to Live in God's Creation* (Nashville, Tenn.: Word, 1998).

6. See chapter 9 on prudence.

7. On the nature of a Christian worldview, see Al Wolters, *Creation Regained* (Grand Rapids, Mich.: Eerdmans, 1985); P. Marshall, S. Griffion, and R. Mouw, eds., *Stained Glass: Worldviews and Social Science* (Lanham, Md.: University Press of America, 1989); and Richard Mouw and Sander Griffion, *Pluralisms and Horizons* (Grand Rapids, Mich.: Eerdmans, 1993).

8. Probably the best introductory text written by an exponent of the theology of liberation is still the early Gustav Gutierrez, A Theology of Liberation (London: S.C.M., 1974).

9. See H. M. Kuitert's comment that "contextual theology" needlessly complicates political analysis, in his Everything Is Politics but Politics Is Not Everything (Grand Rapids, Mich.: Eerdmans 1986), 68–74.

10. Indeed, the theology often gets in the way of a clear political focus. Kuitert suggests that theologians were adapting their theology to politics simply because theology is what they had studied, rather than realizing that, if they had actually wanted political insight, they should instead have studied political science or economics. See Kuitert, Everything Is Politics.

11. Ellul, "Epilogue: On Dialectic," in Jacques Ellul: Interpretive Essays, ed. Clifford C. Christians and Jay M. van Hook (Urbana, Ill.: University of Illinois Press, 1981), 221–308.

12. Cf. Jerry Falwell, "A Look at Government Today," in Listen America! (New York: Doubleday, 1980), 59–70.

13. Ralph Reed, Active Faith (New York: Free Press, 1996); After the Revolution: How the Christian Coalition Is Impacting America (Dallas: Word, 1996).

14. This expression was coined by H. Evan Runner. Its implications are sketched out in H. Vander Goot, ed., Life Is Religion (St. Catherines, Ontario: Paideia Press, 1981), a Festschrift dedicated to Runner. Similar themes occur in the analysis of modern totalitarian movements as quasi-religions. See, for example, Eric Voegelin, Political Religions, trans. T.J. DiNapoli and E.S. Easterly III (Lewiston, N.Y.: Mellen, 1986). The idea that there can be a distinct realm of life called "religious" is also now under question. For an outline, see Paul J. Griffiths, "The Very Idea of Religion," in First Things, May 2000.

15. The theme of idolatry is explored in relation to the family in Tony Walters, A Long Way from Home: A Sociological Exploration of Contemporary Idolatry (Exeter, U.K.: Paternoster, 1979).

16. Ralph Waldo Emerson, Book of Uncommon Prayer (Dallas: Word, 1996), 61.

17. Goudzwaard develops the meaning of idolatry and discusses the modern idols of nation, revolution, material prosperity, and guaranteed security in his Idols of Our Time (Downer's Grove, Ill.: InterVarsity Press, 1984). See also Herb Schlossberg, Idols for Destruction (Chicago: Regnery, 1990), and Robert H. Nelson and Max Stackhouse, eds., Economics as Religion: From Samuelson to Chicago and Beyond (State College, Pa.: Penn. State University Press, 2000).

18. Northrop Frye, "The Critical Path: An Essay on the Social Context of Literary Criticism," Daedalus (spring 1970): 268–342.

19. See the discussions by H. Evan Runner in Scriptural Religion and Political Task (Toronto: Wedge, 1974). On the more explicitly religious dynamics of revolutionary movements, see Christopher Dawson, The Gods of Revolution (New York: Minerva Press, 1975).

CHAPTER SIX

~

Church, State,
and Religious Freedom

The Old Testament

Religious freedom presents problems because religion is not a separate, isolated segment of human existence. It is not merely what people do with their solitude. It is not only acts of worship on a Sunday, or a Sabbath, or a Friday. It is not simply adherence to creeds or doctrines. Religion is one of the fundamental shapers of human life, so religious freedom can allow human life to be shaped in ways that may be destructive, at least, in the eyes of others. It is not simply a good thing; it has costs.

It is also important to remember that most Christian churches have, in the past, not advocated religious freedom. Several Eastern Orthodox Churches still do not accept it, at least as it is understood in the Western world. Many Anglicans and Lutherans accept the idea of an established church, though allowing freedom for others. The Roman Catholic Church did not in principle accept the idea of the equal legal treatment of religions until the Second Vatican Council of the early 1960s. Amongst churches, Protestants have often led the way in religious freedom, but this too has not been universal. It was not a major feature in the Reformation, except among those being persecuted.

Nor does the Bible, at first glance, seem to be fertile ground for defending religious liberty. The core of God's instruction for Israel's life, the Ten Commandments, opens with the words: "You shall have no other gods before me, you shall not make for yourself an idol, you shall not worship them or serve them; for I am a jealous God" (Exod. 20:1–3). The worship of other gods was expressly forbidden. This was not only a moral injunction, it was so central that it could bring capital punishment (Exod. 22:20). However, this inauspicious beginning can be misleading. Even the Old Testament is not as negative about the subject as it might at first appear.

As suggested earlier in the discussion of idolatry, religion—whether true or false—is not only a matter of participating in religious ceremonies or embracing a set of purely theological beliefs; it is not simply the formal act of worshipping God or an idol. It is about the core beliefs that shape human life. Hence, freedom of religion is far more than freedom of worship. It necessarily includes freedom of thought, freedom of assembly, and freedom of speech.[1] Conversely, denying religious freedom can also mean denying these things as well. Religion and worship, whether true or false, are intimately tied to living out what we believe in our lives.

This connection was evident early in Israel's history. The Israelites were not to worship the Canaanite gods, "nor serve, nor do according to their deeds" (Exod. 23:24), for "if you serve their gods, it will surely be a snare to you" (Exod. 23:33). The idea of idolatry as a "snare" recurs throughout Israel's life (Exod. 34:12; Deut. 12:30; Josh. 23:13; Judg. 2:3; Ps. 106:36; Heb. 12:1). For example, the book of Judges describes cycles of Israel's history as it falls into idolatry, then subsequent suffering, then deliverance by God. It repeatedly emphasizes practical actions: "Israel did evil in the sight of the Lord" (Judg. 2:11; 3:7, 12; 4:1; 6:1; 13:1). God's judgment was described as coming because of what Israel did with their lives, not simply because of their formal worship or liturgy.

This emphasis was in turn tied to Israel's special vocation as a nation. The commandments were directed to "You," the people of Israel: the injunctions were given to the nation of Israel as God's chosen nation. That is why God stressed his jealousy for them. Israel was called to be a particular nation whose political and social order rested on belief and trust in Yahweh, an order that would be radically disrupted if other religious ways of life intruded.[2] However, the surrounding nations were left free to follow their own faiths. Israel's neighbors, even those that had religious beliefs and practices that were specifically denounced in the Scriptures, were to be left in peace. The divine freedom to order their communal religious life was extended not only to Israel, but also to all other nations. This was true in spite of the fact that other religious beliefs and practices were often categorically branded as false. Consequently, when Israel was held in captivity in Babylon, when Daniel and others put their lives at risk rather than bow to Nebuchadnezzar's idol, they did not try to stop the Babylonians from doing so. Israel did not seek to impose its religion on others.

This freedom was extended, at least in part, to foreigners who lived among Israel. After Exodus 22:20 announced capital punishment as the required judgment on Israelites who worshiped other gods, the next verses outlined the "law of the stranger": "And you shall not wrong a stranger (foreigner) or oppress him for you were strangers in the land of Egypt. . . . And you shall not oppress a stranger, since you yourselves know the feelings of a stranger, for you were strangers in the land of Egypt" (Exod. 22:21, 23:9. Compare also Lev. 19:33–34). The grounds for the Israelites' toleration of foreigners were that they themselves knew what it was like to be foreigners. In Egypt, despite their other sufferings, they had been permitted to practice their religion. If their experience in Egypt was the pattern, and if they were to refrain from doing any wrong to foreigners, this suggests permission for a foreigner to practice his or her religion in Israel.

There was one important exception which would seem to prove the rule. According to Leviticus 20:2, "Any man from the sons of Israel or from the aliens sojourning in Israel, who gives any of his offspring to Molech, shall surely be put to death." Here the death penalty specifically includes foreigners. The reason is that worship of Molech involved child sacrifice and, while other forms of worship might be tolerated, this could never be. Particularly hideous forms of idolatry apparently needed to be singled out.

Similarly, after the conquest of Canaan, God said: "You may not associate with these nations, these which remain among you, or mention the name of their gods, or make anyone swear by them, or serve them, or bow down to them. But you are to cling to the Lord your God, as you have done to this day" (Josh. 23:6–8). Here, the nations which remained were not to be destroyed or to be forcibly converted. They were simply not be associated with, as, for example, by intermarriage.³ This suggests that the rejection of idolaters and those who followed false religions was seen as a political imperative necessary for preserving the internal life of the chosen nation. If this condition was satisfied, then other religions were left alone.

The commands against false religion were more clearly developed in Israel's early history when the political and priestly functions were most closely intertwined. As the political and priestly elements gradually took on a clearer and more distinct form, there was more toleration of others who practiced other religions. In any case, Israel's goal did not extend beyond the preservation of its own role before God to any general attempt to stamp out idolatry among others.

Christian History

In the New Testament, religious freedom is not particularly discussed but simply seems to have been taken for granted. The cross-cultural nature of the new Gentile and Jewish Christianities, together with the actual task of missionary witness, apparently rested on the assumption that people were free with regards to their faith. The church was now also becoming divorced from national, ethnic, and especially, territorial ties—"neither Jew nor Greek." As the church was now being separated from a specific land, there were now no grounds for excluding other religious believers from a particular territory.[4] It was the church, rather than any particular country or territory, that was the bearer of the Christian faith.

This assumption regarding the freedom of faith was manifest in the vehicle for the expansion of the early Church: preaching. The sermons given in the book of Acts are appeals and invitations to turn to God. They are spiritually and verbally forceful presentations, but there is never a hint that they are or will be accompanied by coercive force. The disciples emphasized that Jesus attracted and invited those who would follow him.

In the earliest days of the church, whether in Ephesus, Alexandria, or Rome, it was, of course, the Christians who were the marginalized and dissenting ones. This gave them a good reason to appeal to religious freedom, since it was the ground for their very own survival. However, early Christian fathers, such as Tertullian, Justin, Athanagoras, Lactantius, and Origen, also consistently advocated religious toleration as a matter of Christian principle.

As the church spread, the Latin-speaking churches of the West (as opposed to some of the Greek, and later, Slavic-speaking churches of the East) sought to keep the role of the church and the roles of the political order distinct. Even when Constantine made Christianity the official religion of the Roman Empire, it was still understood that these were two distinct bodies.[5] The two realms of *sacerdotium* (church) and *regnum* (state) began to emerge. There were henceforth two centers of authority in society, and neither could be reduced to the other. This was not anything like a split between religion and politics. Both centers of authority were seen as *religious*—that is, as divine institutions—but they were understood to have quite distinct roles under God. They had different tasks.

This differentiation into two realms of what was to become "Christendom" had wide and long-lasting effects. However, it was anything but clear as to what the proper boundaries between the two should be, and how they were to be properly related to one another. It was more of a framework in which people asked questions about, for example, pope and emperor, than it was any clear answer to those questions. We should also remember that, even with the best will in the world, the problem is a fiendishly difficult one. Consider the question, "In a conflict between church and state, who decides?"⁶ As it was, there was very often not the best will in the world. Popes and emperors fought over the division, each seeking to expand their powers and assert areas of control over each other.

Despite this continuing confusion and conflict, the division between the two realms contributed to the later growth of religious toleration (and of free societies, and, indeed, democracy) in the West. George Sabine correctly wrote: "The rise of the Christian Church, as a distinct institution entitled to govern the spiritual concerns of mankind in independence of the state, may not unreasonably be described as the most revolutionary event in the history of western Europe, in respect both to politics and to political thought."⁷ It was not that the churches, or the political orders, directly advocated religious freedom—often they didn't. Indeed, Jews and heretics were marginalized and persecuted, and the inquisitions were defended under such a scheme.

But people still always believed that there should be boundaries, and they struggled over centuries to define them. This meant that the church, whatever its lust for civil control, had always to acknowledge that there were forms of political power which it could and should not exercise. And the political orders, whatever their drive to subsume all of human life under their control, had always to acknowledge that there were areas of human life which were necessarily and properly beyond their reach. However much the boundaries were muddied and bloodied, there was an abiding sense that the political order could not be identified with the order of ultimate human concern; that the spiritual core of human life, and the authority this embodied, was a realm beyond civil control. As with Pontius Pilate, the political ruler always faced "another king." The key ingredient in this development was not, in the first place, a doctrine of or an explicit call for freedom. Rather, it was a view of the distinct roles of different institutions. This view, in turn, permeated the culture with the belief that political and ecclesiastical jurisdictions were distinct and limited in their authority, and should always be kept so.

Also, before we are too hard on or smug about those in previous generations, we need to remember what they were actually fighting about. The stakes were very high. When they talked about religious freedom, they were not talking about retaining quaint folk customs on special days of the week, but about the fundamental commitments of human life. When they talked of the church, they were not concerned about interference with an apparently harmless First Methodist over on the corner. They were talking about the single most pervasive institution in society—one with much more influence than the often weak state, which had a head and arms, but very little body. In modern terms, the church composed the "media," since if any news got around, it did so via announcements from the pulpit, the only place where people could and did gather. The church was also the intelligentsia; it ran the universities and the rest of the educational system. Canon law—the law of the church—was more pervasive than the dictates of kings. It usually governed marriage, and therefore shaped what people did with inheritance and property. The church also ran whatever welfare arrangements there might be. It was *this* institution and its relation to the political order with which they were concerned. There are few modern states and very few modern people who would relinquish political control over welfare, marriage, inheritance, property, the media, universities, and the school system to another institution without a literal and possibly bloody fight. In the same circumstances many modern people would do what many of our forebears did.[8]

The same questions of church and state continued in the Protestant Reformation of the sixteenth century. It was then further complicated by the fragmentation of the Christian world—there were now many more churches and many more states to fight about. In this situation, the earliest reformers did not directly advocate religious freedom or toleration. They did, however, wrestle anew with the questions of the limits of political power. And, in a world with a welter of competing authorities, they did renew an emphasis on the role of personal conscience and the freedom of faith. Their spiritual children, especially those in the free churches, and especially in America, took this up in an emphasis on freedom of conscience.

The Anabaptist groups, in particular, struggled against political coercion, and they formed the spring of one of the major streams of Western religious freedom. This tradition continued in Robert Browne, the founder of Congregationalism. The English Baptists, headed by Hanserd Knollys, were consistent from the beginning, while Roger Williams founded the town of Providence as a religious refuge. In 1663, the colony of Rhode Island received a charter from Charles II sanctioning toleration for all religions.[9] Later, similar practices were followed by the Quaker William Penn in Pennsylvania.

As Joseph Lecler, the author of the best work on toleration in the Reformation period, notes, people who are themselves suffering from persecution are usually in favor of toleration. The crucial test is what they do when they themselves have power.[10] Luther failed this test, as did the Congregationalists in New England. It was the Baptists and Quakers who succeeded. In this way, an idea of religious freedom reflecting these Christian origins began to be introduced into the modern world. It took longer yet to have not just freedom for religious groups, but also their legal equality.

Treating different religious bodies equally before the law should not be seen as a compromise of a Christian view of the modern state. Rather, it is a Christian view of the modern state. It does not denigrate the truth of the Christian faith, or of any faith, to have such equality. It simply reflects the fact that government officials have only a specific and limited task. Their task is to do justice for all people within the borders of their country, regardless of who those people are and what they might believe.[11] As a matter of principle, a state shaped by biblical faith should not give special privileges to any religious group.

Although the parallel is inexact, the situation may be compared to a family. Parents may desire and seek that their children grow up to follow their beliefs. Nevertheless, their calling, as parents, is to love all their children regardless of what path they might follow. If one child decides to become, say, an atheist, they may try to persuade him or her, but if they were to refuse to feed dinner to that one child, while still feeding his or her brothers and sisters, they would be abdicating their role as a parent. The task of parents is to care for all the children that have been placed in their hands. Similarly, the task of governments is to deal justly and equally with all the people placed in their hands.

Confusion about Toleration

In stressing a duty to promote religious freedom, we need to look not only at the role of governments, but also to emphasize the importance of personally and socially tolerating religious differences. This is especially true since the term "toleration" has become manipulated and misunderstood. It now has many different purported meanings, some of them bad. Nevertheless, for reasons I hope will become clear, it is something which we need both to revive and practice. What I mean by toleration is putting up with things which we dislike or with which we disagree. This is the view of toleration found in most serious treatments of the matter.[12]

In today's world, toleration often has something of a bad name, though for different, and sometimes contradictory, reasons. For some it smacks of a vague, indiscriminate openness, or relativism, or lack of conviction. It seems merely to paper over the cracks, and in the name of openness, refuses to take questions of truth seriously. In North America the word "tolerance" has recently become something of a code word implying acceptance of new sexual mores such as homosexuality. This has led many to reject the idea outright, and to suspect anybody who advocates toleration of wishy-washiness or surreptitious relativism.

For others, toleration seems merely to be a halfway house, a second best, a sufferance. It is regarded as merely grudging acceptance or a type of paternalism. This is why Founding Father James Madison pushed successfully to have the word "toleration" removed from the final draft of the 1776 Virginia Bill of Rights.[13] In this instance, Madison was correct, since, unlike an individual, the government itself should not simply tolerate different religions, since this would imply that the government was officially disapproving of a religion, though still allowing it to exist. Rather than toleration, a government should grant religious freedom to all in an unbiased way, a theme discussed below.

However, others who criticize toleration are less concerned with the proper role of government than with personal responses to differences. Currently, many who praise diversity insist that we must move beyond mere toleration to real appreciation of, and even celebration of, our differences. They demand that we not merely patiently put up with different views and ways of life, but that we actively rejoice in them. From their perspective, tolerance is seen as narrow-minded and proud, even bigoted.

This latter might be a valid criticism in the case of, say, race. Racial toleration (as toleration is defined above) is not a good thing, since it necessarily implies that, while we might be putting up with it, we are in fact disapproving of another's race. And disapproving of another's race really would be bigotry. But religions are usually not reducible to race or ethnicity. They have real and important differences about the nature of life. Contra modern prejudices, one who has never disagreed with another religion is not openminded, but is simply treating religion as trivial, as if religious beliefs do not matter at all. But we cannot say that all things taught by all religions all the time are all equally true in all respects and all equally good. This would be like saying "all beliefs are true and good." At bottom, a naïve and total acceptance or celebration of belief assumes that religions really have no content except as personal preferences or cultural habits. It thus denigrates all religions. This is one reason that people who describe themselves as "tolerant" can so easily attack and denigrate religions that take a clear position on moral matters such as abortion or adultery (as most do). Behind such attacks often lies the idea that religions should be tolerated because they really don't mean anything, and thus that a religion is fair game for attack the moment it actually does mean anything. It is toleration predicated on a view of religion as vacuous.

One can no more agree with all religions than one can agree with all political stances. While there are very many agreements between religions, each says something different, and the differences are important.[14] And if we were to accept the idea that simply disagreeing with another person is itself inherently narrow-minded, then we would have to view the saying imputed to François-Marie Voltaire, "I disapprove of what you say but I will defend to the death your right to say it," simply as a type of bigotry.

In fact, properly understood, toleration demands a discipline and commitment that many other stances do not. Toleration requires a burden: it is a burden since it means bearing with things which we do not really want. It is really a type of long-suffering, which the apostle Paul described as a gift of the Spirit. Toleration means that we take other views seriously.

Counterfeits of Toleration

If we are tolerant, then we are not indifferent about something. It has to be something we care about. Indifference means that we do not care about something. I am indifferent as to whether someone has red hair—I simply don't care. It is therefore no virtue that I don't try to ban it. This is actually the stance taken toward religion by many secular Westerners, and by some churches. They would like to think of themselves as tolerant, when in fact they basically don't care very much about religious disagreements since they don't think they make much difference. But only when we do believe religious differences are important and that they have an impact on us do questions begin. Genuine toleration is not indifference, but it concerns how we react to something that we really care about.

For example, Roger Williams, a Baptist, had strong religious beliefs and criticisms about almost everything, and he expressed them all the time. He was highly critical, especially of Quakers. However, he was still tolerant of views that differed from his. He did not seek to repress them. People like Williams actually allow more religious toleration than indifferent or skeptical people, and much more than some current trends in "political correctness." These latter often don't care about much, but they require rigid conformity to those things that they actually do care about. Their boundaries of the approved and the allowed are virtually identical. But the extent of toleration is the degree to which we give freedom to those things that we believe are fundamentally wrong.

Nor should relativism (assuming for a moment that relativists exist) be confused with tolerance. A relativist would hold that all views are relative, that some other view could be as true or untrue as his or her own, and that many views are of equal worth. But, in this case, the other's view is no challenge or threat at all—it is merely another stance, neither good nor bad. Relativism is like indifference—the question of disapproval or condemnation never even has a chance to arise.

Nor does skepticism about what we can really know necessarily lead to toleration. There is a strange tendency in the modern age, in popular culture and in philosophers such as Rorty, to think that a skeptical stance is likely to lead to freedom or toleration. But there is no historical or rational reason to believe this. After all, if something cannot actually be known, then why shouldn't we simply impose an answer, even an arbitrary one, for the sake of civil peace and uniformity? This was common practice in the seventeenth century. People might protest that they are being denied an important belief, but since they would be protesting about something that is unknowable, they could easily be ignored and silenced. Uncertainty can easily lead to a call—not for the authorities to allow freedom, but for the dissenters to shut up, or be shut up, rather than persist in pushing troubling speculations about things that cannot be known. In this case, religion is repressed not for specifically theological reasons, but simply for social conformity. This is one of the great dangers of the modern age and one of the usual practices of previous ages. Historically, skeptics have usually repressed religious differences.[15]

Celebration, or approval, is not toleration either. Toleration can only arise where there is already disapproval present. Hence husbands and wives and children should not be tolerated, they should be loved. Perhaps other relatives will need to be tolerated. We do not tolerate things we love or celebrate—we simply love or celebrate them.

Indifference seems safe, but what happens to things we are not indifferent about? Relativism seems benign, but it has no serious differences to contend with. Skepticism seems open, but is also open to repression. Celebration seems marvelous, but we can't celebrate everything. If we acknowledge that there are real and important differences between human beings on religious (and other) matters, and realize that these differences will not soon go away, then we need to face the strengths, and weaknesses, of tolerance.

Genuine Toleration

The important feature of genuine toleration in the modern world is that it focuses precisely on those areas where there is real disagreement. At the same time it calls for peaceful coexistence. Toleration does not require celebration of things which we would rather not celebrate; nor does it fall into the mistake that all views are equal; nor does it trivialize the role of religion in the world, even in public life. But neither does it justify repression.

The key to religious toleration in the modern world is not indifference, relativism, skepticism, or celebration. Nor is it necessarily religious openness. Nor is it a call to confine religion to a private realm or to take it out of politics. Nor is it a claim that religion will be allowed if it does no harm to others. Rather, its focus is on the legal coexistence of differing, and continuing to differ, people and communities.

Genuine toleration means letting others exist freely while seeking, when appropriate, to oppose them by word. Like proper views of human rights, it addresses differences seriously enough to say that they are differences, and that some of these differences are not good. But it forswears the use of force to try to overcome them. It means dealing with religious differences by the power of the word, not the power of the state.

We may hope for a world where there is agreement and acceptance, but it is not likely to be here in the near future. In the meantime, we need to find ways of living alongside each other without destroying one another and without ignoring or trivializing our differences. This is the genius of toleration. Its task is not overcoming our differences, but establishing the possibility of a right to differ. It defends both truth and coexistence. This is why it deserves our support.

Modern Views of Religious Freedom

Locke is usually credited with being the founder of many modern views of religious freedom. While he had several arguments for freedom, including very good ones, he propounded one defective—and still influential—argument that depended on restricting the place of religion in public life. Locke's conception of religion was varied, but was often something solely concerned with a future life in heaven, with no significance below other than from the spiritual duties that would aid the attainment of this heaven.[16] Hence, in this part of Locke's view, the reason that religious discord could and should be overcome was that religious differences were actually irrelevant to social life: "The only business of the church is the salvation of souls: and it in no way concerns the commonwealth or any member of it that this or any other ceremony may be made use of . . . . [R]eligious assemblies . . . [do not] advantage or prejudice the life, liberty, or estate, of any man."[17]

The problem with this influential argument is that, like many modern views of toleration, it is based on giving freedom to something that is thought to be socially irrelevant. It suggests that religion should be tolerated because it has no real public consequence—that, politically, it does not matter. However, this tells us nothing about what to do with religions that do have public consequences, as, of course, the vast majority do. In fact Locke, and those he has shaped with this argument, would be intolerant of such religions. He would not tolerate Catholics, since he thought they would really be servants of a foreign "prince," the Pope. (This idea resurfaced in the U.S. when John F. Kennedy, the first Catholic U.S. president, was running for election in 1960. Many worried that he would be subservient to the Pope.) He would also not tolerate atheists because he thought that, since they would not fear future divine punishment, they could not be trusted to keep their word. Nor would he tolerate those who would not themselves teach the duty of tolerating others. He thought "that all churches were obliged to lay down toleration as the foundation of their own liberty."[18] This meant that Locke's argument only justified tolerating those who agreed with him on fundamental matters.

While Locke also said many other, and good, things about liberty, this part of his argument does not achieve its supposed new realm of toleration—coexistence and peace by expanding the area of freedom. It does so by shrinking and restricting the area of religion. It tolerates only that religion which is thought to be irrelevant to practical human life. This attempt to restrict religion has bedeviled the English-speaking world ever since, especially in what is now called secularism or liberalism.

Liberalism and Public Religion

Much modern liberalism claims that it really has no religious creed itself. This claim is made because its principal feature is something like "a set of beliefs which proceeds from the central assumption that man's essence is his freedom and, therefore, that what chiefly concerns us in this life is to shape the world as we want it."[19] One needs to be careful in criticism of liberalism, since the word "liberalism" is used in many different ways, and here it is not being used in the common American sense of "left-wing." If it simply means a great concern for individual freedom and rights in a constitutional, democratic order, then this author is happy to be called a political liberal. What is meant here is a view that individual choice is the highest goal of politics, and should necessarily trump all question of religious or other belief. It is a form of individualist secularism. It should also be noted that liberals such as William Galston, former domestic adviser to Bill Clinton and Al Gore, have maintained that liberalism, or at least their type of liberalism, is not about elevating the supreme good of choice, but rather about coping with diversity.

However, contemporary liberalism, as described above, is focusing increasingly on individual choice. This focus leads many liberals to emphasize that they do not wish to impose their way of life on anyone else—that they simply desire that everyone should be as free as possible to live out their own way of life with the least hindrance. In this sense it claims to be a neutral philosophy. For Ronald Dworkin, a leading contemporary liberal legal theorist, the liberal state "must be neutral on . . . the question of the good life . . . political decisions must be so far as possible, independent of any particular conception of the good life, or of what gives values to life."[20] Here we confront the common liberal commandment that "you can't impose your beliefs on others (unless your beliefs are liberal)." Given liberalism's emphasis on openness, liberals usually see themselves as exponents of toleration and freedom par excellence. They picture themselves as providing a political setting in which each individual can pursue his or her own freely chosen life, where no view is imposed on another, and where the state is neutral between competing views of what a good life is.

However, in order to do this, many contemporary liberals believe that religious views should play no part in political decision making, and usually, that religion should be excluded from politics. This can even take the form of an attack on the presence of believers, *as believers*, in public life itself. Chapter 1 gave examples of this during the 2000 presidential election campaign. Similar views occur in academic circles. For example, Robert Audi, a Christian, suggests: "It is appropriate, however, that citizens apply a kind of separation of church and state in their public use of religious arguments, especially in advocating laws or public policies that restrict liberty."[21] He adds: "Just as we separate church and state institutionally, we should in certain aspects of our thinking and public conduct, separate religion from law and public policy matters."[22] Here believers are enjoined from even thinking about the political order in terms of their beliefs.

Similar emphases come to the fore in Rawls' contention that political discussion should be confined to "public reason."[23] His approach echoes the Lockean view that religion should be a private matter, but goes beyond it by demanding that we not think and speak about public policy from out of our basic beliefs. Rawls suggests: "To check whether we are following public reason we might ask: how would our argument strike us presented in the form of a Supreme Court opinion?"[24] Here the court has become the standard not only of law, but of what people should say and think about law. Similarly, Rorty remarks: "I take religious toleration to mean the willingness of religious groups to take part in discussions without dragging religion into it."[25] Here liberalism is regarded as such a tolerant view that it need not tolerate other views. However, if we are truly interested in religious freedom, then Carter's response to attempts to exclude religion from public life is exactly to the point: "What is needed is not a requirement that the religiously devout choose a form of dialogue that liberalism accepts, but that liberalism develop a politics that accepts whatever form of dialogue a member of the public offers."[26] We need not a closed liberal society, but a genuine open society.

One of the problems with this type of liberalism is that it fails to see that its parochial claim to be fair to everyone is parochial and only accepted by other liberals. Even when addressing an audience which is all but standing up and yelling, "You are excluding us," many liberals still claim that they provide the basic common denominator, that they offer values which are fair to everybody and with which everybody can agree. Liberalism, in this sense, is not a position which provides the meeting point between others; it is only one more position alongside others.[27] It is not the just means of dealing with differences; it is, rather, yet one more difference concerning public and private life. It needs to be brought alongside, not above. Liberalism's public exclusion of religion should be understood not as a form of respect for religion and religious differences, but, in reality, as trivializing religion and attempting to monopolize the public realm for its own ideology.

Such trivialization could replace a genuinely open society with a homogeneous liberal one. The result would be similar to Canadian George Grant's depiction of liberal society: "[D]ifferences . . . are able to exist only in private activities: how we eat, how we mate, how we practice ceremonies. Some like pizza, some like steaks; some like girls, some like boys; some like synagogue, some like the mass. But we all do it in churches, motels, restaurants indistinguishable from the Atlantic to the Pacific."[28]

The liberal solution is not the best approach to religious freedom. Rather, it takes away the strength, the particularity, the meaning of religions. It excludes them and then says the result is fruitful coexistence. Such liberalism undercuts the very differences, especially religious differences, that it is intended to protect. The result of such undercutting is well described by Rabbi Dennis Prager:

> Liberals are always talking about pluralism, but that is not what they mean. They mean "melting-pot." Pluralism [properly] means that Catholics are Catholics, Jews are Jews, Baptists are Baptists, etc. That's what pluralism means—everyone affirms his values and we all live with civic equality and tolerance. That's my dream. [But] in public school, Jews don't meet Christians. Christians don't meet Hindus. Everybody meets nothing. That is, as I explain

to Jews all the time, why their children so easily inter-marry. Jews don't marry Christians. Non-Jewish Jews marry non-Christian Christians. Jews for nothing marry Christians for nothing. They get along great because they both affirm nothing. They have everything in common—nothing. That's not pluralism. But that is exactly what the liberal world wants. They want a bunch of secular universalists with ethnic surnames.[29]

Instead of becoming "a bunch of secular universalists with ethnic surnames," we need to recognize that religion shapes all of life, and hence, that religious views should be given place in our public life. Governments should not give arbitrary preference to a supposedly neutral, secularist view.[30]

Religion and the Constitution

The conflict between different views of religious freedom, between an equal recognition of the place of religions and the desire to exclude religion from political life, finds expression in U.S. law, especially constitutional law. In discussing this, I will focus only on understandings of the "establishment" clause of the First Amendment of the Constitution, since this has been the cause of most contemporary problems.[31]

I have briefly recounted confusion and struggles in the West on questions of the relation of church and state. The First Amendment to the U.S. Constitution was a crucial step in clarifying this relation.[32] Its first part reads, "Congress shall make no law respecting an establishment of religion. . . ." This demanded that, at a federal level at least, there should not be an established church, such as existed, for example, in England.[33] It also implied that no church should be given special preferences or have a status above that of other churches.

This was a major advance in solving the vexed relation of church and state. It acknowledged, as people in the West had known for millennia, that church and state were separate institutions, but the amendment went much further and clarified the question of exactly how the state should relate to religion, or the church. This clarification was genuine equality—evenhandedness before the law. It did not keep the government from cooperating with or aiding religious bodies, just as it could cooperate with or aid any other bodies in society. The government simply could not elevate one religious body above the others. Gradually, as it became obvious that there were other religions than Christianity present in the country, its provisions were understood to apply not only to Christian denominations but to other religious expressions as well.

This approach has served the United States well for most of its history. But deleterious changes in understanding have come about in recent decades. One key change came in 1947 when Supreme Court Justice Hugo Black used Jefferson's extra-constitutional metaphorical language of "the separation of church and state" as the key to the First Amendment.[34] Not content with propounding the curious notion that a government could somehow be "separate" from something that must necessarily be, at least partially, under its laws, Black added the equally curious claim that the government could not "pass laws which aid one religion . . . (or) aid *all* religions" (emphasis added). This, apparently, meant that no matter if it were evenhanded and nondiscriminatory, still the government could not do anything that might "aid" any religion. Black did not explain why a government should reject a policy simply on the grounds that it was helpful to its citizens. Be that as it may, this shift of interpretation has led to at least five dangerous trends.

First, it set back the whole discussion about the relation of church and state by about 1600 years. Westerners have nearly always believed in some form of what can be called "separation of church and state." As we have seen, this type of notion was present even in the Old Testament. Almost everyone in the West has known that church and state were to be "separate"—that is, they were not the same, and they had distinct roles. The key question over which they had struggled for centuries was the respective roles and relations of each of these bodies. It was to *this* question that the First Amendment stress on nonestablishment gave a clear answer.

But Black's attempt to use "separation" *itself* as the means of clarification of the relation of "church and state" confused the entire issue. The First Amendment was meant to give a solution to the problem of the relation of the distinct institutions of "church and state," not merely to state the problem once again. Black's formulation lost the answer provided by the First Amendment and left the problem open-ended. This open-endedness has allowed many other nonconstitutional views of church and state to intrude.

Second, in treating "separateness" as *itself* the proper relation, it led to the further notion that government cannot be "entangled with" religion. In *Lemon v. Kurtzman* (1971), the Supreme Court announced a three-part test for determining whether something violated the establishment clause: (1) Does it have a secular purpose? (2) Does it have the "primary effect" of either "advancing or inhibiting" religion? (3) Does it entail an "excessive entanglement" between government and religion?[35] This was strange indeed. Churches and state *cannot* be separate or unentangled in this way. Churches and religions operate within state boundaries and under state laws. They are always deeply entangled: if they were not entangled we would never have had to argue for millennia about their respective boundaries. The government is necessarily "entangled" with everything in its territory or else it could never affect anything. It *will* always be entangled with religions and with churches. As the First Amendment itself shows, by saying how they should be related, the question is not whether church and state will be "entangled" but *how* they will be.

Third, the notion that the state cannot "aid" religion leads to further conundrums. If a church is burning down, can a government-supported fire service put the fire out? Can police investigate a burglary at a synagogue? Surely such government action aids the bodies involved. In *Lemon v. Kurtzman*, the Court tried to untangle the questions of "aid" and "entanglement," but inevitably and necessarily, its argument simply became yet another confused symptom of the irresolvable problem it had created. As Michael McConnell has pointed out,

> [T]he [C]ourt has held that religious colleges may receive general purpose government grants, but religious high schools may not; that government may subsidize bus transportation to religious schools but not bus rides for their students on field trips; that government may pay for books but not maps or film projectors; that it may reimburse schools for the cost of state-mandated standardized tests but not state-mandated safety maintenance; and that it may pay for diagnostic, but not therapeutic, services to children at religious schools.[36]

Indeed, in order to justify the State of Nebraska's having a chaplain pray at the beginning of the Legislature's sessions, the Court was reduced to saying that the chaplain's work did not have the primary purpose of advancing religion. This litany of confusion was simply the result of attempts to resolve an incoherent position that government action cannot aid institutions within the territory.

Fourth, if the government somehow cannot be "excessively entangled with" or "advance" religion, then religion would need to be kept out of things where the government is involved. In modern politics, since the state tends to get involved with all aspects of human life, this invariably means that religion must give way to governmental concern in every aspect of life. When the state gets in, religion is supposed to get out. But, since the modern state gets into everything, then religion is squeezed out of more and more areas of life. Hence, an expansive state necessarily means marginalized religion.

Fifth, this approach ignores the fact that religion shapes all of human life.[37] The Court's restrictions on religion have usually been applied only to traditional, more overt, religions such as Christianity, Judaism, Islam, and so forth. They are not applied to newer ideologies such as secularism or liberalism.[38] The ultimate effect is a tendency that the government cannot support "religion," but can support what it describes, for no clear reason, as "secular" causes. In Lemon v. Kurtzman, the Court went so far as to say that all law must have a "secular purpose," but without bothering to clarify what a "secular purpose" might be. Consequently, in disputes between traditional religion and modern secular ideology, the massive power of the U.S. government was placed in the service of the ideology. Another way of expressing this is to say that the way was opened to systematic discrimination in favor of whatever the Court decided to call secular views and against what it decided to call religious views.[39] This helped promote the rapid secularization of American public life. As liberal Supreme Court Justice William O. Douglas said, we are in danger of "preferring those who believe in no religion over those who do believe."[40] Or, as Supreme Court Justice Potter Stewart said, we may be moving toward "the establishment of a religion of secularism."[41]

The peak of the Court's infatuation with the metaphor of "separation" came in the late 1970s and early 1980s, but the situation has improved in recent years.[42] Now, moved to a degree by McConnell's arguments, the Court has begun moving toward the type of position suggested here, stressing the importance of the "neutrality principle" and the problems of "viewpoint discrimination."[43] One of the turning points was Widmar v. Vincent (1981), wherein the Court allowed a Bible study group at the University of Missouri to meet under the same conditions as it allowed other groups. Since then, some other changes have occurred. In the 1993 Lamb's Chapel v. Center Moriches Union Free School District decision, the Court ruled that private groups could not be stopped from using a school's facilities simply because the film it showed discussed "family values" from a religious perspective. In the 1995 Rosenberger v. University of Virginia decision, it said that the University of Virginia could not refuse to fund a student Christian magazine while funding the magazines of other student groups. In June 2000, in Mitchell v. Helms, the Court said that it was constitutional for government to provide computers and other educational materials to religious schools when it provided them on the same basis to secular schools. In the 2001 Good News Bible Club v. Millford, the Court allowed a Christian youth group to meet after regular school hours on public school premises since other groups were allowed to meet then. In addition, Congress passed the Equal Access Protection Act, which said that religious groups should have the same access to public school facilities as any other groups.

In the course of these reviews, the Court also modified the criteria of "separation" used in Lemon v. Kurtzman. In Agostini v. Felton (1997), it refocused its inquiry into three new criteria: (1) whether the statute results in governmental indoctrination, (2) defines its recipients by reference to religion, or (3) creates an excessive entanglement with religion.

While the Court has been moving toward a nonpreferential view, most of its decisions have been decided only by a narrow 5–4 vote.[44] Changes in the Court could easily reverse this trend. Consequently, it is still vitally important to stress the theme of neutrality and replace the self-contradictory "separationist" idea with one that, by stressing equality before the law, deals justly with the full range and integrity of religion in human life.

Education

Since religions are committed to shaping the young, religious conflict in the modern age has focused not usually on churches, synagogues, or mosques, but more commonly on the family and the education system. This system does what bodies like churches used to do—it molds the beliefs of the coming generations. Consequently, the education system tends to be the major arena of conflict between different religious views.

A liberal stress on free individual choice has had major effects on what is taught in schools, and not just in sex education classes. In many schools a supposed liberal ideal is followed by, at least in theory, exposing the children in a full, fair, and balanced way to the moral options that exist, exhorting them to give serious consideration to these options, and then, perhaps, to make a serious commitment to one of them. This approach is applied, of course, only in certain parts of the curriculum; it is not done in physics or mathematics (and certainly not in matters of creation and evolution). But it is frequently applied in politics, ethics, and religion.

However, what a child will actually learn from this approach will be not that one religion, or one option, set before her is true, but that no religion has any compelling claim to be treated as true.[45] Hence, the child learns implicitly that each religion has a claim as good as any other and, therefore, that what is paramount is the priority of her own individual choice.[46] She and her choice are necessarily placed at the center of the moral universe. Insofar as this education works, the pupils become indoctrinated into the worldview of liberalism, into the doctrine of the priority of their own individual choice.

An alternative approach has been to try to be "fair" by having schools simply ignore religion—a fundamental area of human life—entirely.[47] In the context of a similar debate over the role of religion in the English public universities, Sir Walter Moberly correctly noted:

> On the fundamental religious issue (the existence of God), the modern university . . . supposes it is neutral, but it is not. Certainly it neither inculcates nor expressly repudiates belief in God. But what it does is far more deadly than open rejection; it ignores [h]im, . . . If in your organization, your curriculum, and your customs and ways of life, you leave God out, you teach with tremendous force that, for most people and at most times, [h]e does not count. . . . It is a fallacy to suppose that by omitting a subject you teach nothing about it. On the contrary you teach that it is to be omitted. . . . And you teach this not openly and explicitly, which would invite criticism, you simply take it for granted and thereby insinuate it silently, insidiously, and all but irresistibly.[48]

Neither ignoring God, nor simply listing a religion as a possible option of individual choice, ultimately treats religion, and religious differences, in their integrity. It implicitly demeans or rejects them. Hence, we must find means of bringing religious beliefs into the educational system. Given the differences which exist in and over the public schools, this is hard to do. But if state schools are to be genuinely public, then the beliefs of the actual public must find a full and open place there. Public schools should be not merely those to which the state gives money, but schools which reflect the actual public beliefs of Americans.

Since religion is a fundamental shaper of human life, a better response is to structure different schools around different belief systems. There should be a variety of school systems. Given a proper view of the role of government, and a proper view of the Constitution, there is no reason why religious schools should not receive government funding on the same basis as any other schools, whether by vouchers or some other mechanism. Treating religious views equally means treating explicitly religious schools equally. It may be legitimate for government to fund no schools, but, if it funds schools of one belief, and then refuses to fund others, it violates the First Amendment.[49] In the absence of a free, neutral funding of a diversity of schools, we need public schools in which differences of religion are not suppressed in the name of a false "neutrality" but are given place in the calendar, ceremonies, and curriculum.

True Disagreement, True Faith

The problems introduced by the Supreme Court's rejection of equal religious freedom in favor of a secular bias are not confined to education, or to the legal sphere itself. They pervade our public life, as illustrated in chapter 1. We face a situation where many of the people who most shape the culture believe that religious views should be excluded from public life. As George Weigel has said: "Put in the simplest symbolic terms, the people who produce the CBS *Evening News* do not necessarily share the broader cultural and more specifically religious sensibilities of the people who watch the CBS *Evening News*. Survey research seems to have confirmed the existence of a 'new knowledge class,' located primarily in the academy, the prestige press, and the popular entertainment industry, that is deeply secularized. In Peter Berger's pungent phrase, and referring to the Asian subcontinent rather than to the native inhabitants of North America, 'We are a nation of Indians, ruled by Swedes.'"[50]

Even though many religious believers find themselves marginalized in these areas of life, there is no need for wild talk of some secular conspiracy. One of the basic reasons that there are so many secular people in areas that shape our cultural attitude is that Christians—driven by a false understanding of what it means to avoid the world—pulled out of these areas, or else never went into them in the first place. Christians, especially theologically conservative Christians, have wrongly thought that NPR or the *Washington Post* newsroom was not where they were called to be. There is a lot of catching up to do in the means of shaping our culture.

As noted earlier, genuine toleration also implies genuine disagreement. Weigel goes on to say:

> The goal, in short, is not agreement, but disagreement. What passes for disagreement today is usually sheer cacophony. People for the American Way and the various demons it discerns on the religious right do not "disagree." They talk (more likely shout, or still more likely, conduct direct mail campaigns) past each other. Disagreement, [Fr. John Courtney] Murray insisted, was a great accomplishment, because it only happened when a more fundamental consensus on the terms and boundaries of discourse had been achieved. Americans, in short, must re-learn what it means to disagree. Learning to disagree means learning how to conduct public moral argument without requiring confessional admission tickets and without compelling religious believers to wear a large scarlet "A" sewn to their breast when they enter the public square wherein the public's business is conducted.[51]

Notes

1. P. Marshall, ed., *Religious Freedom in the World: A Global Survey of Religious Freedom and Persecution* (Nashville, Tenn.: Broadman and Holman, 2000). Appendices I and II of this survey give criteria to measure religious freedom which reflect international law standards.

2. F. F. Bruce describes this as "practical monotheism" in his *Israel and the Nations* (Grand Rapids, Mich.: Eerdmans, 1963).

3. Judges 3:1 seems to indicate that the nations were "left" by the Lord in order to test Israel.

4. The separation of the Church from a particular territory needs more attention than it has received. Many treatments of Christian social ethics try to move too quickly from the land-based communal ethical life of Israel to our present situation of states, cf. Walter Brueggeman, *The Land: Place as Gift, Promise and Challenge in Biblical Faith* (Philadelphia: Fortress, 1977). The result is often a communalism wherein the cohering, tribal Israelite nation is taken as normative for modern political structures, resulting in advocating a type of tribal socialism. If we wanted to take the tightly woven Israelite life as our pattern for economics, we would probably also need to do so for faith and politics, with dangerous results for religious freedom.

5. Christianity at this phase also became politically intolerant. My point here is not to defend the practice of the Church during this period, but to point out the continuing features that allowed religious freedom to emerge more fully. A full history of religious freedom would, of course, have to point out the great evils done. Nevertheless, the Church was not as bad as many of its modern critics say. On this, for example, see Edward Peters, *Inquisition* (New York: Free Press, 1988).

6. On the difficulties of reconciling different views of religious freedom, Keith Pavlischek, *John Courtney Murray and the Dilemma of Religious Toleration* (Jefferson City, Mo.: Thomas Jefferson University Press, 1999).

7. George Sabine, *History of Political Theory* (New York, Holt, Rinehart and Winston, 1961), 180. David Little adds, "I would underscore that statement several times," in his *Religion, Order and Law* (New York: Harper, 1969), 36. Henry Kissinger notes: "Restraints on government derived from custom, not constitutions, and from the universal Catholic Church, which preserved its own autonomy, thereby laying the basis—quite unintentionally—for pluralism and democratic restraints on state power that evolved centuries later," in *Does America Need a Foreign Policy?* (New York: Simon and Schuster, 2001), 20–21. For background which suggests that this was not "quite unintentional," see Brian Tierney, *Religion, Law and the Growth of Constitutional Thought, 1150–1650* (Cambridge: Cambridge University Press, 1982).

8. Consider, for example, the apocalyptic language often used in our present fights over vouchers for the education system.

9. Roger Williams, *The Bloody Tenent of Persecution* (London, 1644).

10. Joseph Lecler, *Toleration and the Reformation*, 2 vols. (New York: Association Press, 1960), vol. II: 483.

11. Of course, there are some religious expressions that would need to be restricted. A resurrection of Molech-worship involving child sacrifice would need to be banned, and there will always be borderline cases, such as Jehovah's Witnesses and blood transfusions.

12. Bernard Crick well describes tolerance as "the degree to which we accept things of which we disapprove" or "the deliberate forbearing of power that could be used otherwise," in "Toleration in Theory and Practice," in Government and Opposition 6, (1971): 144–171. The philosophical literature bears out his definition.

13. See Douglas F. Kelly, The Emergence of Liberty in the Modern World (Phillipsburg, Pa.: Presbyterian and Reformed Publishing Co., 1992), 133–34.

14. This doesn't mean, of course, that all religions disagree on everything.

15. In the time of the Reformation, authorities often asserted this view by imposing a uniform Church standard in areas where they thought the Bible was silent, as, for example, concerning clergy vestments. These were often called things "indifferent," and, since they were "indifferent," a uniform practice was imposed. See also the excellent article by Richard Tuck on the usual intolerance of skeptical rulers in his "Skepticism and Toleration in the Seventeenth Century," in Justifying Toleration: Conceptual and Historical Perspectives, ed. Susan Mendus (Cambridge: Cambridge University Press, 1988), 21–35.

16. John Locke, A Letter Concerning Toleration, ed. James H. Tully (Indianapolis, Ind.: Hackett, 1983), 26, 42.

17. Locke, A Letter Concerning Toleration, 39.

18. Locke, A Letter Concerning Toleration, 51.

19. George Grant, Technology and Empire (Toronto: Anansi, 1969), 114.

20. Ronald Dworkin, A Matter of Principle (Cambridge: Harvard University Press, 1985), 191. See also Bruce Ackerman, Social Justice in the Liberal State (New Haven, Conn.: Yale University Press, 1980).

21. Robert Audi, "The Place of Religious Argument in a Free and Democratic Society," San Diego Law Review 30, no. 4 (fall 1993): 677–702, 667. See also his Religious Commitment and Secular Reason (Cambridge: Cambridge University Press, 2000), and Robert Audi and Nicholas Wolterstorff, Religion in the Public Square (Lanham, Md.: Rowman & Littlefield, 1997). See also V. Bader, "Religious Pluralism, Secularism or Priority to Democracy?" Political Theory 27 (1999): 597–633.

22. Audi, "The Place of Religious Argument," 691.

23. John Rawls, Political Liberalism (New York: Columbia University Press, 1993), 223–25. Ronald Dworkin argues, in Life's Dominion (New York: Vintage, 1996), that restrictions on abortion may violate the First Amendment's strictures on establishment of religion. I am grateful to Professor Patrick Neal for raising these issues.

24. Rawls, Political Liberalism, 254.

25. "Interview," The Times Literary Supplement, 24 June 1994.

26. Stephen Carter, The Culture of Disbelief: How American Law and Politics Trivialize Religious Devotion (New York: Basic Books, 1993), 230. Both Rawls and Audi

have modified their views considerably in recent years: see Audi, "The Place of Religious Argument," and Rawls, "The Idea of Public Reason Revisited," in *Collected Papers* (Cambridge: Harvard University Press, 1999), 573–615. For commentary, see P. Weithman, ed., *Religion and Contemporary Liberalism* (Notre Dame, Ind.: Notre Dame University Press, 1997); W.E. Connolly, *Why I Am Not a Secularist* (Minneapolis, Minn.: University of Minnesota Press, 1999); Sheldon Wolin, "The Liberal/Democratic Divide? On Rawls' Political Liberalism," *Political Theory* 24 (1996): 97–120; Jonathan Chaplin, "Beyond Liberal Restraint: Defending Religiously Based Arguments in Law and Public Policy," *University of British Columbia Law Review* 33 (2000): 617–46; K. Greenwalt, *Religious Convictions and Political Choice* (Oxford: Oxford University Press, 1988); Robert Song, *Christianity and Liberal Society* (Oxford: Clarendon Press, 1997). However, Audi's and Rawls' modified positions still result in the marginalization of religion: see Wolterstorff, *Religion in the Public Sphere*, and Chaplin, "Beyond Liberal Restraint."

27. What I mean by secularism is the belief that religion should be excluded from public life. For a spirited critique of liberalism on this point, see Stanley Fish, *The Trouble with Principle* (Cambridge, Mass.: Harvard University Press, 2000).

28. Grant, *Technology and Empire*, 26.

29. "Interview," *The Wittenburg Door*, Nov./Dec., 1990.

30. See Roy Clouser, *The Myth of Religious Neutrality* (Notre Dame, Ind.: University of Notre Dame, 1992).

31. In order to clarify the issues here, I have categorized Supreme Court approaches in terms of two approaches. This is obviously a gross oversimplification. A good survey and typology of approaches to First Amendment questions is given by Carl H. Esbeck, "A Typology of Church-State Relations in Current American Thought," in *Religion, Public Life, and the American Polity*, ed. Luis E. Lugo (Knoxville, Tenn.: University of Tennessee Press, 1995), 3–34. I would also particularly recommend the writings of Michael W. McConnell in this area. A summary of these is contained in his "The State of Religious Liberty in the United States," *Public Justice Report* (Sept./Oct. 1995). See also Stephen V. Monsma, *Positive Neutrality: Letting Religious Freedom Ring* (Westport, Conn.: Greenwood Press, 1993).

32. In arguing for a Christian appreciation of the amendment, I am trying to clarify the fact that amongst its roots is Christian belief. However, one cannot argue for a continued public status for the Christian faith in America simply because much of it has been founded by Christians. The founding of a country gives no one any eternal religious "rights" to that country. Otherwise, we would have to argue that the growing Christian populations in, say, Korea and Sudan have no right to reform those countries. We would also have to deny secular people the right to try and reshape the United States. In his otherwise excellent *The Naked Public Square* (Grand Rapids, Mich.: Eerdmans, 1984), Richard Neuhaus seems occasionally to fall into this error. Of course the religious nature of a founding necessarily continues to shape a country powerfully, which is one of Neuhaus' major points.

33. It can be argued that the restriction on Congress establishing a religion was to protect established churches in the states from federal interference. It needs to be added that there were also a variety of different views present among the Founding Fathers themselves when they drafted the amendment: see John Witte, "The American Constitutional Experiment in Religious Rights: The Perennial Quest for Principles," in *Religious Human Rights in Global Perspective: Legal Perspectives*, ed. John Witte and Johan Van Der Vyver (The Hague: Martinus Nijhoff, 1996), 497–557; *Religion and the American Experiment: Essential Rights and Liberties* (Boulder, Colo.: Westview Press, 2000).

34. *Everson v. Board of Education*, 310 U.S. 1 (1947). Jefferson wrote of "separation" in a letter in 1802 to the Danbury Baptist Association. For a good discussion of this, see David Dreisbach, *Thomas Jefferson and the Wall of Separation* (New York: New York University Press, 2000). Jefferson clearly did not intend by "separation" the sort of ideas propounded in its name, since he happily attended a worship service in the House of Representatives just two days after sending this letter. The Library of Congress program on "Religion and the Founding of the American Republic" explores these themes in a marvelous way.

35. *Lemon v. Kurtzman*, 403 U.S. 602 (1971).

36. Michael W. McConnell, "Stuck with a Lemon," *ABA Journal* (February 1997).

37. Supreme Court language on religion also took on a very negative cast, especially in its use of the word "sectarian." See Richard A. Baer Jr., "The Supreme Court's Discriminatory Use of the Term 'Sectarian,'" *The Journal of Law and Politics* 6 (Spring 1990): 449–68.

38. One exception to this has been in the treatment of conscientious objection. The Supreme Court has held that religious exemptions include "whether a given belief that is sincere and meaningful occupies a place in the life of its possessor parallel to that filled by the orthodox belief in God," *Seeger v. United States*, 380 U.S. 163 (1965). In European discussions of laws concerning religion, "secular humanism," or "laicite," is often included under "religion or belief."

39. A point also made in Stephen V. Monsma and J. Christopher Soper's study, *The Challenge of Pluralism: Church and State in Five Democracies* (Lanham, Md.: Rowman & Littlefield, 1997).

40. *Zorach v. Clauson*, 343 U.S. 306 (1952).

41. *Abingdon School District v. Schempp*, 374 U.S. 203 (1963).

42. For a good popular survey of these trends, see Jeffrey Rosen, "Is Nothing Secular?" *New York Times Magazine*, 30 January 2000. Rosen says the court is moving toward "equal treatment." Carl H. Esbeck argues that the Supreme Court has, in the past, seen the First Amendment as a means of defining the institutional role of church and state, and that it makes coherent sense to do so. See his "The Establishment Clause as a Structural Restraint on Governmental Power," *Iowa Law Review* 84, no. 1 (October 1998): 1–112, especially 54–58.

43. See Michael W. McConnell, "Believers as Equal Citizens," 90–106, and Gra-

ham Walker, "Illusory Pluralism, Inexorable Establishment," 111–26 in *Obligations of Citizenship and Demands of Faith: Religious Accommodation in Pluralist Societies*, ed. Nancy L. Rosenblum (Princeton, N.J.: Princeton University Press, 2000); *Mitchell v. Helms*, 2000.

44. *Mitchell v. Helms* was decided by 6–3, but Stephen Breyer's separate concurring opinion was very tentative.

45. There is much more agreement about the place of *explicit* religious practice in public schools. The guide "Religion in the Public Schools: A Joint Statement of Current Law" (April 1995) has the agreement of groups ranging from the National Association of Evangelicals and the Christian Legal Society to the American Civil Liberties Union and People for the American Way.

46. Our goal should not be to *compel* anyone's choice, but we cannot offer all the options as if all were equally true, or equally false.

47. In 1905, Canadian Prime Minister Sir Wilfrid Laurier said of Canada and the United States: "We live by the side of a nation . . . in whose schools, for fear that Christian dogmas in which all do not believe might be taught, Christian morals are not taught. . . . When I observe in this country of ours, a total absence of lynchings and an almost total absence of divorces and murders, I thank heaven that we are living in a country where the young children of the land are taught Christian morals and Christian dogmas," quoted in S. F. Wise and R. C. Brown, eds., *Canada Views the U.S.: Nineteenth Century Political Attitudes* (Seattle, Wash.: University of Washington Press, 1967), 12.

48. Quoted in Carl Horn III, "Secularism and Pluralism in Public Education," *Harvard Journal of Law and Public Policy* 7 (Winter 1984): 177–83.

49. Though, of course, the Court's record in this area has been what McConnell calls "disgraceful."

50. George Weigel, "Achieving Disagreement: From Indifference to Pluralism," *Journal of Law and Religion* 8 (1990): 175–98.

51. Weigel, "Achieving Disagreement," 186.

CHAPTER SEVEN

∾

Politics and Morality

The Difference between Morality and Politics

Americans are deeply divided over what are often called "moral issues." The major such issues include divorce, abortion, pornography, and homosexuality, and they usually arouse far more passion than matters of budgets and foreign policy. Clearly, the expression "moral issues" is vague and misleading, not least because *all* politics is always and necessarily "moral" in some sense. Every political decision, whether on war, trade, gun control, agriculture, environmental policy, education, crime, or taxes, inevitably involves inescapable moral choices. The common mantra that we should never impose morality through politics is either ignorance or demagoguery. There is no politics without moral decisions.

The reason that these particular issues are called "moral" or "ethical" seems to be that, apparently unlike war or crime, they are intertwined with views of personal conduct, especially about sex. And, since much contemporary political theory opposes any attempts to legislate what it calls personal conduct, these issues have become North America's most intense and virulent political battleground. They are treated in terms of military metaphor, most notably the overarching symbol that we are engaged in a culture war.

These battles also usually involve sex, one of the most potent issues in human life. Many observers lament that politics addresses sexual matters, and claim that it diverts energy and attention into a purely personal, not political, matter. But such objections are wrong, since matters sexual are at the heart of human identity and so will always be at the core of society's most fundamental relations. They are also never far from the thoughts of every male and female. Hence, public concern over matters sexual is not obsession, or the product of repressed Puritanism. It is concern over the nature of human beings and human life. Hence, sexual matters always have been and always will be political matters. As theologian Harry Kuitert observed, "Religion, politics and sex . . . are the only subjects worth bothering about." Since moral issues usually involve all three, they will always be explosive.

Views urging some immaculate abstention in government judgment and policy about personal conduct may well be wrong. However, we should still agree that the government is not supposed to be the corrector of all moral evils, including sexual ones. The key question is what sort of morality governments should uphold, and in what areas of human life it should uphold them. Following are some suggestions on how we should address what are currently called moral questions, not by trying to provide any final answers to these controversies, as if anyone could, but merely some ways of approaching them.

The fact that we are focusing on politics, on the purposes and acts of governments, should keep us from at least certain types of moralism. Obviously, if all that is meant by "morality" is that politics always and inevitably involves choices about good and evil, justice and injustice, then we should have no quarrel with such morality. No political action can ever be a purely technical or expert matter, devoid of any normative judgment or consequence. All political decisions depend on views of human nature, human history, and human responsibility.

But in politics we are concerned with more, and less, than morality in general. We focus on particular types of morality—those which are a specific responsibility of governments and states. It is not enough to know, even correctly, that some things, such as family breakdown, spousal abuse, or pornography, are bad. We have to know whether and how they might properly be matters for government action. This means we have to travel through the judicial minefields of family legislation and censorship, and struggle with their myriad unintended consequences.

To take one example, Robert P. Dugan, former director of the public affairs office of the National Association of Evangelicals, argued that "homosexual activity is morally wrong, and . . . our laws . . . have their source in the moral law of God. . . ." Whether or not these statements are true, it would not immediately follow, as Dugan seemed to maintain, that homosexuals should be kept out of the military. After all, when the apostle Paul condemned homosexuality, he put it in the same list as greed, malice, envy, gossip, and pride. These are morally wrong and several are common in the military, as elsewhere, while some, like pride, have been considered military virtues. While many of these vices might damage the military, they are not usually barriers to military service, and governments usually do not make them illegal. Hence, if we want to argue that homosexuality should be a barrier to military service, we would have to say much more than that it is wrong. Many things are wrong. The question is whether it is the type of wrong that governments should be concerned with.

Exactly the same thing may be said about the moralism of the Christian left in economics. Joan Brown Campbell, former General Secretary of the National Council of Churches, claimed that the proposed elimination of the Federal Department of Education "clearly conflicts with the repeated calls of scripture to protect the poor."[1] However, neither Isaiah nor Ezekiel clearly addressed the role of government in education nor commented on whether it should be a state or federal matter, which is what the dispute was about. Campbell gave us no clue as to why we should think that her comments about what the Bible might teach have anything to do with government policy. Furthermore, the immorality of something per se tells us absolutely nothing about government policy. It is immoral not to love, but no government can make us do so.

Nor, on the other hand, must something necessarily be immoral in the first place for governments to need to do something about it. Some actions, such as driving through a red light, would themselves be quite all right if there weren't already a law against them. There's nothing intrinsic to the color red that means it is wrong to drive past it. Many laws concerning traffic were not formulated in order to stamp out evil, but were passed as simple regulations giving rules, sometimes arbitrary ones, in order to make traffic flow more easily. Laws are often regulations of actions which are not intrinsically wrong, but whose regulation can achieve a good public purpose, such as preventing cars from driving into one another. Only after the law is passed do these actions take on a whole new context and become matters of morality.

One example occurs with illegal immigration. While there are doubtless some thugs and thieves among them, as with all people, the majority of illegal immigrants entering the United States from, say, Mexico, Guatemala, and points south, are people who simply desire a better life, and are willing to risk their lives in striving for it. Many do, in fact, die striving. Generally, they are disciplined and hard-working, and many send money back to support needy families. In most respects they are admirable people. They risk life and limb to get a low-paying job. If there were no border then who could object to what they do? It is the fact of a border, a political invention, that makes their action wrong.

America's borders are not divinely located. Like all borders, they are a product of war, compromise, and accident. But if governments are to be able to govern, then there need to be some controls on who can enter a country through these borders. It is because of this necessary *political* restriction that an otherwise praiseworthy activity can become wrong. Illegal immigrants' actions would not be immoral if they were not illegal. This is one reason why we feel ambivalent about them. This ambiguity is shown by the fact that the border patrol tries to stop and capture illegal immigrants, and, at the same time, leaves water out for them so that they will not die in the desert. Morality and politics can have a complex relation.

This also means that we should not think that we can deal with political problems largely by encouraging large numbers of personally principled and compassionate people to go into politics. The effect of such people would depend, in large part, on what their political principles are. Many, especially black, inhabitants of the southern United States and the Republic of South Africa did not in the past rejoice in the fact that they were blessed, or cursed, with the proximity of large numbers of very upright, very pious, theologically conservative politicians. Many of their problems stemmed from just such people. Even good people can do terrible political things: Mohandas Gandhi was a good man and he led a nonviolent struggle against Britain in a just campaign for Indian independence. But he miscalculated politically about the tensions in India. When British India achieved independence, it split immediately into Hindu and Muslim segments (India and Pakistan), and millions fled so as not to be caught on the wrong side. Hundreds of thousands died, millions more became refugees, and the segments have been on the verge of war virtually ever since. This conflict is now also cursed with nuclear weapons. Well-intentioned actions by moral people in themselves achieve nothing. What is required are good statesmen with good political judgment.

Compromise

Many people believe that compromise is a fundamentally evil thing. Indeed, some explicitly describe their stance as "uncompromising," and defend their own correctness by their refusal to compromise. It is often said that one of the major problems today is that politicians always compromise rather than stand on principle.

But compromise is not peculiar to politics; it is a fundamental feature of every aspect of human life. Anybody who is married and has gone through a day without compromising is probably in deep marital trouble. If you live with another person, you have to compromise. You want to do one thing. They want to do another. You want to eat something. They want to eat something else. You want to see one movie. They want to see another. So, if you are a moderately sane person, you'll either split it down the middle, or you'll do one thing today and the other tomorrow. We each try to give a little of what the other wants. That's a major part of what living with another person is about. In biblical history even God is portrayed as compromising. Abraham, Moses, and Samuel argued with God and won (some, like Jonah, didn't). Abraham and God are even described as haggling over the number of righteous people required to save the city of Sodom (Gen. 18:17–32).

Perhaps it could be replied that compromise might be all right in the mundane, day-to-day affairs of personal preference, but not in fundamental matters. This reply is correct. Certainly we should not compromise on fundamental matters and matters of principle. However, we do need to be cautious about what we regard as fundamental matters and principles. For example, a law is not necessarily a fundamental principle. This is true not only of the laws we make now, but also of the laws listed in the Old Testament. The actual law concerning murder in the Torah is not really "Thou shall not kill." This, like the others of the Ten Commandments, is actually not a law but a principle for the law. It is a basic statement about how we should live and treat one another, in the light of which laws can then be made.

Israel developed such laws in its own life. The actual enforceable rules—the laws—concerning killing are described in several parts of the Pentateuch (cf. Deut. 17:8; 19:1–13, 15). These outline, for example, the difference between premeditated and unpremeditated killing, something similar to distinctions between murder and manslaughter. They also detail how many witnesses were needed in order to prove a particularly difficult case, and describe the development of what were called "cities of refuge." Within Israel, if one person killed another without forethought, without planning to, then he or she could flee to one of these cities. If they could get there before their victim's relatives caught up with them to exact retribution, then they could remain free. At first there were to be three cities. Then, later, as Israel grew, more should be added. The underlying idea seems to be that there needed to be a reasonable opportunity for someone to be able to escape.

Israel's practical law, including its criminal code, was complex. It dealt with rules of evidence, questions of malice and premeditation, and possible defenses. It was complex enough that experienced judges had to be appointed to decide if and when an offense had occurred, what type of offense it was, and what the possible penalty should be.[2] It was a developed, varied, multi-layered system of law. In practice, it took a basic principle, such as "Thou shall not kill," and expressed it, in the light of other relevant principles, in the life of Israel. The commandment became expressed in a locally applicable, practical, concrete, enforceable law on killing. The Bible contains not only fundamental principles, but also laws which are the particular local, historical expressions of these basic principles.

Hence, while we should not compromise on the basic principle, "Thou shall not kill," and thus justify the taking of innocent human life, we are called to give this principle concrete form in our own lives and society. This means implementing a principle in a particular, variable, historical situation. Very many different elements, including proper forms of legitimate compromise, can, should, and must enter into the making of laws. A law is not itself a principle, but is usually the particular expression of a principle. Of course, not all compromises are good. Some things should never be compromised. But it is equally true that not all compromise is bad. The key is knowing the difference.

Living with Evil

In areas where governments have no proper authority to act, we are left in the political situation of having to live alongside evils (though we, of course, still can, and should, try to combat such evils by other means, such as personal help, argument, social outreach, and social ostracism). To coexist politically with such forms of evil is not a denial of God's will. It is a different and important aspect of that will. Apart from judgment, the Scriptures also repeatedly emphasize patience. They stress that God will judge, but also that a major part of that judgment will take place in the future.

Jesus told a parable of a man who sowed good seed in his field, but whose enemies planted weeds among it at night. When asked whether the weeds should be uprooted he replied: "No, because you might pull up the wheat with them. Let them grow together until the harvest and then separate them" (Matt. 13:28–30). Jesus went on to explain that this referred to a future judgment when God would separate out evildoers (Matt. 13:36–43). If, as the parable says, God is patient even with those who do evil, so much more should we also strive to live alongside others in political peace.

In fact, Jesus went far beyond describing God's patient acceptance of certain kinds of evil. He said that God not only allows people to live in disobedience, but also still actively cares and provides for them even as they do so. He said: "Love your enemies . . . that you may be children of your father who is in heaven; for [h]e makes [h]is sun to rise on the evil and on the good. And sends the rain on the just and on the unjust" (Matt. 5:45). Here God doesn't simply "tolerate" those who break the commandments; he actively cares for and loves them. The sun's rising is portrayed as a sign of continuing love and care. The rain is welcomed as a gift to all, just and unjust alike.

We should not politically try to uproot all those things that we think are wrong. The state is not to require a particular standard of personal conduct for everyone. Proper civil and political coexistence is not some departure from or dilution of the Christian faith, but should be a direct expression of that faith. It means that in many things we are called to be as patient as God is. The state cannot and will not stamp out all evil; therefore, we must be long-suffering.

In such a situation, we don't have to accept that every lifestyle is good, or that it doesn't matter what anyone believes or does. We are not called to be relativists. We are simply acknowledging that the government is not called to resolve all matters. The question is not only whether people are doing the right things; it is whether or not it is the government's job and within the government's authority to support or stop them.

There is an old prayer, attributed to almost everyone, that has become so used that it is hackneyed. But it is still cuts to the core of human judgment and responsibility, including political judgment and responsibility—"Lord, give me the courage to change the things I can, the patience to bear the things I cannot, and the wisdom to know the difference." We need to know the political difference.

Imposing Our Views on Others

Where would modern political talk be without the "eleventh commandment" that "you can't impose your beliefs on others"? This cliché is a staple especially of those who wish to impose a policy of (misdefined) toleration or a view of human autonomy on everyone else (see chapter 6). It is a major theme in the pro-choice position on abortion. Some pro-choice people may agree that abortion is wrong and that many sincere people are strongly opposed to it. They may say that they personally are opposed to abortion. But they then often argue that while people may have strong views on the subject, it is a matter on which there is deep division and deep disagreement, and so say, "We can't impose our view on other people. For ourselves we may choose not to have an abortion, but it's not something that we can demand of anybody else. People must choose for themselves." That is why proponents of this position want the label "pro-choice," not "pro-abortion."

Similar arguments are widespread in disputes over pornography, euthanasia, drugs, and teenage pregnancy. In each of these cases many (especially those intent on changing traditional attitudes) will lament a problem and perhaps say that people are doing something very wrong. However they will then immediately add, "But we can't impose our values on others and so we must allow them to be free to do what they want."

Many people are confused in the face of this argument. On the one hand, they sense that there is an implicit political agenda behind many of these demands and so resist it. On the other hand, they remember the times that Christians and others have tried to compel dissidents to believe something, sometimes by imprisonment and force, and certainly don't want to repeat that tragedy. Hence, people can want both to agree and disagree, and feel trapped. In addition, our society has another cliché, which is that we should not judge others, and people want to avoid at all costs the charge of being "intolerant."

In one sense it is right to say both yes and no to these arguments and impulses. There are areas where we definitely should try to impose our morality or legislate our views and there are areas where we should not. There are many, very different, types and levels of morality and conduct: some are appropriate for politics and some not; some are matters of personal taste, while others are matters of life and death, and therefore politically central. We shouldn't try to tell people what they should put on their pizza. It's a matter of taste, and, unless someone is about to die of food allergies, people should be free to make up their own minds about what they want for lunch.

But differences on, for example, slavery, are not matters of taste or personal predilection. They are judgments about the fundamental nature of human freedom and of human rights. They are judgments about the basis of political order and the responsibility of the state itself. An answer to the question of slavery must always be imposed in any society, for it is necessarily a question of the authority of life and death of one human being over another. A slaveholder cannot say, "Well, if you don't believe in slavery then don't have slaves, but don't try to impose your views on me." (This example is not at all fanciful; it is precisely the argument the Southern slaveholders used—they were the first to argue that someone else's values should not be imposed on them.) But, if the slaveholders' argument is granted, most arguments of human freedom from constraint must be granted. One human being could claim the right to kill another without someone else's morality being imposed on him or her, and thus can claim the right to do anything to another.

In reality, everybody, except anarchists, believes that some things should be imposed by the government and some should not be. Bill Clinton was quite willing (as he should have been) to urge Congress to impose his views about what "just taxation" is on everybody. Pat Robertson correctly believes the government has no business telling people where to worship. Each of them agrees that some views, but not others, should be legislated. What is purely personal should be free. What is properly political must be imposed.

Given that some views must always be imposed, the brain-dead slogan that "you can't impose your views on others" can be seen as, at most, a half-truth, and therefore, a distortion and manipulation.[3] It assumes the very thing that is in dispute and which first needs to be shown—that the issue in question clearly is one of those things that are purely personal rather than political. It tries to hijack the debate by surreptitiously introducing the conclusions of one side of the argument. The key question is not whether we can impose views. We know it is right to impose views that are properly political, and not those that are personal. The key question is, What is properly political? What is properly a sphere of government action?

The issue where these arguments occur most frequently is abortion. The assertion that "you can't impose your views" regarding abortion declares dogmatically, from the outset, that abortion is a purely personal rather than an political matter. But this claim is precisely what the debate is all about. The assertion sidesteps the issue.

This confused debate highlights once more a central theme of this book, which is that we need to understand what states and governments have and have not the duty and authority to do. This is not an abstract question of interest and consequence only to academics and pedants. It lies at the heart of issues that threaten to tear the United States apart. The question is not whether we can "impose our views" on others. The question is, in what areas of human life can the state properly impose or not impose views, and what kind of views can it impose?

In areas properly within its jurisdiction, like taxes and the taking of human life, the government can and should demand that human beings act in certain ways, and it should use its coercive power to see that they do. In areas which are not within its jurisdiction, like worship in churches, it should not act, even if people are doing things many others believe are wrong. Hence, when we deal with what are generally called moral issues, the question which should always be before us is not "Can we impose our morality?" but "Is this a proper function of government?" If it isn't, the government should stay out of it. If it is, the government may and must impose a view.

This chapter has stressed that the fact that someone may be doing something bad is not itself grounds for government action. Individuals, families, churches, unions, and businesses have their own rights and responsibility and need to have the political freedom to exercise that responsibility. If governments were to correct everything, we would have a totalitarian system where no one except the state was free to make any real decisions at all. Genuine politics would simply disappear.

This theme of diverse and differentiated responsibility gives a foundation to the modern idea of human rights—that human beings must necessarily be free of political control in many areas of their life regardless of whether we, or the government, like or dislike what they are doing (see chapter 4). The mere fact that greed and lust, and waste and pornography, are evil is not in and of itself any grounds for any government action.

In this particular sense we should agree that it is not the task of government to enforce morality. The government's task is not to compel everything that is right or moral, but to enforce the particular part of morality that we call justice—which lies at the core of genuine political morality. Governments must respect the proper independence of others—respect independent human callings, human responsibilities, human rights. Human rights are one way of referring to an area of human decision and responsibility properly beyond the authority and power of governments.

However, while stressing the importance of human freedom and human responsibility, even for bad decisions, we must also stress the importance of justice between people (see chapter 3). Rights point to human freedoms, and justice points to the way in which human freedoms are related to each another in the public sphere. Relations between independent people, institutions, organizations, and things are always subject to the demands of public justice. What people do cannot always be treated as simply their own affair. Real freedoms must always be exercised in the context of relations with others. Consequently, while we should always highly value free expression and the right of people to control their own lives, we should not accept the idea that, for example, all censorship is always and forever wrong, or that abortion should never be subject to legislation. These, like every human activity, should be judged in terms of how they affect just relations between people.

Abortion

Most of these issues come to focus in abortion. Even if we believe that abortion is killing our offspring, there are still many questions regarding the state's role in controlling it.[4] Even a human right to life is not absolute. For example, though the situations are not parallel, soldiers can legitimately be asked to give their lives in a just war. Or, if someone needs a kidney transplant to survive, we do not, presumably, believe that we should force someone else to donate one of their own kidneys to save another's life. It might be very good to donate a kidney, but it should not be compulsory. Human life itself is not an absolute, but along with everything else in the world, must be weighed in the scales of justice. In the case of a kidney transplant, we are allowing one person's right to their bodily integrity to override another person's need to something essential to their life. Life itself does not trump everything.

Similar limits arise with the claim that a woman has a right to control her body. In a general sense, this is obviously an important freedom to be protected, and therefore, there would need to be an important reason to override it. If a person really cannot decide about what happens to her body, she is usually not free to decide much else. But there is the crucial question of whether an unborn child actually is only a part of a woman's body or whether, instead, it should be regarded as a new human life. And, clearly, there are also many others who are affected by a decision about abortion—the father, the doctors, even the people who will pay for it. Abortion never involves just one person. Any claim otherwise is empirically false.

In view of the fact that governments must be concerned with things that are not purely private—that is, things which have important effects on others—and because abortion always and necessarily involves at least an unborn child and her mother—that is, more than one human life—it can never be treated as merely a matter of personal choice. Governments must have a responsibility here, as they do in the matter of owning slaves, which cannot be a matter of personal choice either. No human being has an inherent authority to dispose of another. Virtually every school of political thought asserts that the taking of human life is a responsibility which must be politically controlled. Consequently, limits on abortion are not "imposing personal morality" on other people for the simple reason that an abortion decision is not a personal one, except in the tautological sense that all decisions are obviously made by persons. Rather, they are attempts to ensure that the relations between different human beings are just. No government can do anything less. Consequently, governments must weigh both the rights of the mother and of the unborn child (and of other parties involved), and, since the most fundamental basic claim of the unborn child, its life, is at stake, there must be very weighty grounds on the side of the mother if an abortion should take place. A decision about abortion cannot be solely a private, personal decision, or even solely a medical decision. As it involves more than one human life, it necessarily needs to be a judicial decision, though with most evidence offered on personal and medical grounds.

This chapter has emphasized the importance of compromise; but, in stressing this with respect to abortion, this is not to suggest that compromise is relevant in this issue but not in others. Questions of compromise arise in any and every political circumstance from tax law to traffic control to war. However, because our society is so divided on abortion, questions of compromise come to the fore repeatedly and are often debated in a bitter fashion.

We cannot condone, nor easily acquiesce in, the taking of human life; hence we must always resist abortion. But laws are never made purely abstractly, without regard to our situation, and so we need also to consider what laws can be achieved and defended now. Or, perhaps more to the point in the current United States, we must consider how current bad laws and their effects can be changed and limited. The Catholic Church has given careful scrutiny to the principles of abortion law, and the possibilities of the current situation. A good reflection of this is given in Pope John Paul II's *Evangelium Vitae*:

> When it is not possible to overturn or completely abrogate a pro-abortion law, an elected official, whose absolute personal opposition to procured abortion was well known, could licitly support proposals aimed at limiting the harm done by such a law and at lessening its negative consequences at the level of general opinion and public morality. This does not in fact represent an illicit cooperation with an unjust law, but rather a legitimate and proper attempt to limit its evil aspects.

This gives, with a precision not present in official Protestant and Orthodox formulations, a partial guide to addressing abortion law.

There are other legal features that should be considered. A law is not a theological or philosophical principle, nor is it only the legal expression of a principle. Laws are, among many things, binding rules made by governments with the threat of force to compel obedience (this is not intended to be a full description of law). Many factors are properly involved in the making of law.

First, any law must conform to the Constitution. In the practical short-term, this means that the Supreme Court must find the law constitutional. Hence, simply trying to pass a law which we think is good when, by our best estimates, it will be struck down by the Court, will be, in the shorter term, a futile, even self-defeating, exercise. Such a proposed law may perhaps be a useful symbol (and symbols are important), but it is not going to be the law of the land in the near future. Of course, Supreme Courts change, and there is the possibility that it may hold a law constitutional at a later date. But this does not invalidate the requirement of the Court upholding the law. It merely says that it may be achieved later. We still always face the practical necessity of conforming to the Court's view of the Constitution.

Second, the proposal must be achievable—that is, can we actually have it passed into law? Do we have the votes or can we get them? A supposedly better law which cannot get through Congress or a state legislature is not going to be a law. Perhaps it will be a law in the future, but not now. Meanwhile, we may have to weaken it in order to get enough votes to pass it. But, a weak law can be better than no law at all. Of course, a proposed possible law could be watered down so much that it could be worse than nothing. In this case, we should drop it and try another day (meanwhile working to change the legislature.) But the fact remains that without votes it will never be a law. An unachievable bill is no law at all.

Third, a law must be enforceable. If a law cannot be enforced, it will wither and decay. If the population refuses to follow a law, it will not have force.[5] For example, in Canada in the 1980s, abortion was largely illegal. However, Henry Morgentaler, the country's leading abortionist, was repeatedly tried and acquitted by juries, though there was never any doubt that he was in fact performing abortions. Canadian public opinion, at least as expressed in repeated jury decisions, would not enforce the penalties of the existing law. Later, the Canadian Supreme Court struck down the law. But, at this point, even reinstating the previous law would have made little difference—the justice system seemed incapable of securing convictions under such a law.[6] In a democracy, the law must be accepted by the public at large. This doesn't mean that everybody has always to agree (after all, some people disobey laws about bank robbery). No law is ever followed by everybody. But it does mean that the law has to be broadly in tune with public opinion and public sentiment.

It is certainly true that laws also have an educational function. Laws shape society by giving standards of conduct, not only by enforcing conduct. Abortion laws, or the lack of them, always send strong messages. But this is true only if the law manages to be a law—enforceable and accepted by the public at large. A law which fails to achieve constitutionality and enforceability will also fail in any possible educational function. Indeed it is likely to give the wrong message. If the law is not being upheld, its failure is likely to encourage people to think that trying to enforce it is wrong.

Possible Legal Changes

One way to move forward despite these difficulties is in the debate over what are called "partial-birth" abortions. Even in an already grotesque area, such abortions have a particular horror. Many pro-life activists have given major attention to outlawing this practice, and many otherwise pro-choice politicians, such as former Senator Patrick Moynihan, have also condemned it. The Senate and the House of Representatives passed legislation outlawing the procedure, but President Clinton always vetoed it.

Some pro-life groups worry about such legislation if it simply outlaws partial-birth abortions. Their concerns are twofold. One is that, especially since the Supreme Court has struck down state laws, any proposed new law may need to contain exceptions which drastically weaken it.[7] Also, such abortions are only a small percentage of the abortions performed yearly in the United States. In short, the proposed law leaves most of the abortion industry intact.

However, the legislation can have beneficial effects. First, it would stop a small number of abortions. Others would certainly continue, but we should not refuse to stop some because we cannot stop all. Secondly, it focuses attention on the actual nature of the procedure and so puts its defenders very much on the defensive. It means that they cannot say that this is simply a medical procedure carried out on an amorphous blob of tissue. It is close to what even present law defines as an act of murder. This gives a powerful message about the nature of abortion and educates the public for further steps.

There are other laws that are constitutionally achievable, supported by public opinion, and that can educate the public. One is the Urban Victims of Violence Act, making it a crime to harm a fetus in circumstances other than abortion. Under such a law, an assault on a pregnant woman is treated as an assault on her unborn child as well. Another is the Child Custody Prevention Act, which would make it a federal crime to transport a minor across state lines to procure an abortion if it circumvented a state law requiring parental notification before an abortion. A third is the Born-Alive Infants Protection Act, which would protect children who have survived an abortion. Finally, there can be guidelines that forbid research that results in the destruction of human embryos. To these can be added the growing nationwide trend to have mandatory waiting periods and counseling before an abortion. Each of these can both limit abortion and educate the public.

In none of these examples should attempts to develop a law, even if successful, be seen as the end of the matter. Such legislative attempts must be seen as initial steps in an overall campaign. As in any conflict, we should not shy away from small wins because they are not the final victory. Already one effect of these efforts is that pro-life views in the population, as shown in opinion polls, are steadily increasing, especially amongst the young and women.

Alternatives to Abortion

Rhetoric about abortion in the United States is dominated by claims that it is an individual right.[8] Hence, it is often treated as if it were only an individual mother's concern wherein only her individual rights are involved. The consequence of this individualism is a great tendency for, especially, single mothers to be left alone with the consequence of their own decision. Treating abortion as an individual right means that birth is increasingly treated as an individual responsibility, and then, as an individual consequence. A woman may make the decision on her own but, when she has made the decision, she is equally often left on her own. She is dumped by fathers and feminists. If she suffers grief after abortion, that's her problem. If she raises her child, that's her problem. You make your decision and you, individually, must live with the consequences. Fathers, or parents, or other relatives, or the community at large, are usually regarded as intruders in the legal decision, and so should be kept out of it. There is a parallel tendency for the father, or parents, or other relatives, or the community at large to ignore what happens to a mother when she aborts or bears her child. She is isolated both in responsibility and in consequence. American law now says, in effect, that fathers have no legal say in any decision about abortion, and, in parallel, the state makes little effort to ensure that fathers support mothers and children. Our tendency is to isolate the mother and child both in law and in society.

This can be contrasted with some European practices, which tend to be focused less on individual rights in decisions about abortion, and consequently, focused less on individually coping with the results of that decision.[9] These different approaches help produce different rates of abortion, even apart from whether or not the law actively forbids abortion. The ethos of the law shapes people's behavior. For example, the Netherlands, despite having an awful abortion law, as well as other medically related laws, has a lower abortion rate because of its support structures for families. Forbidding or allowing abortion is only one part of the equation. Hence, apart from laws which allow and forbid, we should consider conditions which help people take alternative actions.

Also, many abortions come about because a man refuses to accept responsibility for a child, and demands that a reluctant woman have an abortion or face desertion. Polls consistently show that support for abortion is higher among men than among women.[10] This calls for changing views of pregnancy and childhood. It means changing the widespread social attitudes that see children as a hindrance to a self-fulfilled life. As the American Catholic bishops said in the their 1995 pastoral letter, *Faithful for Life: A Moral Reflection*, "We are bound to our children, not because we chose them, but because we were given them. . . . To live in fidelity we have to rearrange our lives, yield control, and forfeit some choices." We must work to help women and families bring up in a healthy way the children to whom they have given birth. This requires helping single women and poor women who cannot easily afford another child. This requires action by churches and individuals in adoption, employment, child care, and housing.

If laws are passed that are in opposition to the hearts, lives, and commitments of the population at large, then those laws may have little effect. But direct action in direct support of our neighbor can make important differences. After all, the vast majority of people's problems are met, in the first place, by families, friends, and churches, not by governments. We must seek to pass laws that constrict and restrict the practice of abortion or other evils, and help shape a society in which these laws can have effect. Meanwhile, we must seek to supplement and support political efforts by direct, compassionate actions in support of women and children facing desperate need.

As the example of abortion shows, there is no simple answer to the issues of morality and politics. They require both a clear and disciplined view of the proper role of the state, combined with a willingness to work personally, and in community, directly with those in need.

Notes

1. Robert Dugan, *Washington Insight*, March, 1993; Joan Brown Campbell, "Letter to President Clinton," 26 September 1995.

2. Though not so complex, apparently, as to require lawyers.

3. This is not the same as the common view that we should be left free to do what we want as long as we do not harm others, as articulated by, for example, John Stuart Mill in his *On Liberty*. There are types of harm to others which should be allowed. For example, in a competitive market, a growing company with new techniques or a new technology may drive other companies out of business. The bankruptcy of Trans-World Airlines, or any other large corporation, leaves people unemployed, which is certainly a form of harm. Even without bankruptcy, companies can see their markets shrink, and lay off employees. Similarly, people who live in unhealthy ways raise other peoples' medical costs in shared health plans, whether through Medicare or HMOs. "Harm" is not itself the criterion; the question is whether it is the type of harm that can properly occur in just relations.

4. It is not my aim here to deal with all the questions of "right to life," but to illustrate a way of approaching a moral question like abortion. A good, brief discussion on the issue of the unborn child is Oliver O'Donovan, *The Christian and the Unborn*

Child (Bramcote, U.K.: Grove Books, 1975). O'Donovan acknowledges, but does not address, the complex political difficulties that abortion raises.

5. This was the situation during the prohibition of alcohol in the United States. Alcohol consumption remained high and the criminal gangs who supplied it became even more powerful. The law didn't "take hold."

6. I analyze this decision in "Some Political Implications of the Abortion Decision," in *The Issue Is Life*, ed. D. O'Leary (Burlington, Ontario: Welch, 1988), 14–27.

7. *Steinberg v. Carhart* (2000) struck down Nebraska's law, one of approximately thirty such state laws.

8. My concerns here and in the earlier discussion of abortion reflect the statement, "The America We Seek: A Statement of Pro-Life Principle and Concern," *National Review*, 25 March 1996. This statement was developed by the Ethics and Public Policy Center.

9. See the discussion by Mary Ann Glendon in her *Abortion and Divorce in Western Law* (Cambridge, Mass.: Harvard University Press, 1987).

10. James Davison Hunter, *Before the Shooting Begins: Searching for Democracy in America's Culture Wars* (New York: Free Press, 1994), 72–74.

CHAPTER EIGHT

~

International Relations

Religion and International Relations

Previous chapters described religion as a basic commitment. But even if, for the moment, we restrict ourselves to a more traditional sense of religion, its importance in the international world is also becoming increasingly apparent as, with the passing of European colonialism, more of the world's cultures and religions—hitherto politically marginal for a century or more—have reasserted themselves.[1] The clearest example of this is the Islamic world stretching from Morocco on the Atlantic through Indonesia and the Philippines on the Pacific Rim. Islam has shaped civilizations, including the most powerful ones in the world, for over thirteen hundred years. It did not simply pack its bags and give up because European powers had taken over its heartland for a century. Bin Laden terrorism is not typical of Islam; indeed, it is a perversion, but it is symptomatic of the ferment which still continues in the Muslim world in general. It is part of the resurgent power of a world religion, one which will continue to shape the world in the coming centuries.[2] Similar patterns are occurring with Hinduism in India and Nepal, and Buddhism in Sri Lanka and Burma.

Along these lines, we should rethink our conception of the "West." At one level, the West is a civilization that has been shaped by Christianity, although it is now often post–Christian. The West in this sense includes both Latin America and much of Eastern Europe, and shows continuing common features with, along with differences from, the rest of the world. Similarly, we should not think of the rest of the world solely in terms of Western ideas of globalization, development, secularization, or liberation, or the old vocabulary of First and Third Worlds. In order to understand the world, we need to take religion seriously, something that many political analysts still refuse to do.

One major cause of this comparative neglect of religion is the prevalence in the Western world of what may be called secular myopia, which can be described as an inability even to see, much less understand, the role of religion in human life.[3] This myopia is particularly widespread amongst what the English describe as "the chattering classes." As Luttwak has written:

> Policymakers, diplomats, journalists, and scholars who are ready to over-interpret economic causality, who are apt to dissect social differentiations even more finely, and who will minutely categorize political affiliations, are still in the habit of disregarding the role of religion, religious institutions, and religious motivations in explaining politics and even in reporting their concrete modalities.[4]

This secular myopia was one reason for America's unpreparedness for the terrorist attacks on September 11, 2001. But this is only the latest of several instances. One was U.S. ignorance of the views and power of the Ayatollah Khomeini's followers when they came to power in Iran in 1979. Luttwak notes that there was only one proposal for the CIA to examine "the attitude and activities of the more prominent religious leaders" in Iran, and that even this proposal was vetoed as mere "sociology," intelligence-speak for irrelevant academic verbiage. Consequently, as the Shah's regime was collapsing about them, many U.S. political analysts kept insisting that everything was fine. Following their training, they examined factors such as economic variables, class structure, and the military, and concluded that, since these relevant power groups supported the Shah, then he was comparatively safe. There were, of course, mullahs arousing Islamic sentiment, but analysts had been taught that such religious drives were akin to folk memories, were destined to disappear with modernization and globalization, and were irrelevant to the real structures of political power. Similarly, "in Vietnam, every demographic, economic, ethnic, social, and, of course, military aspect of the conflict was subject to detailed scrutiny, but the deep religious cleavages that afflicted South Vietnam were hardly noticed." The "tensions between the dominant Catholic minority [and] a resentful Buddhist majority . . . were largely ignored until Buddhist monks finally had to resort to flaming self-immolations in public squares, precisely to attract the attention of Americans so greatly attentive to everything else in Vietnam that was impeccably secular."[5] Parallel, though less striking tales can be told of Bosnia, Lebanon, the Philippines, Nicaragua, India, Israel and the Palestinians, Sudan, and Indonesia. Indeed, politics shaped by religion is one of the most powerful trends of the age, from the Palestinians to Chechnya, from Nigeria to India.

The neglect of this trend often comes not necessarily by ignoring particular patterns or events, although this happens too, but by redefining them. Americans, in particular, are prone to redefine religion through the nebulous catch-all term "ethnic." For example, Chester Crocker gave an excellent lecture to the Foreign Policy Research Institute entitled "How to Think about Ethnic Conflict."[6] However, even he described the Northern Ireland and India–Pakistan conflicts as ethnic. But India and Pakistan comprise hundreds of ethnicities, and are separate countries only because of their different *religions*, not ethnicities. Ireland is divided for the same reason. Other recent examples include the *Economist's* description of the slaughter of fifty-four Buddhists in Sri Lanka as perhaps "the first sign of ethnic cleansing," and fights between Christians and Muslims in Nigeria as "cultural."[7] Similarly, the *International Herald Tribune* expressed the fear that an Indian victory in Kashmir would lead to the "ethnic cleansing" of Muslims, while the *New Republic* contrasted the Sudanese conflict between a "predominantly Muslim north and a predominantly Christian south" with a Western dream of a "multiethnic democracy."[8] Many of these depictions seem to take their cue from descriptions of the former Yugoslavia, wherein Bosnian Muslims and war between Orthodox, Catholics, and Muslims were routinely described as ethnic. We have now coined the term "*ethnic* cleansing" to describe the murder of Muslims.

Our press coverage and political analysis often also have an introverted focus on a type of Western Enlightenment culture, as though this constituted the common opinion of humankind, or the common opinion of reasonable humankind, or at least the common opinion of Americans. Consequently, movements overseas are assimilated to Western categories. Hence, Jewish, Islamic, or Hindu militants are often described as right-wing, whatever that might mean. But what is a right-wing or left-wing view of the place of "infidel" Western troops in the Islamic holy land of Saudi Arabia, or attempts to build a Hindu temple on the site of the Babri mosque in Ayodhya, or to build a Jewish Third Temple near the Islamic Al-Aksa mosque in Jerusalem? None of these schemes has anything to do with categories of left and right (terms derived from the seating arrangements in the French Assembly after its revolution). Their meaning can only be grasped by understanding their deep-seated religious context. And such understanding is doubly urgent since these projects could precipitate war between nuclear powers.

When the vocabulary of left and right has run its tired course, we are commonly left with that old standby, "fundamentalist," a word dredged from the American past, and of dubious provenance and meaning even there. Using the term "fundamentalist" is currently a sign of intellectual laziness—a refusal to take seriously what people say they actually believe. "Fundamentalist" is now shorthand for "religious obsessive," therefore someone to be categorized rather than heard, observed rather than comprehended, dismissed rather than read.[9]

When ethnicity and psychology fail to subsume religion, a common alternative is to treat it as the sublimation of drives which can really be explained by poverty, economic change, or the stresses of modernity. Of course, these factors play a role—no part of human life is sealed off from any other. But all too often what we encounter is *a priori* methodological commitment to treat religion as secondary, as an evanescent and derivative phenomenon which can be explained, but never be used to explain.

All of these trends came to the fore in attempts to understand bin Laden and Al Qaeda. Bin Laden has always been forthright about his goals, and his deeds confirm his actions. Unfortunately, public statements by most U.S. commentators seemed to ignore both. Instead, Al Qaeda's intentions were filtered through a grid of parochial Western nostrums about the nature of religion, the causes of war, and the Middle East, all in an attempt to portray the war as another conflict between heirs of the Enlightenment.

We were told that this was not a war about religion, a claim that is transparently ludicrous. Certainly, bin Laden's views were not those of the majority of Muslims around the world. Certainly, the U.S. has not been waging war to defend a particular religion. It has defended Christians, Muslims, Jews, Buddhists, Hindus, atheists, and others from terror. But there is no hiding the fact that bin Laden, his lieutenants, and his foot soldiers repeatedly stated their aim to impose their version of Islam on, first, the Muslim world, and then, the rest of the world. They wanted each country to accept or be forced into submission to their version of Islamic *sharia* law.

Their public statements, strategy, recruitment, and prayers have shown a religious devotion. They do not lament inequality, decry poverty, or call for democracy. They do not rant about globalization or consumerism or capitalism. They explicitly name and target Christianity, Judaism, and moderate Islam.

As he repeated in his 1998 *Al-Jazeera* interview, "There are two parties to the conflict: World Christianity, which is allied with Jews and Zionism, led by the United States, Britain and Israel. The second party is the Islamic world." When he merged with Egypt's Islamic jihad in 1998, they formed the "World Islamic Front for Holy War against Jews and Crusaders," about the closest thing Al Qaeda has to an official name. He argued that the collapse of the Islamic world in the face of "Christendom," ongoing since the failure of the second Ottoman siege of Vienna in 1683, could only be explained by Muslims' apostasy from true Islam and only reversed by its embrace.

But many analysts argued that this was not religion but terrorism, not religion but frustrated desires for self-determination, not religion but opposition to American foreign policy. These misconceptions have been shaped either by the view that religion cannot be bad, or that it cannot be important.

But religions are not solely focused on abstractions, with no regard for the brutal realities of daily human life. They are teachings about how we should live, and so they shape life, for good and ill. Religion is no more all good or bad than politics is all good or bad. It brings saintly sacrifices that even the most jaded secularist recognizes. But it also produces jihads and inquisitions. By all means call this inauthentic religion, perverted religion, hijacked religion. But, at the cost of blinding ourselves, let us never forget that it is religion.

If we take religion seriously in international affairs, then we may also learn about a wide range of other things, including freedom of all kinds.[10] It was pointed out by religion scholars long before Samuel Huntington's important work on the "Clash of Civilizations" that chronic armed conflict in the world is concentrated on the boundaries of the traditional religions.[11] The Middle East, the southern Sahara, the Balkans, the Caucasus, Central Asia, and South Asia are where Islam, Christianity, Judaism, Buddhism, and Hinduism intersect. They are also the sites of most wars in the last fifty years. The point here is not *why* people fight, but *where* they fight. These are usually not explicitly religious wars. But, since religion shapes culture, people at these boundaries have different histories and different views of human life, and hence are more likely to oppose one another. Regardless of the many and varied reasons for conflict, these are the areas where conflict likely occurs. They are religious fault zones, and hence sites of political instability.

Religion also shapes forms of government.[12] In Eastern Europe, authoritarian governments have found it easier to continue in areas where the Orthodox churches, with a history of cooperation with the state, have held sway.[13] Traditionally Orthodox countries such as Russia, Serbia, and Greece have also voiced support for one another in the face of NATO's bombing of Serbia in 1999. The new boundaries of Eastern and Western Europe may fall along the old divide between Orthodox and Catholic/Protestant. Huntington has argued that changed attitudes toward freedom within the Roman Catholic Church since the Second Vatican Council have produced a "third wave of democracy." This has helped depose dictators in much of the world, especially in the Philippines, Spain, Portugal, Eastern Europe, and Latin America.[14] The major upsurge of evangelicalism in the world is, in most places, a catalyst for democracy.[15]

In any concern for democracy we should also attend more to religion. For example, the attention to China's courageous pro-democracy activists is certainly deserved, but it must be remembered that their following is still quite small. Yet there has been little attention to China's dissident churches, which at a conservative estimate number some thirty-five million (apart from fifteen million in the official churches) and are growing rapidly. *The Far East Economic Review*, in a 1997 cover story entitled "God Is Back," reported one Beijing official as saying, "If God had the face of a seventy-year old man, we wouldn't care if he was back. But he has the face of millions of twenty-year-olds, so we are worried."[16] The Chinese government currently seems far more scared of religious movements such as Falun Gong than of more overtly political movements, and represses them mercilessly. The rapid growth of the only nationwide movements in China not under government control merits systematic political attention.

In East Asia, the economic dynamo of the world for much of the last few decades, economic growth has been strongest in areas which have been shaped by a Confucian ethic. They have often combined Confucianism with authoritarian government, and the jury is still out as to whether they can continue to do so. But it is becoming impossible to understand the factors of economic development here or elsewhere without taking religious factors into account. Berger maintains that Weber's celebrated thesis on the positive effects of Protestantism on the development of an industrial economy is still acutely relevant in the modern world, especially in Latin America. He writes that "Max Weber is alive and well and living in Guatemala."[17]

I am not saying that religion, simply understood, is the factor that explains everything. But I am saying that the role of religion is key in addressing conflict, persecution, political order, and economic development.[18] It is relevant to almost every international question.[19] Despite Western secular predictions and hopes in the 1960s and 1970s, there is no sign that this influence is diminishing. The trends point in the other direction. It is absurd to ignore it.

Apart from the growth of radical Islam, the Balkan conflicts, the rise of the Welfare and Virtue parties in Turkey, and the BJP party in India, the following religious trends at the beginning of the millennium also merit political reflection and attention:

1. The rapid and alarming upsurge of intolerance (official and unofficial) against minority religions ("cults") in Eastern and Western Europe.
2. The pattern of violence and warfare along the sub-Saharan boundary from Nigeria to Ethiopia. This traces a Christian/Muslim divide.
3. The rapid growth of Christianity in Korea (now over 30 percent of the population), China (a minimum of fifty million, up from one million in 1980), Taiwan, and Indonesia.
4. Tensions in Nigeria and Indonesia. There is widespread religious violence in the north and central regions of Nigeria, often caused by the introduction of a radical Islamic *sharia* law, with several thousand dead in recent years, and fears that there could be a religious war. In Indonesia, rising religious strife precedes and has some separate dynamics from recent anti-Chinese violence. In this case, radical Islam threatens to undermine what has been one of the world's best examples of interreligious toleration and cooperation. In both of these regional powers there is instability and violence that could spread far beyond the religious communities themselves.
5. The current exodus of Christians from the Middle East: over a million in the last five years. Currently some 3 percent of Palestinians are Christians, compared to an estimated 25 percent fifty years ago. Similar movements have taken place out of Egypt, Syria, Lebanon, Turkey, and Iraq.
6. The emergence of Orthodoxy as a unifying symbol in the Balkans, Greece, and parts of the former Soviet Union.
7. The increasing prominence of religion in the conflicts between India and Pakistan, now enhanced by nuclear weapons.
8. The rapid growth of charismatic Protestantism (and, now, Catholicism) in Latin America.

Religion is a vital factor in these trends, and these trends are vital features of the modern world.

Idealism and Realism

With the fifteenth- and sixteenth-century breakdown of Western Christendom as a uniting element in Europe, and with the emergence of distinct states, the question of actual international (or, more properly, interstate) relations, of how states do and should relate to one another, took on more force. People soon tried to supply answers. In the sixteenth century, Machiavelli suggested war and manipulative diplomacy. Other influential proposals included the post–Reformation treaties, such as those of Augsburg and Westphalia, trying to provide a peaceful religious division of the continent. In the early seventeenth century, the work of Hugo Grotius further developed the idea of treaties and international law. From this beginning has grown a modern plethora of embassies, trade agreements, treaties, and international organizations. These have flourished especially in the latter part of the twentieth century. Meanwhile, the older practices of war, imperialism, and domination have, of course, continued unabated and with a larger death toll.

Seventeenth-century Europe found some peace from its religious wars in the agreements of the Treaty of Westphalia of 1648. Similarly, nineteenth-century Europe found some security at the end of the Napoleonic wars in the Treaty of Vienna. This maintained a semblance of peace in much of Europe for the rest of that century by trying to balance states, and possible alliances of states, against one another. Out of this partial success came the idea of a "balance of power." The idea of this balance is that states will usually try to dominate one another if they are able to get away with it. Consequently, one useful way to maintain peace would be to ensure that states, and possible alliances of states, are roughly equal in military power so that none can, with confidence, turn on or attack its neighbors. From this balance-of-power idea also comes the modern theory of nuclear deterrence—maintaining defensible nuclear arms with which one can retaliate against a nuclear attack so that no country can hope to benefit itself via a nuclear first strike on another. In such a situation it is hoped that nuclear powers will tend to balance each other out so that none can see any benefit in a nuclear attack on another.

Another offshoot of the balance-of-power idea is the approach called "realism" in international relations. Realism stresses that human beings and states, or at least, politically strong human beings and states, seek their national interest by whatever power they have available, and that this explains most of how states relate to one another. States will seek to be autonomous, to achieve their own interests, and expand their sphere of influence as much as they can. This theory teaches that international relations have been, are, and will be, a power struggle. In its final analysis, the most important power in international relations is military power, and so each state must try to maintain sufficient armed force to defend and promote its interests. States that do not do so will not survive in the long run—they will disappear or fall under the control of others.

From out of the competing international law tradition has come what tends to be called a more "idealistic" view of international relations. This view stresses binding treaties between states, the importance of international legal agencies (such as the International Court of Justice in The Hague) to mediate disputes, and international political bodies such as the United Nations. While not necessarily being credulous about the capacity of states for evil, these views hold that there is much more to international relations than power struggles. Countries will often have at least some minimal sense of justice, and they are willing to maintain compromises with others on that basis.

Closely related to these idealistic theories is the theory of "functionalism" in international relations. Functionalists typically advocate developing interdependence, especially economic interdependence, between states. Their ground for doing so is that states which have extensive trade links, investments in one another, and a division of labor between them are unlikely to fight because they have many mutual interests. In any conflict, both sides would inevitably lose a great deal.[20] Such functionalism has provided one of the basic rationales for the development of the European Community and was important in the ideology of the Clinton presidency, such as it was, that obsessively stressed trade links as the key to democracy, human rights, and peace.

Theories of "imperialism," especially economic imperialism, are still also widespread. They have remained almost an orthodoxy of much of the Left, even in the postcommunist era. One variant of this view stems from Vladimir Lenin and another (with important differences) from the turn-of-the-century English economist, J. A. Hobson. These theories basically hold that the rich countries have made, maintained, and kept their wealth because they have exploited and drawn wealth out of the countries which are now poor. While today, political empires have largely ceased to exist, this view maintains that "economic empires," basically financial, trade, and investment links managed through multinational corporations, still continue a pattern of exploitation, thus explaining most of the continuing poverty in the Third World. It is the theory that underlies much of the protest against globalization, the World Bank, the World Trade Organization, and the G-8 summits.

There are other views of international relations, but most are really actually social science methods for analyzing how nations behave. Furthermore, the theories we have mentioned are not incompatible, for there can be both idealistic and realistic theories of imperialism. Functionalism can also fit either of the schemes, though it is stressed more by the idealists. Consequently, this chapter will focus on the polarity of realistic and idealistic views of international relations.

A simple polarity between idealism and realism is, of course, a naïve and simplistic way of looking at the matter, and the terms themselves are hardly adequate. Who, after all, wants to be called merely a naïve idealist, and who does not want to be reckoned a tough realist? Indeed, Herbert Butterfield remarked that realism is less a school of thought than a self-interested boast. And what realist wants to be characterized as a person with no ideals? Nevertheless, this polarity does illuminate some of the current major views about international relations, and it corresponds fairly well to major differences about the use of military power.

There is something in both idealism and realism that should appeal to us. As far as realism is concerned, human beings are fallen; a desire for power— to be like God—is at the root of the fall, and human perfection is not to be expected in this world. Consequently we should not act as if the world were or could be run on goodwill and amity. Indeed, realist theory rests on a long tradition of reflection about politics stretching back at least as far as St. Augustine. One of the most articulate twentieth-century exponents of such realism in America was the great theologian, Reinhold Niebuhr.[21]

But we cannot let the matter rest with realism. Hunger for power is not the only thing to be said about action in the world.[22] Human beings are still called to do justice, and having not lost the image of God, still seek it. We cannot avoid trying to create and maintain just relations between nations. In this sense we have to be idealistic. Even realists acknowledge this fact, sometimes grudgingly, sometimes naïvely, when they say that unless states can militarily maintain themselves, all other values will be lost. In so doing, they acknowledge the moral drive which lies behind their own theory, as, indeed, it lay behind Machiavelli's.

Consequently, in international relations we must be both idealistic and realistic. Governments are given the authority to coerce, and they need to have and use it in a fallen world. A government which does not maintain its ability to defend its citizens is not only naïve, but is also shirking a divine responsibility (which is perhaps another way of saying the same thing). It will allow war and oppression. But the necessity of the ability to defend one's legitimate interests does not in itself provide much guidance about the other actions governments ought to take. Maintaining an ability to act does not tell us how to act. In this sense, realism can never be more than a partial guide to international conduct, for it merely cautions us to prepare for the dangers that face us. It gives us only partial direction as to what we should try to achieve, or how we can achieve it, in the face of these dangers.

The responsibility to seek just international relations is not some woolly mandate to construct an ideal international order, as though there were some given, fixed state of affairs that is just and which, when achieved, abolishes the need for further action. It is not a mandate to expect a utopia or attempt to construct one. It is not some goal to be achieved; it is not a final, international realm of peace to be delivered; it is not an ultimate realm of international amity that will come about. It is simply a way to be followed, a standard of conduct. It is not something that can only exist in some ideal, transcendent world of peace-loving states. It is a guide right here, right now, precisely in an all-too-broken world of despotic self-seeking states.

We are not called to be unrealistic, assuming that there will be universal goodwill when this is all too clearly not the case. Any search for justice has to be intensely realistic about the world. We act in an unremittingly brutal and selfish world. However, we can never retreat into self-interest and mere realism simply because the world is wicked. Rather, precisely because the world is wicked, we must carefully harness our ability to act properly in a realm suffused with evil.

Justice is a fundamental aspect of the way that the world is made. Hence, its reality is manifested empirically in what states actually do. This is shown in balance-of-power relations. Any balance of power, if it is to secure long-standing peace, needs to be more than a merely military standoff. If one state feels unjustly suppressed, then it will try to change the situation and upset the balance. Felt injustice leads to instability. Any successful balance-of-power arrangement is one which the participants accept as having some legitimacy, one whose arrangements can be justified. Such arrangements might not be their first choice for their position in the world, but they will accept it if it provides a relatively just place for themselves and their neighbors. This implies that there must be a consensus in any balance-of-power arrangement. Without such a consensus, then every difference, dispute, or disagreement can become a test of ultimate strength, no useful negotiations are possible, and the system becomes unstable. Hence, a sense of justice is an essential component of international relations—it is part of the fundamental reality in which we live. It is not a pipe dream but an essential aspect of all politics.

Another aspect of justice is that we must not idolize the doctrine of national sovereignty. Briefly put, the strongest doctrine of sovereignty asserts that, subject only to the constraints of its own legal order, a state can do what it likes, and nobody else can legitimately stop it. We must also resist any ultimate claims to sovereignty for the simple reason that only God can be a final sovereign. This statement is not some piece of theological sleight of hand disguising two very different meanings of the term "sovereign," since the sovereignty of God has always been of immediate political relevance. Because God is the final sovereign, there can never be a final authority in anything on earth itself.

This does not mean that, for example, the United States should subordinate its foreign policy to the United Nations, or any other international body. This is for the simple reason that these bodies are not final sovereigns either, even apart from the fact that they frequently act at the behest of tyrannical and brutal powers. But it does mean that states should recognize that they are subject to an order of responsibility higher than their own immediate self-interest (this is one of the things that just-war theory is meant to point out). This awareness of the limits of sovereignty, coupled with our earlier discussion of the rule of law, should lead us to the realization that treaties and international law are, for all their failings, an important and irreplaceable element of our response to international conflicts in the modern age.

There is also among Americans, and particularly among conservative American Christians, a strong streak of political isolationism. This is easily overcome when the United States itself is attacked, but, when faced with tragedies such as the wars in Bosnia or Sudan, it manifests itself in complaints that the United States should not be involved there or, for that matter, anywhere else beyond its borders, unless some matter of crucial national interest is at stake. The caution inherent in this view of the role of government is valuable: our children should not easily be put in harm's way. It also recognizes that the government is not a pragmatic instrument for problem solving in the international arena, any more than it is in the domestic arena. Governments are charged primarily with the responsibility of defending the inhabitants of their territory. States are not Boy Scouts, looking out for good deeds to do. Nor is the military a humanitarian agency for correcting wrongs. It is also hard to accept and justify casualties and pursue a strong and costly war effort if something of great moment to the country is not at stake. People of an isolationist bent are correct in recognizing all these.

However, the state's goal can never simply be its own interest, or even the interest of its citizens—if that interest is understood as immediate self-interest. Indeed, in a morally ordered world, no person or human institution can define its task purely by self-interest. The government's task, and proper interest, is always to do justice—something which may transcend its own interest, narrowly understood. This is why national interest is not the only ground for international action. It also brings us to the question of war.

War

The question of warfare has been a central and divisive element of views of politics from the beginning of the Church, and before that, in Judaism.[23] People's views have ranged from launching crusades to seeking peace, to simply going along with whatever a government might ask. But there are two longstanding Christian approaches to warfare. These are the pacifist and the just-war traditions.

The pacifist or nonviolent tradition holds that people (or sometimes only Christians) cannot engage in any warfare or violence. Even within this broad framework, there is a range of disagreements.[24] These include whether police functions should always be rejected in the same way as military functions, or whether it is proper to serve in noncombatant roles, such as medical officers or air raid wardens, or whether all people, or only believers, must forsake violence.

Key biblical texts for the pacifist view obviously include the Sermon on the Mount—"blessed are the meek," "turn the other cheek," "love your enemies and pray for those who persecute you" (Matt. 5). Coupled with these views is the verse "all who take the sword will perish by the sword" (Matt. 26:52). The pacifist asks how, faced with such clear and unequivocal injunctions, anybody could justify doing violence to anybody, including their enemies. When dealing with the fact that God seems to urge Israel to (certain) wars in the Old Testament and that these are called "wars of the Lord" (cf. Num. 21:14, Josh. 3:5), many pacifists respond that Jesus is the culmination of God's revelation to us, so that what he says and lives must supersede all that has gone before.

But there are also New Testament writings on the authority of the state such as "he who is in authority . . . is God's servant for your good . . . he does not bear the sword in vain" (Rom. 13:3, 4). A pacifist response to this is often to say that therefore the state cannot be part of the gospel given by Jesus Christ.[25] Government is seen only as part of God the Father's preserving grace in which sin is restrained. While we may be thankful for the divine order of the state, there is nothing specifically Christlike about it and we should not participate in its fallen order.

However, the distinction between an order of preservation and an order of redemption has major weaknesses. For one thing, it seems to imply that different members of the Trinity have different views of the rule—that God the Father defends it, and that God the Son rejects it. Also, the distinction between Matthew 5 and Romans 13 is not one between an order of the gospel and an order of preservation, but a distinction between ordinary persons and those who hold the specific authority of government office. In the letter to the Romans, Paul told his readers to leave "vengeance" to God (Rom. 12:9), and very shortly thereafter wrote that governments are (one of) God's means to carry out that vengeance (Rom. 13:4). We do not use coercion against others partly because God has established the government to do so. (See the discussion of the New Testament and politics in chapter 3.) Romans 13 and 1 Peter 2:13–17 suggest that governments are divinely given and that essential to their responsibility in a sinful world is the use of coercion. They indicate that the use of force, while terrible and to be avoided where possible, is something authorized for governments. While we should not hate our enemies or do violence to our neighbor, even in retaliation, this personal conduct is distinct from the proper judicial function of justly deterring and "paying back" evildoers. Similarly, a judge is not retaliating, not refusing to turn the other cheek, but carrying out an office.

Since the Sermon on the Mount forbids personal self-defense, classical just-war theory has usually not been developed on the basis of a right to defend oneself but on the basis of a duty to defend third parties, which necessarily means defending innocent human life. The defense of the innocent is the core of political responsibility. Hence, the government's role is not to protect itself per se, but rather to protect those who are entrusted to its care. It cannot stand aside and let them be assaulted and killed. It is precisely for this reason that just-war theory emphasizes that only a legitimate government can properly wage a just war. This restriction is not an obsession with legalism or the status quo. Rather, it is a fundamental part of an attempt to have a universal and integral ethical stance. This is one reason that Thomas Aquinas begins his classic exposition of just-war theory with the question of legitimate authority.

Given that the use of force by governments seems consistently recognized in the Bible, just-war theorists look for biblical guidance, and as the New Testament does not involve wars, then the Old Testament provides most guidance. In the wars of Israel we find several limits on war. With certain restrictions, all those over twenty could be drafted (Num. 1:2, 3), but usually only selected people were (Num. 31:3–6). Those exempt from the draft (Deut. 20:1–8) included: those who had built a new house but had not dedicated it or enjoyed it; those who had planted a vineyard and not enjoyed its fruit; those who had "betrothed a wife and not taken her," since they would have a divided mind (this is depicted beautifully in the King James' Version rendering of Deuteronomy 24:5, "When a man taketh a new wife, he shall not go out in the host, neither shall he be charged with any business; he shall be free at home one year, and shall cheer up his wife" [KJV]); "the fearful and faint hearted"; the Levites (priests).

This suggests that neither marriage, housing, nor farming could be swept up into a total war effort. They had their own place that must be respected. The needs of the state even in war cannot always override the needs of others. Other features of war include:

- Israel was to declare war or offer peace before any attack could be undertaken (Deut. 23:9–14).
- Captured women could not be made slaves nor kept as permanent captives, but they could be married (Deut. 21:10–14).
- Legitimate war must be defensive only. Israel was forbidden to use more than a small number of horses (Deut. 17:16), and therefore, chariots, since horses and chariots were weapons used in offense.
- Israel could not cut down fruit trees even during a siege. They could use only non-fruit trees and then only as many as they needed, since, "are the trees in the field men, that they should be besieged by thee?" The war could not be against the earth, not even the enemies' earth (Deut. 20:19, 20).

These types of examples have been theoretically synthesized in the idea of a "just war." Just-war theory accepts and defends the limited and proper use of governmental force against injustice. The basic criteria of a just war are:

1. That the *intention* of the war is good. Its goal must not be gain but a just peace.
2. The *cause* must be justified. It must be a battle against injustice—commonly and historically meaning the defense of one's own territory.
3. The *means* must be limited. This usually implies that:
   a) Noncombatants, neutrals and third parties must not be harmed.
   b) Existing laws and treaties (e.g., the Geneva Conventions on the rules of war) must be honored.
   c) The means must be proportionate to the goals. The war must not do more harm than good: you don't kill a thousand to save a dozen.
   d) The enemy must know the terms on which peace can be achieved.
4. The war must be winnable; we should not engage in futile warfare but only fight to achieve a realizable goal.
5. The war must be a matter of last resort. All other means must have been seriously tried.
6. Only a duly constituted government can wage such a war. Private citizens cannot do so.

This is not a shopping list of unrelated items, but has an intrinsic and cumulative logic. This logic is that our neighbors, even our enemies, must, as much as possible, be cared for. Hence, if we do harm them, then it can only be with a very powerful justification, and we must always ask: for what cause? with what intention? and within what limits? While this basic overview is widely shared, there are various divisions within just-war theory, especially on whether a just war must meet all of the criteria outlined or only a substantial part of them. As Weigel has said, the just-war tradition is not an "algebra"—a formula giving indubitable right answers—but "something analogous to a recipe . . . it helps us think in publicly accessible, reasonably grounded moral categories about building a measure of order in international life."[26]

It is often argued, especially by pacifists, that, for its first three and a half centuries, the Christian Church was pacifist. However, there is not a great deal of evidence either way, and what evidence there is is often ambiguous. What is clear is that it was only in the fourth century, with the first official "Christian" Roman Emperor, Constantine, that just-war views became ascendant. This association between just-war views and the political accommodation of Christianity to the Roman Empire makes many suspect that the Church was selling its soul in accepting this view of war.

However, we should not assume that new things in the Church are necessarily wrong things. At the time of Constantine, whatever the defects of the supposed "Christianization" of the Empire, Christians, hitherto suppressed and persecuted, were now faced with the actual responsibility of holding political power. A pacifist view might be cogent among people who could not affect political events anyway. But it can begin to appear insufficient when those same people have to decide about the actual use of government power. The Church faced a new situation. Hence, just-war theories can be understood not as a sellout to imperial power, though that may have taken place as well, but as a consistent elaboration of the Church's teaching as it faced new responsibilities, including putting limits on imperial power. Just-war theory placed limits on the Empire that had not existed before. Since that time, just-war views have become almost the orthodoxy of the Church, and have become the dominant view among Christians in the twentieth century.

Just-war views are often castigated as unrealistic because many countries do not respect them. Certainly, it is true that just-war criteria have often been ignored or twisted for unjust ends. However, this does not invalidate them any more than the fact that most people have never been persuaded to be pacifists invalidates that tradition. The fact that we violate any and all other commandments does not invalidate them, either. Even the best guides are no guarantee that people will follow them. No commandment carries within itself a guarantee that it will be respected.

There are also major achievements of just-war theory that must be recognized, such as the development of international law and of military codes of conduct, either domestic or international, like the Geneva Conventions. At the time of the 1991 Gulf War against Iraq, the U.S. had a major and important public debate about the relevance of just-war criteria to the American-led allied intervention. In the attacks on Afghanistan in 2001, questions of just conduct in war permeated discussions of the bombing. The just-war tradition is often under strain, and frequently neglected, but it remains an important element of the modern world, especially in American military analyses.

Commandments, Not Prophecies

In concluding this brief discussion of international relations it is worth emphasizing that one approach that must be avoided is the tendency among many fundamentalist, and some evangelicals, to approach international relations by trying to analyze it in terms of the meaning of biblical prophecies. Proponents of this view often try to match current events with biblical texts in order to discern what God might be doing. This tendency came to the fore strongly in the Gulf War when a coalition of forces, led by the United States, liberated Kuwait from occupation by the Iraqi army. Certain preachers argued that figures such as Saddam Hussein and nations such as Iraq are prefigured in the Bible: indeed the juxtaposition of Baghdad and Babylon seemed to cry out for some such link. During this time, John Walvoord's book from the 1970s, *Armageddon, Oil and the Middle East Crisis*, was reprinted with a run of a half-million copies.

This approach identifies an event supposedly foretold in the Bible, whether an assault on Israel or the war around Iraq. Its proponents then support the policy of (usually) the U.S. or Israel, believing that these policies will bring about the fulfillment of the prophecy. However, even if we were to accept this mode of biblical interpretation, just because something might fulfill a prophecy, this still doesn't make it right to do.

Suppose, for example, to take a common "prophetic" scenario, the Russians were about to attack Israel and thus, perhaps, trigger a whole set of biblically ordained events. Would we be justified in supporting Israel on the basis of biblical prediction? Why not instead support the Russians, as this could equally bring about prophetic fulfillment? Should some Russian invasion be defended just because it might, eventually, help bring about a desired end? One might as well support Hussein on the grounds that he, too, might be fulfilling biblical prophecy.

Some might protest that their aim is not to support just anyone whose action may inadvertently bring about the desired end result, but rather to support those who are trying to achieve what the Bible has said will come about. However, this is also a dubious procedure, as may be illustrated from the Bible itself. At the end of Chronicles (2 Chron. 26:17) it is said that God brought the King of Babylon up against Israel and gave Israel into Babylon's hand (Isa. 47:6). This was partly to give the land the Sabbath rest that had been promised (2 Chron. 36:21). Clearly the Babylonians are depicted as carrying out God's purposes. But Babylon was also depicted as doing terrible evil, enslaving a people, and burning down the house of God. Jeremiah proclaimed God's judgment against Babylon for its misdeeds. In this description, God is described as using the evil that people do, but also condemning that evil. This means that, although God may bring good out of evil, there is never any excuse to participate in that evil. Even if we were correct about the meaning of prophecies, this in itself provides absolutely no justification for any particular attempt to fulfill them. It provides no guidance for action.

International responsibility does not mean trying to find out what God might supposedly bring about, but rather following the commandments that we are given. It is not our task to determine a final outcome, but to try to obey the commandments. This is as true in international relations as anything else. Biblically, it is God who weaves the strands of history. We are to seek justice with our neighbors, including neighbors in Israel, in Afghanistan, in Russia, in Kuwait, and in Iraq. A call to peace and justice, not any predictive prophecy, is the criterion for judging any human action, including any international action.[27]

Notes

1. This section relies on B. Zylstra's "The Society of the Future in Political Perspective" (paper presented at the Annual Meeting of the Canadian Sociological and Anthropological Association, Halifax, 28 May 1981).

2. For a good, brief overview, see Bernard Lewis, "The Return of Islam," in *Islam and the West* (New York: Oxford University Press, 1993), 133–54. On the negative effects of "Political Islam," see Habib C. Malik, "Political Islam and the Roots of Violence," in *The Influence of Faith: Religious Groups and U.S. Foreign Policy*, ed. Elliott Abrams (Lanham, Md.: Rowman & Littlefield, 2001), 113–48.

3. This section draws on my "Religion and Global Affairs: Disregarding Religion," *SAIS Review* 18 (1998): 13–18.

4. Edward Luttwak, "The Missing Dimension," in *Religion: The Missing Dimension of Statecraft*, ed. J. Johnston and C. Sampson (New York: Oxford University Press, 1994), 8–19. Some of the material in this section is drawn from my essay "The Importance of Religious Freedom," in *Religious Freedom in the World*, ed. P. Marshall (Nashville, Tenn.: Broadman and Holman, 2000), 9–13. See also R. Scott Appleby, *The Ambivalence of the Sacred: Religion, Violence and Reconciliation* (Lanham, Md.: Rowman & Littlefield, 2000); Mark Juergensmeyer, *The New Cold War? Religious Nationalism Confronts the Secular State* (Berkeley, Calif.: University of California Press, 1993).

5. Luttwak, "The Missing Dimension."

6. Chester Crocker, "How to Think about Ethnic Conflict," *Wire* 7, no. 10 (September 1999).

7. "Cries of Battle," *Economist*, 25 September 1999; "Nigeria's Ethnic Violence," 31 July 1999.

8. "Pakistan Ought to Concentrate on Pulling Itself Together," *International Herald Tribune*, 14 July 1999; Michael O'Hanlon, "Saving Lives with Force," *The New Republic*, 12 July 1999.

9. There are attempts to give a more precise meaning to "fundamentalism," notably in the series on fundamentalism edited by Martin E. Marty and R. Scott Appleby, *Fundamentalisms Observed; Fundamentalisms and Society; Fundamentalisms and the State; Accounting for Fundamentalism; Fundamentalism Comprehended* (Chicago: University of Chicago Press, 1991, 1993, 1993, 1994, 1995), but the term generally remains vague and pejorative. For a good critique of Marty and Appleby's methodology, see Paul Freston, *Evangelicals and Politics in Asia, Africa, and Latin America* (Cambridge: Cambridge University Press, 2001).

10. See also John Carlson and Eric Owens, eds., *The Sacred and the Sovereign: Rethinking Religion and International Politics* (Washington, D.C.: Georgetown University Press, forthcoming).

11. Samuel P. Huntington, "The Clash of Civilizations," *Foreign Affairs* (Summer 1993): 22–49, and *The Clash of Civilization and the Crisis of World Order* (New York: Simon and Shuster, 1996).

12. Daniel Philpott, *Revolutions in Sovereignty* (Princeton, N.J.: Princeton University Press, 2001), argues that religion, especially the Protestant Reformation, was essential to the development of the modern state system, embodied in the treaty of Westphalia.

13. See William Pfaff, "The Absence of Empire," *The New Yorker*, 10 August 1992; David Koyzis, "Imaging God and His Kingdom: Eastern Orthodoxy's Iconic Political Ethic," *Review of Politics* 55 (1993): 267–89.

14. Samuel P. Huntington, in his *The Third Wave: Democratization in the Late Twentieth Century* (Norman, Okla.: University of Oklahoma Press, 1991), argues for

the importance of religion, especially Catholicism, in the spread of democracy. Some thoughtful essays on this are also given Johnston and Sampson, *Religion*.

15. For an overview, see David Martin, "The People's Church: The Global Evangelical Upsurge and Its Political Consequences," *Books and Culture* (January/February 2000).

16. "China: God Is Back," *Far East Economic Review*, 6 June 1996.

17. See Peter L. Berger, ed., *The Desecularization of the World: Resurgent Religion and World Politics* (Grand Rapids, Mich.: Eerdmans, 1999), 16.

18. See the essays in Marshall, *Religious Freedom in the World*. On religion and human rights, and American campaigns to fight religious persecution, see Allen D. Hertzke and Daniel Philpott, "Defending the Faiths," *The National Interest* (fall 2000): 74–81.

19. See also Susanne Rudolph and James Piscatori, eds., *Transnational Religion and Failing States* (Boulder, Colo.: Westview Press, 1997).

20. See David Mitrany, *The Functional Theory of Politics* (London: M. Robertson, for the London School of Economics and Political Science, 1975).

21. Niebuhr was a prolific author; see his *Christianity and Power Politics* (New York: Scribner's, 1940); *Christian Realism and Political Problems* (New York: Scribner's, 1953).

22. For a good, brief critique of realism, see Richard Wolin, "Reasons of State, State of Reason," *The New Republic*, 4 June 2001.

23. See Paul Ramsey, *War and the Christian Conscience* (Durham, N.C.: Duke University Press, 1961); *The Just War: Force and Political Responsibility* (New York: Scribner's, 1968); Michael Walzer, *Just and Unjust Wars* (New York: Basic Books, 1977); George Weigel, *Tranquillitas Ordinis* (New York: Oxford University Press, 1987); Kenneth Thompson, ed., *Ethics and International Relations* (New Brunswick, N.J.: Transaction, 1985); Rowland H. Bainton, *Christian Attitudes toward War and Peace* (Nashville, Tenn.: Abingdon, 1960).

24. See John Howard Yoder, *Nevertheless: Varieties of Christian Pacifism* (Scottsdale, Pa.: Herald Press, 1971).

25. See John Howard Yoder, *The Politics of Jesus* (Grand Rapids. Mich.: Eerdmans, 1972), 199 ff. The same criticism can be made of Richard B. Hays, *The Moral Vision of the New Testament* (San Francisco: Harper, 1996), 330–31.

26. George Weigel, "Just War and Counterterrorism: Views from the Catholic Church," *Right Reasons*, 2001.

27. See Elliott Abrams, *The Influence of Faith*.

CHAPTER 9

~

Concluding Reflections

This book has outlined some general ideas relevant to political life. I hope they are a little more than ideological prescriptions and pious generalities. However, engagement in politics, or serious thinking about politics, requires far more than these beginning exegetically shaped reflections. One thing required is philosophic reflection on political life, thinking about the nature of history, good and evil, power, law, mercy, and justice. Another is, as described in chapter 5, actual knowledge of the world. While biblical exegesis is a touchstone for such reflection, it cannot substitute for it.[1]

In classical political philosophy and theology, several of these themes are discussed in terms of prudence, or its political expression, statesmanship. Unfortunately, mentioning prudence in the modern world invites misunderstanding, since much of its meaning in Aristotelian and classical Western and Christian thought has been lost. It is often treated simply as a type of utilitarianism or pragmatism, as if it were judging an act or policy merely by its consequences. It is sometimes merged with realism, especially in international relations, and treated as a type of flinty-eyed self-interest. It can also equate with timidity and self-preservation, the preserve of the small-minded. In colloquial use it is captured in comedian Michael Myers' parodies of George Bush, Sr., contemplating action but then withdrawing with a mumbled, "But wouldn't be prudent, wouldn't be prudent."

Especially in some Christian circles there is misunderstanding of and antipathy to prudence. Some consider it as the opposite of genuine Christian ethics, and believe it evades absolute commands and refuses to trust that the consequences of our actions lie ultimately in God's hands. To quote Josef Pieper: "To the contemporary mind, prudence seems less a prerequisite to goodness than an evasion of it."[2]

But there are good reasons why prudence has been considered a virtue. One of its facets is a true grasp of the world—what it is and what is possible within it. Because the world is God's creation, this requires knowing that the world is not as a happenstance thing but is an actual creation.[3] This also means that good intentions are never enough. We certainly need good intentions—if this means a desire for what is good—but these must be attuned to real situations, to the possibilities of concrete human action. Consequently, the classical opposites of prudence included thoughtlessness and vacillation.

The knowledge involved in prudence concerns not only the universal conditions of human life, but also a grasp of particular situations, of the contingencies of our historical moment. This, in turn, requires not the ability to recall a mountain of facts, but a willingness to be taught by experience, to listen to and take advice, an openness to the unexpected, and good judgment about the future—especially whether an action will achieve its goal. These are not solely matters of skill and discipline, though they are involved, but also concern the condition of our heart and soul. They also require physical alertness and good health.[4] Even if we are experienced and taught, prudence will not provide certainty about what will happen, so courage is also a key part of prudence. We will always be, as Thomas Aquinas says, anxious about our actions.[5] Uncertainty underlies action in the political world, and no amount of knowledge or piety will change this. This is why discipline, awareness, experience, and courage are vital parts of prudence.

We also need to be careful about how we speak and argue. While this book outlines views that flow from religious beliefs, this does not imply that such language and modes of argument should usually be used in addressing a wider public. Instead, we should try to express ourselves in ways accessible to and amenable to those who have other, or no, religious faith, or who think that their, or another's, faith is, or should be, irrelevant to politics. This is not to suggest hiding, lying, or dissembling, but merely that in our language we must attempt to reach out to others.

This is not because "religious" talk is somehow inherently illegitimate in the public realm. We should not succumb to contemporary attempts to outlaw nonliberal (often called "religious") language from public discourse. As Carter says: "We do no credit to the ideal of religious freedom when we talk as though religious belief is something of which public-spirited adults should be ashamed."[6] Nor is it possible to separate our fundamental beliefs about the nature of law and life, hope and evil, history and justice, from our thinking about public policy.

However, while we should resist any cultural imperialism that suggests a quasi-official, secularist theory of knowledge for American public policy, it is often not a good idea to use explicitly religious language or argument in political debate. The reason is not epistemological subtlety, but effectiveness (though these are connected). Quite simply, many people do not understand, or else resist, religious conceptions in public discourse. Whatever words may be used, or ideas intended, there is often a widespread, ingrained prejudice that sees an incipient theocracy whenever God might appear in public. This view is ignorant and prejudiced, but it is there. And, since communication means speaking in a way that can be heard, then such views must be accommodated. It is similar to saying that it is a bad idea in America to give a general political speech in Swedish: lots of people don't understand Swedish so they will not know what you are talking about.[7]

This can be hard, as it can be difficult to "translate" from one idiom to another or from one world view to another. Doubtless, something will always be lost. But this is a necessary requirement for operating in a public realm, a realm open to all and inhabited by all. Every political argument, article, or speech always requires a rhetorical strategy to reach those who read or see or hear. After all, what is communicated in any setting is not what we say, or intend to say, but what is heard.[8]

A further feature of American religion, one which has been touched upon several times throughout this book, is a desire for spontaneity, rapid renewal, and successful crusades. But, apart from some wars, politics is seldom quick in its long-term effects. On this one can do little better than quote Jean Bethke Elshtain's words about the shootings at Columbine High School in May 1999. Commenting on the hope among many Christians that the courageous death of a teenager like Cassie Bernall might lead to religious revival and spiritual renewal across the country, Elshtain pointed out that even the inner life itself is a product of discipline and institutions:

> Unfortunately, the hearts, the flowers, and the doves with flapping wings on the Cassie websites are too insubstantial to provide a perdurable message of spiritual formation. The inner life is an enterprise of time and work. Changes of heart really do happen, and they are important, but large and sustaining cultural projects must be built on more than fervor and feeling. If Max Weber was right that politics is the slow boring of hard boards, we should not expect any

single event or any single act of heroism to carry the day. Political and cultural change is effected when people hang in for the long haul, and institutions—places of work, schools, governments, families—are thereby transformed. Websites and rallies will not do it. Conversion experiences without the sturdy wisdom of traditions and institution will not suffice.[9]

Similarly, because of the nature of idolatry, we must beware of thinking that politics presents primarily a set of goals or a blueprint for a new order. Either of these can easily lead us to turn away from one idol to embrace another. New goals, whether increasing income or eradicating pornography, can easily become programs to which everything else is subordinated, and by which everything else is judged. An idol is a good thing in creation that has been made into a god. A blueprint, or a goal, can become so fixed or rigid that its implementation becomes unjust. An idol is a "graven image," something carved in stone. Our own response to our political circumstances is not itself the word of God, and should never be carved in stone. All programs for an ideal society must be treated skeptically. From the Constantinian hope of a Christian Empire, to the Puritan "city set on a hill" in New England, to the Jesuit state of Paraguay, to the utopian communes of the nineteenth and twentieth centuries, the history of Christendom, and nearly every political view, is littered with failed political dreams. Politics does not provide easy, clear, and simple solutions. It simply means taking up our responsibility for what governments do.

Political change requires ongoing work: writing, lobbying, organizing, entering a race, testing new ideas, drafting new policies. Just like the rest of life, it is often slow, grinding, and frustrating: day after day, week after week, year after year. As Jim Skillen has written, "Politics is not something done in a moment of passion with simple moral zealousness. Politics is more like raising a family, or running a business or stewarding a company. It requires lifelong commitment, patience, steadiness, and great attention to detail day after day."

But this work is not without hope, and we cannot succumb to the political cynicism that has been pervasive amongst Americans. Cynicism is a vice only of the comfortable, one reason that it disappears when there is a real threat, such as in war. Cynicism allows us to stand aloof and shrug, but only because we know that there will be some food on the table tomorrow. Most of us do not fear the police at the door. We do not face imminent death in war. Those who do face such threats may certainly be drawn to despair, but they are never cynical about the importance of governments. They will surrender most of what they hold dear to change the political order in which they live. In recent years, in countries as diverse as Poland and the Philippines, explicitly religious movements, as well as others, have deposed dictators and ushered in genuine democracy and freedom.

Even with success, political action does not bring utopias. It does not conquer sin or change human nature. But it can make a difference between rampant crime and safe neighborhoods; between hungry families and economic security; between victory or defeat in war. And only those who have never been mugged, never been hungry, or never been at war will think these differences are trivial.

Notes

1. See, for example, Oliver O'Donovan, *The Desire of the Nations: Rediscovering the Roots of Political Theology* (Cambridge: Cambridge University Press, 1996). A good sourcebook in Christian political thought is now available, see Oliver O'Donovan and Joan Lockwood O'Donovan, eds., *From Irenaeus to Grotius: A Sourcebook in Christian Political Thought* (Grand Rapids, Mich.: Eerdmans, 1999). See also Luis Lugo, ed., *Religion, Pluralism and Public Life: Abraham Kuyper's Legacy for the Twenty-first Century* (Grand Rapids, Mich.: Eerdmans, 2000); K. Grasso et al., eds., *Catholicism, Liberalism and Communitaranism* (Lanham, Md.: Rowman & Littlefield, 1995); Robert Song, *Christianity and Liberal Society* (Oxford: Oxford University Press, 1997); the four volumes of Daniel J. Elazer's *The Covenant Tradition of Politics* (Rutgers, N.J.: Transaction, 1995–1998); Michael Walzer, Menachem Lorberbaum, Noam J. Zihar, Yair Lorberbaum, eds., *The Jewish Political Tradition*, vol. I (New Haven, Conn.: Yale University Press, 2000); David Novak, *Covenantal Rights* (Princeton, N.J.: Princeton University Press, 2000); the "New Natural Law Theory," associated with John Finnis, Germain Grisez, and Robert George. In a more sociological vein, see John Milbank's *Theology and Social Theory* (Oxford: Blackwell, 1990) and the writings of other members of the "radical orthodoxy" project in John Milbank, et al., eds., *Radical Orthodoxy* (London: Routledge, 1999). On Christian approaches to political science, see T. W. Heilke and A. Woodiwiss, *The Re-Enchantment of Political Science: Christian Scholars Engage Their Discipline* (Lanham, Md.: Rowman & Littlefield, 2001), and on law see Michael W. McConnell, Robert F. Cochran, Angela C. Carmella, eds., *Christian Perspectives on Legal Thought* (New Haven, Conn.: Yale University Press, 2001).

2. Josef Pieper, *The Four Cardinal Virtues: Prudence, Justice, Fortitude, Temperance* (Notre Dame, Ind.: University of Notre Dame Press, 1966), 4. The following comments on prudence, at least the Thomistic account of it, rely on Pieper.

3. Pieper, *The Four Cardinal Virtues*, 7–9.

4. Pieper, *The Four Cardinal Virtues*, 17.

5. Pieper, *The Four Cardinal Virtues*, 18.

6. Stephen Carter, *The Culture of Disbelief: How American Law and Politics Trivialize Religion* (New York: Anchor, 1996).

7. Both Robert Audi and John Rawls have interpreted a principle of "equal respect" to mean that we should only offer reasons that other citizens can reasonably be expected to know and understand. Chaplin suggests that this implies "a low opinion" of citizens' "capacities to enter imaginatively into another citizen's thoughts . . . and patiently to forbear with a view they cannot yet . . . fully grasp," Jonathan Chaplin, "Beyond Liberal Restraint: Defending Religiously Based Arguments in Law and Public Policy," *University of British Columbia Law Review* 33 (2000): 637–38. However, I share this low opinion, not necessarily of citizens' capacities, but of the possibility of their being well-employed in contemporary political discourse, especially in political campaigns. In this situation, I am not arguing for a principle of "equal respect" (especially in terms of Audi's "secular" or Rawls' "public"), but for the practical possibility of actually being heard and understood. See also Richard Mouw, *Uncommon Decency: Christian Civility in an Uncivil World* (Downer's Grove, Ill.: InterVarsity Press, 1999).

8. See Kent Greenawalt, *Private Consciences and Public Reasons* (New York: Oxford University Press, 1995); Robert P. George and Christopher Wolfe, eds., *Natural Law and Public Reason* (Washington, D.C.: Georgetown University Press, 2000).

9. Jean Bethke Elshtain, "Heartland of Darkness," *The New Republic*, 17 January 2000.

Index

~

About the Author

Paul Marshall is Senior Fellow at the Claremont Institute for the Study of Statesmanship and Political Philosophy in Claremont, California.

He is also a Senior Fellow at the Center for Religious Freedom, Freedom House, Washington, D.C., and has testified many times before Congress, lectured at the U.S. State Department, the Helsinki Commission, and the Asylum Bureaus of the I.N.S., and spoken on human rights at the Chinese Academy of Social Sciences, Beijing. He has also lectured in Australia, Austria, Belarus, Canada, Cyprus, England, Indonesia, Israel, Korea, Lebanon, Malaysia, the Netherlands, Nigeria, the Philippines, South Africa, Spain, Sudan, Switzerland, and Thailand.

He is the author of the best-selling, award-winning survey of worldwide religious persecution, *Their Blood Cries Out*, released in 1997. In speeches introducing the International Religious Freedom Act in the U.S. Senate, his book was described as "a powerful and persuasive analysis" and an "exhaustive" survey, "which simply cannot be ignored." He is also the general editor of *Religious Freedom in the World: A Global Report on Freedom and Persecution* (2000) and author and editor of nineteen other books and booklets, including *Islam at the Crossroads: Understanding Its Beliefs, History and Conflicts* (2002); *The Talibanization of Nigeria* (2002); *Heaven Is Not My Home* (1998); *A Kind of Life Imposed on Man: Vocation and Social Order from Tyndale to Locke* (1996). He has also published forty scholarly articles, twenty briefs to government bodies, and hundreds of popular articles. His writings have been translated into Arabic, Chinese, Dutch, German, Japanese, Korean, Malay, Russian, and Spanish.

He is in frequent demand for lectures and media appearances including interviews on ABC *Evening News*, the Australian Broadcasting Corporation, the BBC, the Canadian Broadcasting Corporation, CBS *Evening News*, CNN, Fox, PBS, and the South African Broadcasting Corporation. His work has been the subject of articles in the *Boston Globe*, the *Christian Science Monitor*, *Christianity Today*, the *Dallas Morning News*, *First Things*, *Globe and Mail*, the *Los Angeles Times*, the *New Republic*, the *New York Times*, *Reader's Digest*, the *Wall St. Journal*, *Washington Times*, the *Weekly Standard*, and several hundred other newspapers and magazines.

Visiting professorships include the Catholic University, Washington, D.C.; the European University for the Humanities, Belarus; the Faculties of Law and of Philosophy of the Free University, Amsterdam; Fuller Theological Seminary; Institute for Christian Studies, Toronto; J. Omar Good Distinguished Visiting Professor, Juniata College, Pa.; Satya Wacana University, Indonesia; and Adjunct Professor in the Graduate Program in Philosophy at Rutgers University, and Satya Wacana University, Indonesia..

He has also been an Overseas Research Fellow for the Human Sciences Research Council of South Africa; Senior Fellow at the Institute of Religion and Democracy; exploration geologist in the Canadian Arctic; forest fire fighter in British Columbia, and an advisor to the Council of Yukon Indians. His hobbies include shark diving and photography.